CHICAGO PUBLIC LIBRARY

R00515 56622

C0-DXA-211

```
LB         Jessup, Dorothy
2844.53    Kerr.
.U62
N4875      Teachers, unions,
1985         and change
```

FORM 125M

EDUCATION & PHILOSOPHY

The Chicago Public Library

Received DEC 3 2 1986

© THE BAKER & TAYLOR CO.

TEACHERS, UNIONS, AND CHANGE

TEACHERS, UNIONS, AND CHANGE

A Comparative Study

Dorothy Kerr Jessup

Library of Congress Cataloging in Publication Data

Jessup, Dorothy Kerr.
    Teachers, unions, and change.

    Bibliography: p.
    1. Teachers' unions—New York (State)—Case studies.
I. Title.
LB2844.53.U62N4875   1985   331.88'113711'009747   84-26441
ISBN 0-03-002858-2 (alk. paper)

Research for this report was made possible through grants from the
National Institute of Education (Grant No. 9-0165)
and the
SUNY Research Foundation (Grant No. 426-7911A).

Published in 1985 by Praeger Publishers
CBS Educational and Professional Publishing
a Division of CBS Inc.
521 Fifth Avenue, New York, NY 10175 USA

© 1985 by Praeger Publishers

All rights reserved

56789 052 987654321

Printed in the United States of America
on acid-free paper

ACKNOWLEDGMENTS

This research was supported by grants from the National Institute of Education and the SUNY Research Foundation. But the research would not have been possible without the cooperation of the teachers, administrators, and school board members who participated in the study. Many of these people contributed valuable insights helpful in interpreting the research findings. Since anonymity was promised for the school districts involved, it is not possible to include individual names here. However, I want to take this opportunity to thank them collectively for the time and attention they so generously provided.

CONTENTS

ACKNOWLEDGMENTS v

1 INTRODUCTION 1
   The Background Literature and Research Questions 3
   Data and Methods 5
   A Theoretical Framework 6
   The Teachers' Union as an Organizational Type 7
   The External Environment 7
   Organizational Goals 9
   Internal Structural Constraints 11
   The Union's Impact on the School 14
   What the Case Studies Will Show 15

2 CEDARTON 19
   Background 20
   Teachers' Organizations 25
   The Teachers' Association 25
   Changes in the Teachers' Association during the 1960s 26
   The Early Union 29
   Union Issues 29
   Period of Organizational Conflict 32
   Organizational Merger 33
   The Strike Period 35
   The 1973 Contract Negotiations 35
   The Strike 41
   The Strike Settlement 46
   Impact of the Strike 47
   The Poststrike Period 49
   Issues during the Poststrike Period 51
   Changes in Administration 54
   The Union in the 1970s 56
   Organizational Structure and Leadership 56
   Membership Participation and Support 62
   Degree of Organizational Solidarity 63
   Relationships of the CFC to the Statewide Organization 64

The Late 1970s		65
Negotiations: 1976 and 1979		65
Noncontractual Gains		68
Discussion and Analysis of the CFC Position in the Late 1970s		75
Cedarton in 1979		83
3 MIDDLEBURY		**87**
Background		88
Teachers' Organizations		95
Changes in the Teachers' Organization		95
Attempts toward Professional Negotiations		96
The Move toward Unionization		100
Union Leadership and Factionalism		102
The Late 1960s and Early 1970s		105
Negotiations in the Late 1960s		105
Changing External Conditions		109
Changes in Union Goals and Leadership		113
The Strike Period		114
Contract Negotiations in 1972 and 1973: Underlying Issues		114
The Conduct of Negotiations in 1973		117
The Strike		120
Administrators' Reactions during the Strike		123
Community Relations during the Strike		124
The Strike Settlement		126
Impact of the Strike		128
The Poststrike Period		129
The Union in the 1970s		132
Organizational Structure and Leadership		132
Membership Participation and Factionalism		137
Relationship of the MTF to the Statewide Organization		138
Union Issues in the Middle and Late 1970s		140
The Late 1970s		142
Negotiations: 1976 and 1979		142
Noncontractual Developments		144
Discussion and Analysis of the MFT Position in the Late 1970s		148
The Teacher Center		160
Middlebury in 1979		161

4 OAKVILLE	**165**
Background	166
Teachers' Organizations	169
Negotiations and Bargaining Issues, 1968-1973	172
The Early 1970s	175
The Union in the 1970s	177
Middle and Late 1970s	179
Changes in Administration	179
Administrator-Staff Relations	181
Negotiations in the Late 1970s	182
Oakville in 1979	**184**
5 CONCLUSIONS: CHANGES AND IMPACTS	**187**
Changes in the Unions	**187**
The Rise of Teacher Militancy	188
The Logic of Unionization	191
Early Union Goals	192
Changes in Union Goals	194
District Differences in Sustaining Professional Goals	198
Analysis of Different Union Patterns in Middlebury and Cedarton	199
Impact of the Unions on Teachers	**203**
Impact of the Unions on the School System	**207**
Union Impact on School Management	207
Teacher Participation in School Decisions	214
The Issue of Teacher Protection	217
Overview	225
APPENDIX	**227**
Table 1 – Membership in Teachers' Organizations: Percentage Changes from 1969 to 1979	229
Table 2 – Union Activism: Percentages of Members Very Active in Unions, 1969 and 1979	229
Table 3 – Teacher Participation and Support for Strikes in Early 1970s: Percentage Distributions by School District	230
Table 4 – Activists' Perceptions of Organizational Emphasis on Various Issues: Percentages Reporting Emphasis on Each Issue, 1969 and 1979	231

Table 5 — Activists' Perceptions of Organizational Emphasis on Various Issues: Percentages Reporting "Much Emphasis" in 1979   232

Table 6 — Members' Perceptions of Organizational Emphasis on Various Issues: Percentages Reporting "Much Emphasis" in 1979   233

Table 7 — Activists' Perceptions of Organizational Effectiveness in Various Areas: Percentages Reporting Own Organization as Effective, 1969 and 1979   234

Table 8 — Members' Perceptions of Organizational Effectiveness in Various Areas: Percentages Reporting Own Organization as Effective, 1969 and 1979   235

Table 9 — Teacher Perceptions of Changes in Welfare and Working Conditions since 1969 — by School District: Percentages Indicating Changes in Each Direction   236

Table 10 — Teacher Perceptions of Changes in Relations with Administrators and School Boards since 1969 — by School District and Grade Level Taught: Percentages Indicating Changes in Each Direction   237

Table 11 — Teacher Perceptions of Changes in Quality of Staff and Staff Participation in School Decisions since 1969 — by School District and Grade Level Taught: Percentages Indicating Changes in Each Direction   238

Table 12 — Ideological Orientations of Union Activists, Comparisons between 1969 and 1979: Percentage Distributions on a Liberalism-Conservatism Scale   239

Table 13 — Ideological Orientations of District Teaching Staffs, Comparisons between 1969 and 1979: Percentage Distributions on a Liberalism-Conservatism Scale   239

REFERENCES   241

ABOUT THE AUTHOR   245

1

INTRODUCTION

Twenty-five years ago, 5,000 New York City teachers went on strike for a day for the right to "collective bargaining." A year later, the United Federation of Teachers (UFT), newly affiliated with the American Federation of Teachers (AFT) and the AFL-CIO, won an election according it the right to represent New York teachers, and in 1962, the UFT called a strike supported by more than 20,000 city teachers. While teachers' unions had been in existence since the turn of the century, it was not until the 1960s that *most* teachers within a given district voted for union representation and supported a strike, or that a school district formally established collective bargaining with teachers.

These events were the starting point of a major transformation in teachers' organizational orientations throughout the United States. The number of teachers affiliated with the American Federation of Teachers and organized labor increased, nationally, from about 56,000 in 1960 to 450,000 in 1979 (Bureau of Labor Statistics 1980). Teachers' strikes have become far more common, increasing from only five in 1965 to 138 in 1976 (National Center for Education Statistics 1978). Most states now have collective bargaining legislation mandating a negotiated contract between local school boards and public school teachers. Furthermore, teachers' organizations affiliated with the National Education Association (NEA), while not identifying themselves as "unions," began in the late 1960s to act more and more like their union counterparts, using the same mechanisms of bargaining, contracts, and strikes to attain similar goals.

Such changes have not been generally well received by the public, and the public image of the teacher as a "dedicated professional" has consequently suffered. Most laymen — as well as many school board members, administrators, and even teachers — have failed to understand either the kinds of concerns underlying the teacher movement or the social conditions affecting its development. The popular assumption has been that initial motivations for the movement were purely economic, and that teachers' claims regarding broader concerns were only "window dressing" designed to attract public sympathy for their cause. Such skepticism has caused many to view teachers' unions with suspicion, to blame a wide variety of school problems on unionism, and to become increasingly critical — even bitter — toward teachers.

The real issues underlying the teacher movement are, in fact, deeper and more complex than most people have recognized. The purpose of this book is to provide insights into the situations, events, and concerns that gave rise to the teacher movement in the 1960s and that pressed it toward changes during the 1970s. The issues initially at stake included not only salaries — which, by comparison to similar professions, were excedingly low in 1960 — but also heavy workloads. In addition — and perhaps even more important to the movement — were teachers' feelings of being subject to unfair, arbitrary treatment by administrators and school boards, and their sense of powerlessness in influencing decisions that affected their teaching environments. Such problems contributed to low teacher morale, frustration, and to the anger that led to their militancy.

The focus of this study is upon the origins and development of teacher unionism in three small suburban and rural school districts between the mid-1960s and late 1970s — districts one would not have expected to have been prone to militancy. Teacher unionism is generally assumed to be an urban phenomenon, and in fact, teacher unionization has been more common and more often studied in large, urban school districts. However, teachers in smaller districts have also frequently unionized, and even conducted major strikes, in spite of their more conservative leanings. A major advantage of selecting small districts for study is that the key issues, participants, and events are more easily identified than in larger districts, where the picture becomes more complicated. Put another way, in small districts such as those studied here, the human aspects of the struggle are more readily highlighted.

THE BACKGROUND LITERATURE
AND RESEARCH QUESTIONS

In spite of an extensive literature on teacher unionism, our understanding of the phenomenon is, in fact, still very limited. The bulk of the literature consists of impressionistic accounts or polemics reflecting strong biases for or against unionism; research-based inquiries into the nature of the movement have been far fewer. Furthermore, a large number of the research studies have addressed questions primarily related to teacher motivations for supporting unionism and strikes and the social correlates of such support (Cole 1969; Rosenthal 1969; Corwin 1970; Jessup 1971, 1978; Waganaar 1974; Ritterband 1974; Bruno and Nelken 1975; Nasstrom and Brelsford 1976; Fox and Wince 1976). Or, they have analyzed teachers' strikes, but not unions (for example, Vagts and Stone 1969). Research on the development of the movement has been limited mainly to studies of collective bargaining and its impact (for example, Perry and Wildman 1970; McDonnell and Pasal 1979; Retsinas 1982; Johnson 1983), with a large number of such studies focusing on questions of economic impact only (Kasper 1970; Thornton 1971; Baird and Landon 1972; Lipsky and Drotning 1973; Gustman and Segal 1978; Holmes 1979). Some studies, such as Ravitch (1974) and Grimshaw (1979), have considered unionism in its relation to other historical and political developments within school systems, but their focus has been upon analysis of these broader developments, not on understanding the dynamics of the union movement itself. Others, such as Donley (1976) focus more directly upon the movement, but more in terms of its early history and broad national trends than upon its recent development or organizational dynamics. Kerchner and Mitchell (1981) have systematically analyzed the development and impact of collective bargaining relationships, but they do not examine changes in, or the impact of, unions as organizations in respect to their goals, leadership, or other activities. To date, there has been no systematic research investigating changes within unions or of how unions operate within school systems.

My interest in analyzing changes in the teacher union movement derives from the observation that there may be inherent contradictions in the forces motivating and sustaining the movement (see Lortie 1975; Cooper and Bussey 1980). These contradictions are evident in much of the research cited above. For example, both

Rosenthal (1969) and Corwin (1970) suggest the importance of substantive educational concerns and teachers' desire to strengthen their professional authority within school systems as important factors helping to mobilize teacher militancy. Yet research by others (for example, Perry and Wildman 1970) indicates that collective bargaining settlements have generally not given such issues priority. Such contradictions between claims of teacher concern for educational issues and actual contract provisions have led some critics (for example, Dreeben 1972) to conclude that teachers were either not genuinely concerned with such issues or that these concerns bore no significant relation to their militancy.

My own, earlier work (see Jessup 1978) suggested that teacher expressions of concern for educational and authority-related issues may indeed have been genuine and relevant to their militancy, but that both the teacher organizations and the collective bargaining process are subject to internal and external constraints that restrict or alter the direction of union activity. Such constraints include, for example, the political necessity for the organization to build and sustain a large, supportive membership and to develop membership solidarity. The need to establish solidarity may tend to relegate complex educational issues (on which teachers differ widely) to lower levels of organizational priority simply because economic issues provide a clearer basis for consensus within the organization. Lortie (1973) has suggested that economic issues may represent the relatively narrow "common denominator" on which all teachers can agree, given the wide variety of occupational roles and interests represented within their ranks.

Another limit to what teachers' organizations can accomplish is the fact that school boards have generally refused to acknowledge educational program or policy issues as legitimate matters for negotiation. They have staunchly defended their own ultimate authority over school system decision making against any inroads by teacher groups (see Kerchner and Mitchell 1981). These attitudes within school boards serve to discourage teachers' organizations from assigning priority to educational or authority issues because doing so inevitably leads to impasse. Because teacher organizations cannot survive without some measure of success in negotiations, leaders focus their energies more on the kinds of issues for which bargaining is likely to yield tangible results.

As a consequence of such constraints, we would expect shifts in organizational activity and goals to occur in order that some goals be met. However, we would also expect the educational and professional concerns identified by Corwin, Rosenthal, and me to remain viable among at least some members of the organization, especially if these concerns were an original impetus to teacher unionization. Teacher organizations may, therefore, be subject to continuing demands from within their own membership to respond to such concerns.

These observations concerning probable contradictory pressures affecting teacher organizations raise a number of questions concerning the development of the teacher movement over time. Have teacher organizations modified their goals? If so, in what ways, for what reasons, and with what outcomes? Have underlying issues changed? For example, do teachers continue to express concern over educational and authority issues within the framework of their organizations, and, if so, under what conditions and with what outcomes? What has been the impact of organized teacher militancy upon the actual operation of school systems? Have there been changes, for example, in authority relationships between teachers and administrators? Lortie (1973) has stressed the need for intensive research addressing such questions. Research into these kinds of questions can contribute not only to improved understanding of the dynamics of teacher organizations but also to a better general understanding of problems teachers face and of the internal dynamics of local school systems.

DATA AND METHODS

The research is based upon intensive study of teachers' organizations in three small school districts located in southern New York State. The study was conducted in two phases: the first phase in 1968-69, with a more detailed follow-up in 1978-79. My original selection of school districts was based upon the presence of union chapters (affiliated with the AFT) in each of them since 1967, when unionization outside large city school districts was still uncommon.

Data were drawn from several sources. Mailed questionnaires were administered to teachers in all three districts in both 1969 and 1979. The 1969 survey sample consisted of 270, representing over 50 percent of the teaching staff in each district. The 1979 sample consisted of 207, representing over 50 percent of all teachers in two districts and 39 percent in the third. The lower response rate in the third district is attributed to the greater sensitivity of that staff to investigation because of a general insecurity described in the case study.

At both phases of the study, interviews were conducted with leaders of teachers' organizations, rank-and-file members, and significant informal teacher leaders. In 1968-69, 21 such interviews were conducted, and 37 were conducted in 1978-79. In the second phase (1978-79) interviews were also conducted with 20 school administrators and 25 school board members. Four outside respondents (two attorneys and two representatives from New York State United Teachers) were also interviewed in 1979, making a total of 86 interviews in 1978-79. The interviews were in-depth and semistructured, utilizing probing techniques. Most lasted from one to two hours, and a few lasted as long as five hours. The research also included examination of pertinent union documents, including contracts, mediators' reports, and various memoranda pertaining to contract negotiations. The results of these investigations are organized into three comparative case studies.

Names of the school districts and principal actors have been changed in order to provide anonymity. The school districts are called Cedarton, Middlebury, and Oakville. All fictitious names of people are marked with an asterisk.

A THEORETICAL FRAMEWORK

We will be focusing attention in the case studies upon changes in the unions in three general areas: the nature of organizational goals, the nature of leadership, and the union's role in the school system. In a later chapter, we shall also address questions related to the impact of the unions upon the school systems.

The analysis of change and impact presented in these chapters draws upon a theoretical framework that views local unions within the context of their organizational, social, and economic environments, for example, in terms of external and internal pressures exerted upon them beyond their own members' control. In comparing the three unions, I will attempt to show how such pressures interacted with deliberate organizational choices to produce at some times similar, at other times different, outcomes.

This theoretical framework takes into consideration a description of the teachers' union as an organizational type, the union's external environment (the school district), its organizational goals, structural constraints within the union itself, and its impact on the school system in which it exists.

The Teachers' Union as an Organizational Type

A teachers' union is an occupational association attached to an institution (a school system) where relatively highly trained, semiprofessional personnel constitute a majority of the staff, but it is also linked either informally or by formal affiliation to state and national labor organizations in which, traditionally, most members have not had professional or semiprofessional status. In this respect (and perhaps mainly in this respect), it differs from the traditional teachers' association, which was affiliated with a national organization (the NEA) composed entirely of professionally trained educators. As a labor union, members are by definition employed by the host institution to which it is attached (the school system), and issues relating to conditions of employment in the school district are the central reason for the union's existence. Its main function is to mobilize employees within the workplace in order to exert pressures on school managers to improve unsatisfactory conditions and to maintain those which are satisfactory. The labor union is, thus, an organization that stands essentially in opposition to management, that is, in a conflict relationship. Such a relationship represents a distinct departure from what had been established in the older, "professional" teachers' associations where teacher-administrator relationships were traditionally defined as sharing common concerns.

The External Environment

Of central importance in analysis of the teachers' union is the local school system, as the occupational site where union members are employed, including its administration, with whom the union must deal in the handling of routine activities, and its school board, as the agent with whom it must negotiate to attain its goals. Another important part of this external environment is the community that contains the school system, whose residents raise taxes to support it and elect school board members to manage it.

Significant outside organizations directly influencing the union include state legal structures, the union's "parent" organizations at the state and national levels, parallel organizations, and competing teachers' organizations. State legal structures pass legislation that can be viewed as both influencing the goals and activities of the teachers' unions and resulting from them. Of key importance here is New York's Taylor Law, enacted in 1967, which mandated collective negotiations for all public employees, established grievance and mediation mechanisms, and prohibited teacher strikes. This legislation was an outcome of lobbying by major public employee organizations within the state. It also influenced the content of bargaining by setting guidelines for negotiations. Parent organizations — the AFT and its state affiliate, New York State United Teachers (NYSUT) — influenced the emergence of the unions we shall be examining by offering an alternative to the NEA. They also influenced local teachers' perceptions of what constituted legitimate union goals and provided direct support in handling grievances and in negotiations. Parallel organizations — other local unions — provided supportive and informal networks. Competing organizations — usually, local teachers' associations maintaining affiliation with the NEA — exerted pressure on local unions to justify their goals and activities, in competition for membership.

The relationships of each local union to these various outside groups are also importantly affected by broad social trends. These include economic conditions, population shifts, and changes in social attitudes. An atmosphere of economic scarcity threatens teachers' job security and constrains school boards to grant fewer benefits in bargaining. Population shifts affect the growth and stability of the school system. In New York State, population mobility out of the state combined with a declining birth rate produced declining student enrollments leading to substantial retrenchment of teacher positions — an important circumstance in two of the districts studied.

Changing social attitudes also have special significance, in view of the high vulnerability of school systems to public pressure arising from local community control (Selznick 1949; Sieber 1967).

Changing perceptions of the adequacy of school programs and competency of the teaching faculty exert pressure on school boards to conduct more stringent evaluations, to be more cautious in granting tenure, and, in some cases, to press for dismissal of tenured teachers. Such actions raise teacher sensitivity and are likely to produce tensions between teachers, administrators, and school boards.

Within the more immediate school environments, special problems arise in respect to authority relations between administrators and teachers, both in terms of creating pressures toward teacher unionization or other forms of militancy and in terms of tensions arising from such militancy. One such problem relevant to this study is the decreased accessibility of administrators to teachers that accompanied the school system expansion during the 1960s. Ambiguity and conflict in authority relations between administrators and teachers also arise because teaching is a partially, but not completely, professionalized occupation that takes place in a partially bureaucratized organization where spheres of authority have not been clearly defined (see Gouldner 1954; Blau and Scott 1962; Corwin 1965, 1970; Dreeben 1973). Such tensions contribute, as Corwin (1970) noted, to increased teacher dissatisfaction and militancy. We may also expect to find new tensions produced in some instances as a result of increased teacher militancy, arising from the more adversarial stance of unionized teachers toward administrators.

Organizational Goals

Because the major, original purpose of the union is to mobilize workers to maintain satisfactory, and change unsatisfactory, conditions related to their work, an understanding of the nature of the goals for which they believe they mobilize becomes central to understanding the organization. Two traditions influence members' definitions of legitimate goals for a teachers' union: the labor union tradition, having an ideology emphasizing broad social goals, particularly stressing the importance of raising workers' consciousness and energies to press collectively for improvement in their own work situations (Cole 1969), and the professional tradition, having an ideology stressing the importance of service to clients (in this case, students) and responsibility of the occupational group for the quality of this service (Goode 1973).

Historically, workers in professional and semiprofessional occupations have, in fact, pursued goals associated with both these traditions (Carr-Saunders and Wilson 1933). Nevertheless, the two sets of goals are at times incompatible because, it has been argued, the pursuit of ends associated with self-interest is contradictory to norms emphasizing service to others (Parsons 1951). On the one hand, teachers are particularly vulnerable (and sensitive) to public criticism for pursuing self-interested goals, because of their marginal status as professionals; furthermore, they have real, client-centered concerns associated with strains in their teaching situation. On the other hand, they have only recently come to the collective realization that their economic status is lower than that of other occupational groups having similar levels of training and that the economic differential can in large part be attributed to other workers' having claimed more for themselves (Cole 1969). Thus, a new ethic at times conflicts with the service ethic, which emphasizes client welfare.

The teachers' union is, therefore, faced with pressures from within its own ranks to emphasize both teacher welfare and client-service goals. Contradictions between these goals are less easily resolved than in professional associations (such as the American Medical Association or the American Bar Association) that govern their own affairs because the teacher union's success in achieving its goals depends ultimately upon convincing management of the desirability of these goals. Under circumstances in which public distrust and budget exigencies severely limit the possibility of making arrangements that satisfactorily balance various interests, resolution will be especially difficult. The union is, therefore, forced into a defensive position in reconciling inherent contradictions in its goals. This defensive position becomes an important factor in the union's determination of priorities.

Other reasons also cause conflicting organizational goals (Perrow 1970). In addition to fulfilling organizational purposes of the types just identified, unions must concern themselves, on the one hand, with establishing and sustaining relations to external organizations (such as engaging in negotiations and attending state conventions) and, on the other, with maintaining the stability and continuity of the organization itself (such as building and sustaining membership). These different sets of goals often tend to come into conflict. Goals related to maintaining the organization (for example, avoidance of dissension among membership ranks) may constrain leaders to be cautious, avoiding risks that may be necessary to attain stated organizational goals (for example, strengthening teacher voice in policy making). Conflicts may also arise simply because of limits of time and energy. Differences in how such conflicting goals are handled by union leaders will be an important theme in this inquiry.

Internal Structural Constraints

Special problems arise for the union because it is a voluntary, democratic, and independent association, yet it has to establish a power base and long-range stability in order to achieve its goals. These imperatives impinge upon it in ways that can be expected ultimately to transform the organization, in terms of both its structure and goals, to an entity considerably less democratic and more conservative and narrow in focus than that originally envisioned or even currently desired by its members.

As in all voluntary associations, membership enrollment and participation are routinely problematic for the organization (Barber 1950). Unions, however, have a further problem in this respect in that membership support is interpreted as a sign of its potential to mobilize employees to strike or otherwise collectively oppose management. Because the union's bargaining power in negotiations with management rests ultimately on management perceptions of its potential to strike, the relative size of the membership base is a crucial factor, and building membership takes on major importance as an organizational goal, often taking priority over stated goals (Michels 1962).

The principle of democracy has a special tradition in the labor movement. Yet in practice, most labor unions (like most voluntary associations) tend toward oligarchy in their top leadership (Michels 1962; Barber 1950). This tendency arises initially from difficulties in recruiting members to leadership roles and from the organization's need to maintain leaders who have developed experience and expertise in handling its affairs (Michels 1962; Barber 1950). Leaders who develop such expertise come to enjoy special status within their occupational group and are, thus, motivated to maintain their positions. In order to maintain its legitimacy as a democratic organization, the leadership must respond to its membership on issues of importance to the latter. Both the semblance of democracy and membership solidarity are of crucial importance because the union leadership is particularly vulnerable to criticism from management and from the competing employee organizations. However, because union members have other (family and occupational) primary role obligations (Gouldner 1947) and because their participation in the union is voluntary, attendance at meetings is always problematic. In fact, decisions generally are made by a small leadership group and are only presented on occasion to the membership for ratification. Furthermore, mechanisms for the expression of dissenting views are not encouraged because of the importance of maintaining a semblance of unity on ideological issues. Membership input in determining union activity and goals, therefore, tends to be low.

In principle, the local teachers' union has a high measure of autonomy in determining its goals and activities in accordance with district problems. It may, in principle, be chartered as an independent union or it may affiliate with the AFT, its parent organization, the AFL-CIO, and the state subsidiaries of these two organizations. Because union locals exist within hostile environments (Michels 1962), almost all elect to affiliate with these larger unions for external support in building their power. In doing so, however, their autonomy is eroded. Local union leaders tend to depend on state and national "experts" for advice in determining goals, tactics, and the legitimacy of issues brought to the bargaining table. These experts generally have earned their status through experience in organizing industrial labor unions — not in teaching. Thus, they have little familiarity with classroom and authority-related problems peculiar to teaching, and tend to take a perspective emphasizing features of the teaching situation held in common with industrial workers (Cole 1969). This perspective not only minimizes the importance of problems specific to teachers, thus diverting the local union from attending to such concerns in setting priorities among goals, it also emphasizes the differences in interest between teachers (envisioned as labor) and administrators (management). In fact, teachers and administrators share many common interests and concerns by virtue of their training, their occupational purposes, and their common status as public employees in the communities they serve. The perception of labor-management dichotomy, however, imposed by a traditional labor perspective overlooks this commonality of interest.

These constraints — the need to build membership, the tendency toward oligarchy in leadership, and ties to larger labor organizations — combine to limit the union to those activities and goals for which membership unity and parent organization support can be most easily achieved. There is, thus, a tendency for the teachers' union to give most emphasis to conservative goals — that is, those that have traditionally been accepted as legitimate labor union goals — especially where teachers' job security is at stake. Such goals can also be expected to be accorded greater legitimacy by school boards in collective bargaining because they encroach less than professional goals on what school board members perceive to be their exclusive sphere of authority in formulating school district policy (Gross, Mason, and McEachern 1958). As a result, goals that have not traditionally fallen within the prerogative of labor (for example, decisions over policies affecting teaching processes) will tend to be neglected.

Such conservative tendencies may be attenuated, however, by other features in the organization's informal structure. These include:

unusual qualities in leadership (for example, a charismatic leader with strong personal commitment to professional goals may be able to sustain membership support for such goals even in the face of the above tendencies);
unusually strong commitment to professional norms among members of the union, influencing the degree of internal emphasis on professional goals;
mechanisms within the occupational community (Lipset, Trow, and Coleman 1956) for reinforcing professional commitment and/or clarifying issues of common concern (for example, opportunities for informal gathering of union members permitting extensive discussion of occupational problems or the formation of factions that mobilize support for particular issues within membership ranks). Such mechanisms enhance more democratic membership participation in the union because of the opportunity for more complete discussion of organizational issues.

Interplay among these factors can be expected to influence both the types of goals granted priority within the union and the extent to which goals related to sustaining the organization are given priority over stated organizational goals.

The Union's Impact on the School

The successful achievement of union goals may have both positive and negative consequences for the school system to which it is so closely tied. Positive consequences may result not only from achievement of educational (or professional) goals but also from achievement of teacher welfare goals. Desirable effects of the latter may be unanticipated and unrecognized (Merton 1936). For example, a possible positive effect of union efforts to protect job security may be that these efforts help to preserve small class sizes and certain specialized services. Protection of job security may also be important in terms of sustaining teacher morale. In these ways, the union may contribute to maintaining organizational stability — an important function in view of the school's vulnerability to public pressure. Achievement of union goals may also have negative consequences. Union contracts designed to protect teacher rights may include reduced flexibility in staff arrangements and thereby interfere with optimum program planning.

Questions arise concerning the impact of teacher unionism per se upon administrator and school board relations with teachers. Regardless of the union's success or failure in achieving its own goals, the degree to which it has been successful in establishing itself as an organization within the school system will in itself have an impact upon such relationships. For example, how does the union's adversarial relationship to school management affect day-to-day teacher-administrator relations? An organizational adversarial relationship might be expected to increase hostility and distrust in personal relations. It might also contribute to smoother relations in that it encourages teachers and administrators to clarify their respective spheres of authority. The presence of the union may serve further to constrain administrators to listen and attend more carefully to teachers' suggestions and complaints, because the administrators may wish to avoid confrontations with the union over teacher grievances.

Questions also arise about the impact of the union on the school when the union has been unsuccessful in achieving its stated goals. If formation of unions and collective bargaining procedures represent mechanisms through which the teaching staff may resolve unsatisfactory school conditions, what is the effect upon the staff when such mechanisms have not been effective? Do they continue to press for recognition of these issues as legitimate union goals, or do they develop alternate mechanisms for coping with such issues outside the union? How do unresolved issues affect teachers' support for the union, and how do they affect teacher-management relations — do they intensify hostility?

WHAT THE CASE STUDIES WILL SHOW

In the case studies that follow, we shall see how each of the teachers' organizations studied began as an undemanding "association" having rather limited purposes and how these associations began, during the 1960s, to initiate compliant, informal talks with their local school boards in order to convey their wishes concerning salaries and fringe benefits — in what Kerchner and Mitchell (1981) have called the "Meet and Confer" era. We shall then see how various external circumstances — proliferating bureaucracy, a hostile school board, and rising teacher expectations — induced association leaders to press for more substantial negotiating rights. We shall see how all three school boards resisted this pressure, insisting on maintaining "management prerogatives," and how school board resistance to negotiations was a major reason, in all three cases, for the rise of a teacher "union." The enactment of state legislation, mandating collective bargaining for teachers and specifying its content, eased board resistance to bargaining in only one of the three case studies; in the other two, the confrontation over bargaining resulted in an extended period of conflict between teachers and the boards. In the one case where initial bargaining relationships were better, conflict intensified over time, as the composition of the school board changed.†

---

†The parallels to Kerchner and Mitchell's (1981) "generational" phases are at times striking — especially in respect to the evolution of the teachers' organizations in their early stages and to alternating patterns of accommodation and conflict between teachers and boards (see also Mitchell et al. 1981). However, my findings do not indicate a high degree of consistency in the sequence of phases. In one case, for example, the first high conflict phase occurred several years after the onset of serious negotiations. In another case, the union moved gradually from one form of accommodation into another, without an intervening period of conflict. Leadership philosophies, as well as school board and community receptivity to the unions, appear to have contributed to varying

The period of conflict, in all three districts, included a teachers' strike — although the strikes varied in duration and intensity. A common theme in reasons for teachers striking was their desire to be recognized as equal partners in negotiating processes. In each case, the major strike issue was not economic, but a struggle over the scope of bargaining — again consistent with Kerchner and Mitchell's (1981) findings.

In all three cases, the strikes were followed by a period of increased polarization between teachers, school boards, and administrators. At various times, before or after the strikes, teachers' groups polarized from administrators, as well. By the late 1970s, we find, in all three, new patterns of greater accommodation emerging, with variations in degree and style.

We shall see how in all three cases, the unions themselves changed in response to external and internal pressures and circumstances. A particular focus of interest is the contrasting pattern of change between two of the districts — Cedarton and Middlebury — in respect to leadership, organizational goals, and definitions of the union's role in the school system. While both these districts were subject to fairly severe economic pressures (budget cuts and teacher retrenchment), we shall see in the case of Middlebury (our second case study) how professional and educational concerns emphasized by the union in the 1960s were eroded by economic pressures, internal organizational conflict, and community antagonisms, transforming what started out as an idealistic and professionally oriented union into a fairly traditional, protective labor organization by the late 1970s. By contrast, in Cedarton (our first case study), we shall see how different leadership patterns and a more receptive community enabled the union to more effectively balance educational and other professional concerns with teacher welfare concerns so that by the late 1970s, the union had established itself as an effective force contributing to district stability and aiding the articulation of teacher concerns with educational concerns in school district planning.

The third case study, Oakville, diverges somewhat from the first two in that it is a smaller, rural, school system, which underwent less drastic population changes. Teacher vulnerability to a hostile school board initially motivated unionization. Therefore, protective

---

patterns of accommodation and account for the difference between my findings and Kerchner and Mitchell's.

concerns were always paramount in Oakville. We shall see how, as school board hostility gradually subsided, the union, administrators, and school board developed informal patterns of accommodation in which union-management boundaries became less distinct.

We have noted that organizations develop, change, and act in interplay with forces in their environment. The stories of the three teacher unions that follow — of how they emerged and changed over time — portray a dynamic interaction between these three, small organizations and three sometimes recalcitrant, sometimes responsive school communities. Each story takes place against a backdrop of broad social developments — economic, demographic, and ideological — which seems at times to powerfully pervade individual, localized actions and events. To some extent, therefore, these appear to be stories of individual teacher leaders, administrators, and community leaders playing out their historic roles in response to a changing world beyond their control. We shall also see, however, how each of the three unions responded quite differently to external situations on the basis of deliberate, organizational choices. Differing styles of leadership and differing definitions of union functions and goals led to different patterns of union interaction with the school and community environment. Thus, in spite of many broad similarities in the development of these unions over time, we shall see that by the late 1970s each also developed its own distinct shape and direction.

2

CEDARTON

The story of the Cedarton teachers' union is a story of teachers' struggle for recognition as legitimate participants in decisions affecting their work and their welfare. This struggle took place within the context of rapid school district expansion. A small, informally run school was transformed within 15 years into a large, complex school system. Its rapid transformation was accompanied by multiple problems and increased public demands for budget tightening and teacher accountability. On the one hand, such problems and pressures combined with reduced avenues of communication with administrators to frustrate the teaching staff. On the other, teachers' rising consciousness of issues related to their own welfare — accelerated by the union movement elsewhere within the state and nation — sensitized them to the need for effective organizational representation.

This case study will show how school board resistance to recognizing the legitimacy of elected teacher representatives and their right to negotiate pushed a relatively conservative teaching faculty toward increasing militancy. It will show how a bitter strike that failed in terms of gaining its immediate objectives succeeded in terms of gaining community respect for the union and, ultimately, in gaining school board recognition of the union. The study will also show how the development of better relations between the school board and teachers' union following the strike allowed an ongoing dialogue between union, administrators, and the board to emerge. Despite severe external pressures on the school system during the 1970s — budgetary cutbacks, a sudden, unanticipated population decline following earlier expansion, and the necessity for teacher retrenchment — this dialogue became the basis for sustaining good staff-community relations and for the effective resolution of numerous internal problems.

By contrast to the Middlebury study, the Cedarton case study will show how the union moved gradually and consistently from an organization having a fairly traditional definition of purpose into a highly respected, effective, and professionally responsible organization that was able to successfully articulate teacher welfare functions with educational and professional concerns. The broader scope in effectiveness of this union can be attributed, in part, to its ability to sustain high caliber leadership and, in part, to leaders' ability to recognize and solve some basic problems neglected by leaders in Middlebury. Today, apart from effectively fulfilling its labor union functions, this union, called the Cedarton Faculty Congress, plays a major informal role in the successful operation of the school district.

BACKGROUND

Cedarton, until the mid-1950s, was a small, stable rural community lying beyond the suburban region surrounding New York City. A single school building accommodated all its pupils, from kindergarten through high school. In 1950, the school district had a total staff of about 30 teachers and a graduating class of 27 students. Through the early 1950s, the school system operated under a single administrator, a supervising principal named Victoria Long.* As the district expanded during the 1950s and 1960s, it hired additional administrators (mainly as building principals) but Long continued as chief school administrator through the late 1960s.

Respondents recalled Long's administration as a period when a spirit of mutual cooperation and sense of common purpose ("educating children") prevailed. Many characterized Long as an educator — in contrast to later administrators whom they viewed as more management and cost oriented. They reported her to have been highly respected within the community and the school and, therefore, able to exercise considerable personal authority while allowing extensive involvement of community and staff in school decisions.

As one respondent said:

> Miss Long was at the helm. She ran the district, but . . . she knew her teachers. To use a cornball expression, it was like a family. Everyone knew [everyone else]. . . . She involved you. . . . You felt you were part of something.

Long maintained good informal contact with teachers and was thereby well informed about school problems; she was also generally responsive to teacher concerns.

As long as the community remained stable, Long was in a position to deliver school board support for meeting school needs. Until the 1960s, few board members had more than a high school education, and those who did acknowledged Long as a professional educator and so deferred to her judgment in educational matters. Some respondents also noted that during most of Long's administration the importance of what was considered educationally sound could be taken for granted; concern for either costs or community reaction was minimal. Money for schools was relatively plentiful through the mid-1960s; the district's tax base, relative to expenditures, was favorable and real estate taxes were low. Interest groups opposing Long's educational philosophy had yet to emerge.

During the 1950s and early 1960s, suburban expansion in the New York City region caught up with Cedarton. Its large parcels of undeveloped land and its location near a major highway made the town ideal for mass real estate development. As several large, cheaply constructed developments were built during the late 1950s, the resultant influx of young, growing families struck the school system hard. "We just started to explode," stated one respondent. A new school building opened in 1955 to house the elementary grades, and by 1957 it was already on double session. By 1958, an annex to this building had been constructed and an additional elementary building had been opened; by 1961, Cedarton had added a third elementary school and a high school. Three more buildings were opened by 1969. Within 15 years, the school system expanded from one to seven buildings and from a student population of fewer than 500 to more than 5,000.

The district added many new teachers each year. Because teachers at that time were generally in short supply, many of those hired were young, inexperienced people who entered teaching with the intention of soon leaving to enter another career or to marry and have children. Thus, during the 1960s, the district experienced high staff turnover. An administrator respondent noted that he sometimes wondered how anything else got done — so much time was spent simply in hiring new personnel. Between 1954 and 1969, the total number of full time teachers in the Cedarton schools rose from 30 to more than 250.

With a larger faculty and more buildings came changes in district administration — not only a larger administrative staff, but also the nature of administrators, including Long herself, to maintain the kinds of personal contact previously established with the teaching staff; divisions between administrators and teachers became pronounced. During this period administrators also were in short supply. Rapid expansion of the district's administrative staff, therefore, resulted in a number of administrators being hired at the middle-management levels (as building principals) who had little administrative experience but little background in classroom teaching. Furthermore, there was considerable turnover among principals in this period, especially in the high school. These factors appear to have contributed to less effective management of school problems during the 1960s and early 1970s than might have been present under more experienced and stable administrative leadership at the building levels.

Population changes in the district affected the school board during the 1960s. High status, well-educated residents became increasingly dominant on Cedarton school boards. As an administrator put it, "You saw . . . (more) lawyers, IBM-ers, and less of the guy who worked for the Water Company." But there was also an influx of blue-collar families moving into the early residential developments, as the middle class vacated these for newer, more desirable housing. The new working class residents were in many ways similar (in income, education, and attitudes) to the "old guard" residents who predated district expansion. By the late 1960s, these two working class groups, combined, made up about half the district's population, with middle class residents making up the other half. Clearer division in community attitudes toward the schools began to emerge. A teacher respondent explained:

> You had two very different factions of people starting to play with this whole thing. People who were well educated, who wanted very, very high performance — great expectations, great accountability,

very business oriented. And you had a lot of other people who were very down to earth, in many cases less educated, less expectations . . . nuts and bolts people. . . . A lot of different attitudes about what education is or where it should be going, what it should cost, and what it should do.

School budgets rose sharply and were reflected in higher property taxes. Whereas middle class residents tended to be generally supportive of rising school expenditures as necessary for maintaining high standards, the working class segments of the community wanted school expenditures reduced. They became increasingly vocal, criticizing what they regarded as frills and featherbedding in school programs, staffing and salaries, and some "progressive" offerings. These groups never dominated either the school board or even audiences at open board meetings, but they had sufficient representation and were vocal enough that the board could not ignore them. Middle class residents, although generally more supportive of both school budgets and programs, had their own criticisms, and on certain issues were even more vocal than the working class — for example, on problems related to administration and student discipline in the high school. During the late 1960s, therefore, school board members were far more subject than their predecessors to community pressures both to control school expenditures and to assume accountability for what took place in the schools.

These changes profoundly affected the way the school board operated. Board members began increasingly to question Long's decisions. They found her informal administrative style inappropriate for a large district — outmoded in terms of modern management principles. Several apparently viewed the district as "out of control, needing direction" and felt that they, as a board, should exert more authority in running the district.

Several respondents who worked under Long commented on how these changes affected her ability to effectively administer the school system. One commented: "Toward the end, I think the growth of the district was overwhelming to her. She found it very tough. . . . The system was larger, less personalized, couldn't be a one-man show any more." Another said:

> Victoria was terribly effective at doing what she did the way she did it, but . . . things were definitely getting out of hand for her, out of control. She no longer could do what she did so well. She knew she

couldn't keep it together. There were bigger forces than she wanted to deal with or was able to deal with. It was very obvious to those who had been there that it was no longer her game, her place.

In 1968 Long retired early, by choice.

The school board deliberately sought to replace Long with a superintendent having extensive formal training in school administration and scientific management. They hired a relatively young man named Andrew Wilson* who had little previous administrative experience, but who held far better formal credentials than Long in terms of appropriate professional degrees. Wilson introduced management objectives to the school system. In direct contrast to Long's informal style, Wilson emphasized efficiency, coordination, organizational planning, and cost-oriented budgeting — in short, a more businesslike approach. A respondent described Wilson's administration as follows:

> He was very much a business manager. He represented the new breed. . . . It was a larger district, there were more teachers, more people concerned. He wanted to run it in a different way. . . . It was a drastic change. He tried to establish more firm and clear channels of communication, rules, evaluative procedures . . . accountability and all of that.

Many teachers viewed Wilson and the changes he brought with considerable resentment. They viewed the application of management principles to running the schools as inappropriate, preferring Long's more personal style and what they perceived as her greater availability, responsiveness, and more purely educational focus. Several respondents, however, noted that many changes associated with Wilson's administration were essentially related to the general direction of change in the district at the time — that it was so much larger, that costs were rising, that informal communication between teachers and administrators had begun to break down — so that introduction of a more formal administrative system was probably necessary.

Wilson was faced with many difficult problems. No groundwork had been set for a change in administration — Long had never delegated much responsibility. When she left, mistrust rapidly arose between teachers, administrators, and the school board. Problems also arose within the buildings related to the district's continued rapid growth: high staff turnover, curriculum changes, and student discipline. Such problems were especially severe in the high school. During Wilson's first year, two new buildings were opened. Finally, the district suffered its first school budget defeats (wherein the public voted against proposed school budgets) for two successive years right after Wilson arrived. This last factor, alone, imposed severe limitations on his administration, forcing a greater concern with the tax rate. In Wilson's second year, after a period of tremendous growth, the school board initiated some cuts in programs, services, and personnel.

TEACHERS' ORGANIZATIONS

The Teachers' Association

Even during the good years of Long's administration, and for as long as any respondent could recall, Cedarton had had a teachers' organization. Until 1973, it was a "Teachers' Association" affiliated with the NEA. Before the mid-1960s, it had been primarily a social organization, to which administrators as well as teachers belonged. It sponsored occasional speakers but had little involvement in local, district affairs and did not attempt to represent teacher interests per se except in the matter of salaries. Before the 1960s, there had been little need for a strong teachers' organization, because most personnel problems were resolved (by Long) on an informal, personal level. Even though a few cases were reported of teachers having been treated unfairly, such problems did not arise frequently during these years.

The officers of the association changed often — almost annually, circulating among an active group within the teaching staff, thus showing little stability either in the leadership group or in the occupants of particular positions.

In the early 1960s, the association formed a salary committee. This met annually with representatives of the school board to discuss teacher salaries for the following year — a privilege granted the association by the board as an extension of good will, and not in any sense formalized as a right. The committee offered salary proposals by way of suggestions — not as demands. Still, according to respondent recollections, salary discussions were at times quite heated.

The manner in which salaries were settled in those meetings clearly illustrates the authority Victoria Long exercised with the board. A former association officer who had served on the salary committee described her role as follows:

> The critical stage always came at the end. . . . Victoria never entered [the discussion] until the eleventh hour. Her timing was always perfect. She'd come in at the last hour and she'd say, "You're here, and you're there, and I'm telling you, *this* is fair. . . . This is how it's going to be."

Written contracts in the early 1960s were quite informal, containing little beyond salary schedules. Details about teaching duties and working conditions (for example, lunch duty, hall duty, playground duty, length of school day) were not included — they were simply understood to be what they had been in previous years. Board policy was regarded as more important than a contract, and the boards set their own policy, under Long's direction.

Changes in the Teachers' Association during the 1960s

During the 1960s, a number of changes took place in the Teachers' Association. The organization began to involve itself more directly in school district affairs. Its constitution was revised, on several occasions. It excluded administrators from membership in the association, as increased disparities between teacher and administrator interests became apparent. It made provisions to improve teacher representation and communication within the organization and the district by having more frequent membership meetings, by establishing building representatives as officers of the organization, and by instituting monthly meetings between association officers, the supervising principal, and board president. It also established simple, informal grievance procedures whereby teachers who felt in some way offended could present their cases before the school board. The association still had no grievance committee: what constituted a grievance was not clearly defined, and the final decision in resolving teacher complaints still lay strictly with the school board.

The association also attempted to play a more forceful role in contract negotiations, even before 1967 when formalized negotiations were first mandated by the New York State Taylor Law.

Particularly in connection with negotiations, the Cedarton Teachers' Association (CTA) began to establish stronger ties with the statewide branch of the NEA, its parent organization. The state branch (NYSTA) had begun to provide advisory services regarding contract negotiations to local teacher associations as early as 1965. Starting in the mid-1960s, the CTA invited NYSTA representatives to sit in, as consultants, on some negotiating sessions with the board.

Long found these developments distasteful. As the association pressed for more formal contract provisions, particularly after the Taylor Law, she left negotiations more and more to the school board. But the board, even after the enactment of the Taylor Law, did not take negotiations seriously. A respondent active on the association negotiating team in the late 1960s reported:

> They still had not made the transition from "This is what I'm offering you and if you don't like it that's tough" to "Now we have to talk about it and arrive at some kind of consensus." . . . They really dug in, constantly said, "Why should you think you have anything to say about that? You're just a teacher."

And now conflicts Long had previously resolved in good faith began to linger, causing teachers to become irritated. There was, for example, a conflict that focused upon protection of nontenured teachers. In the words of a former association officer:

> People were being dismissed for what we would have to challenge in terms of fairness. . . . I remember being in at least two or three major hassles over people who had been released, and by their records, had been treated unfairly. . . . And the board was always the final point. The best you could do with the board at that time was to get a reconsideration of the dismissal. They usually were quite good about reexamination, but they never reversed a decision.

Several of these dismissals were based on personality conflicts with administrators (particularly building principals). The problem, essentially, appeared to be that reasons for dismissal had never been specified, leaving ample room for discriminatory treatment. Although formal evaluation procedures were followed for all probationary (nontenured) teachers, some teachers who had consistently received good evaluations were denied tenure, and two teachers regarded by colleagues as fine teachers were denied tenure with no clear explanation. The association could not get any specific "language" protective of nontenured teachers written into the contract.

Although salary levels in Cedarton had been relatively high, salary increases for the school district were not keeping pace with increases elsewhere in the county. The salary issue became another area of conflict.

A third conflict area was class size. Teachers wanted clear restrictions on class size; board members strenuously resisted such restrictions, claiming that because class sizes crucially affected school budgets, the board had to reserve the flexibility to raise class sizes as necessary. To some teacher respondents, the board's attitude on class size was an indication of a shift in priorities from a primary concern with setting sound educational standards to a concern for the budget.

This period of growing dissatisfaction among the teaching staff reflected the problems associated with rapid growth and deteriorating teacher-administrator relations in the district. It was also a period when teacher organizations elsewhere were gaining strength. New York City and other school districts in the metropolitan area had already greatly improved their ability to protect and advance teacher interests through successful collective negotiations. Hence, the inability of Cedarton Teachers' Association to negotiate effectively to resolve key local issues became the focus of increasing criticism from within the organization's own ranks. Newer teachers, some of whom had taught in districts having stronger teachers' organizations before coming to Cedarton, were especially critical. A former association officer explained:

> They were critical, basically, because of the ineffectiveness of the traditional system. . . . The fact that you couldn't really negotiate anything that was worth a damn, or make changes that were dramatic enough to do anything for yourself. You literally were still at the mercy of someone's final say. . . . They knew there was another way.

Some of these critics began to talk union, perceiving the central factor in New York City teachers' success to have been their affiliation with organized labor. Most association members, however, were still resistant to the idea of union affiliation as unbecoming to their professional status, and they resisted its implied adversarial relationship with administrators and the board. In 1967, a small group of Cedarton teachers decided to break away from the CTA to form a union chapter affiliated with the American Federation of Teachers (AFT).

The Early Union

None of the teachers involved in founding the Cedarton Federation of Teachers (CFT) had been active in a teachers' union elsewhere, although all had been active, for at least a short while, in the Cedarton Teachers' Association. The influence of unionism from outside the district was, therefore, mainly felt through union literature they were beginning to read and through contacts they deliberately sought out.

In 1969, at the time data were first gathered for this research and two years after the founding of the union, the CFT had 33 members, from a teaching staff of more than 250. Most members were males teaching in the high school; many were relatively new to the district. It was, however, a very active membership. Attendance at meetings generally was about 30 — almost the equivalent of typical attendance at association meetings, although the latter group had about eight times the membership.

Those who assumed leadership roles in the union were, from the time of its founding, articulate people, highly respected by their colleagues. This characterization was offered by a wide range of respondents, including administrators and association officers as well as their own members. An administrator commented in 1969, "The people who organized the union were extremely capable people, and they had . . . a strong feeling for what they thought was important in their profession." An association officer maintained, "They were sharp people. They had good heads. They knew how to do what they were going to do." The Cedarton union's ability to maintain highly respected, able teachers in leadership positions later became a key factor in its gaining broader support. At the time of its emergence in 1967, however, Long, most of her administration, and the school board were offended by it and refused to give it credence.

Union Issues

Union activists interviewed in 1969 provided a wide variety of reasons for having founded the Cedarton union chapter. There were, however, important common themes. Central to these was the perception that teachers needed a stronger organization.

Union activists had two major criticisms of the association: its inability to negotiate what they regarded as an adequate contract, and its inability to protect teachers against arbitrary treatment and unfair dismissal. They attributed the weakness of the association's contract not only to its leaders' inability to negotiate effectively, but also to its reliance on outside advisors from their parent organization (NYSTA) who themselves had virtually no previous experience in negotiations. Furthermore, they believed most association leaders (at both local and state levels) maintained too close ties with administration, in terms of old loyalties, and were too steeped in paternalistic attitudes to permit them to stand firmly in opposition to administration in cases where teacher and administrator interests diverged.

By contrast, they felt that affiliation with the union would have two major advantages: first, that it would provide them access to advisors experienced in labor negotiations, and, second, that it would permit them to stand in opposition to administrators, where necessary — because the union was free of the traditional ties that limited the association and because differences in employee and management interests were more openly recognized by the union.

Most union activists I interviewed in Cedarton in 1969 openly expressed a strong welfare orientation in their discussion of union goals — meaning that they saw the central purpose of the union to be to improve teacher welfare through provision of better benefits, working conditions, and job protection.† These respondents, however, also reported other kinds of concerns to have been important to the formation of the union, and, in fact, all union activist respondents spent far more time and spoke with more intensity on these other concerns than they did on issues of welfare.

The nonwelfare issues union respondents raised centered mainly on problems related to school administration, including the following:

ineffective administrative leadership, particularly in the high school, where there had been a high level of turnover in the principal's position,

---

†See Table 4, Appendix. Note especially the contrast to Middlebury, where union activists in 1969 were less highly oriented to welfare issues.

inadequate channels of communication through which teachers might bring school problems at the classroom or building level to the attention of the superintendent and school board,

insufficient input by teachers in determining school district policies because of inadequate consultation with teachers on the part of administrators, and/or tendencies to ignore teacher recommendations, and

lack of appropriate administrative supervision and support for new, inexperienced teachers.

They attributed ineffective administrative leadership in part to inexperience and turnover in administrative personnel, but also, in larger part, to other factors. They felt most building principals were out of touch with classroom problems because they lacked adequate background in classroom teaching, were too far removed from the classroom, and were too subject to the authority of central administration and pressure from parents and school board members. They believed that a major key to improving administrative leadership, therefore, lay in making administrators more accountable to teachers, both through increasing teacher participation in their initial selection and through improving communication and teacher participation in school decision making.

The frequency with which union respondents offered similar explanations regarding such administrative problems indicated that the union had extensively discussed the points listed above. This critical perspective on administration constituted a strong motif appearing in all the interviews with union activists in Cedarton. Their goals were not, therefore, simply to improve teacher benefits and job protection; they wanted to change the structure of relations between teachers, administrators, and school boards. Many CFT activists identified themselves with an ideological current within the AFT at that time, emphasizing the importance of collegiality, or "democracy in the workplace." The first president of the CFT explained to me in 1969:

> The average teacher who was involved in founding the union also was very much concerned with having a voice — you must have heard this a thousand times — having a voice in actually running the school and helping to make policy decisions. This is to me the major issue. This is the reason why we came into existence. . . . We want to elect our

principals. We want to start gradually by electing our department chairmen; we finally want to elect our principals.

During the late 1960s and early 1970s, the union offered many specific proposals to the faculty and the school administration for meeting problems their members identified. In addition to specific suggestions for strengthening the contract in terms of improving teacher benefits, union proposals included suggestions for electing building principals and establishing a council composed of teachers, administrators, school board members, and students to formulate school district policy. For new teachers, the union advocated clearer evaluation procedures (to strengthen due process) and an internship program. In addition, it advocated reducing class size and suggested improvements in educational programs. Many of these proposals were ignored.

Period of Organizational Conflict

Shortly after the formation of the union in 1967, the new organization challenged the association by petitioning for a collective bargaining election. In accordance with the Taylor Law, the winning organization would represent all teachers in the bargaining unit in negotiations. On the first challenge, the union won approximately 30 percent of the vote, with its supporters appearing to have been concentrated mainly in the high school. From 1967 to 1972, the two organizations engaged in bitter conflict. During these years, the union initiated additional challenges, each time increasing its percentage of the vote. The association continued to retain a clear majority of the teaching staff and, therefore, remained the official bargaining agent. The union also continued to be sharply critical of association leaders for their weakness in negotiating contracts and in protecting teacher rights.

During these years, association leaders were, however, able to successfully negotiate many things the union pushed for, particularly in teacher welfare areas. An association officer reported, "Their arguments . . . often became the association's position." Between 1967 and 1972, association leaders were able to obtain an improved salary schedule and clearer delineation of teachers' duties. They were still, however, unable to obtain a satisfactory grievance procedure, and they were in other ways frustrated in negotiating a satisfactory contract. The board continued to resist any real "give and take" during negotiations and refused to negotiate many items that districts elsewhere were beginning to include in their contracts. On those items board members did negotiate, they insisted on so many qualifying phrases in contract wording (for example, wherever feasible, insofar as possible) that the matters spelled out continued largely to be within board discretion.

Association leaders felt unable to negotiate from a position of strength, because of divisions within the teaching staff. On the one hand, the association membership was divided about how strongly they should push the board in negotiations, with many old timers still reluctant to challenge traditional authority relations. On the other, increasing numbers of younger association members were defecting to the union because the association was not militant enough. An association officer explained:

> Any time it came to a crisis in negotiations — of whether you were going to accept the board's offer or whether you were willing to go the next step, to reject the board's offer — always, what it came to, when it came to a total show of forces we could never go the next step.... It was an extremely difficult thing to marshall any kind of militancy, any kind of force that would have had any real teeth to it.... The board knew the internal struggle that we had.... They knew we couldn't marshall the strength at any point to put our foot in the door and make it stick.

The NYSTA representatives whom they had invited as consultants were of no great help. An association activist reported: "NYSTA was totally ineffectual.... NYSTA representatives sat in on negotiations ... but they were totally unprepared. They didn't have bargaining experience. There weren't many people around who did."

Organizational Merger

Teachers' association leaders began to talk among themselves about the possibility of inviting their union opponents to join with them, for it was becoming increasingly obvious to some that the conflict between the two organizations was self-defeating. A representative of this viewpoint explained:

I saw that was the only direction that could help the district at that point. . . . It was not a hard decision for me. I felt their [union leaders] heads were pretty solid. These people were well-organized, respected members of the staff . . . and I saw the two [organizations] as having the same goals.

But others in the CTA strongly resisted making overtures to the union. A 1972 association officer reported:

It was a tough time for certain personalities because of their philosophical commitments. . . . Embracing a philosophy that had anything to do with unionism was very, very difficult to accept. . . . It was a blue-collar type thing, a working man's role, and how could you possibly equate yourself as a classroom teacher and a professional with an ordinary labor union?

In the winter of 1972, the union challenged the CTA again for collective bargaining representation, and this time came within eight votes of winning the election. The close vote apparently shook association leaders badly. They now had to face the possibility of losing in a subsequent challenge. This motivated many who had previously resisted the idea of merger with the union to change their position. The close vote also put the union in a difficult position, for under the Taylor Law it was restrained from making a further challenge for several years.

In the spring of 1972, the statewide affiliates of the NEA (NYSTA) and the AFT (ESTF) announced plans to join forces to form a single state teachers' organization. Anticipating the probable merger of their parent organizations, resistance to merger at the local level dropped substantially on both sides, and the memberships of both organizations voted to endorse consolidation.

Representatives of the two groups met to write a new constitution and to nominate a new slate of officers, deliberately drawing strong candidates from both former organizations. A resistant faction within the old association ran an opposing slate, but the merged slate won overwhelming faculty support in the election. The new organization was named the Cedarton Faculty Congress (CFC).

The man chosen as president of the CFC, a high school science teacher named James Nelson,* had formerly served as vice president of the union. Other union officers, including its former president, assumed key leadership positions within the new organization from the outset. By contrast, those who had assumed active roles within the association for the most part retired from leadership positions, with the result that the officers recruited for the merged organization from the association were more likely to be newer faces than those recruited from the union. Those identified with the union were, therefore, more visible to outsiders than those recruited from the association. Because of their greater experience in leadership positions and because most union people came from the high school, union activists may also have exerted a dominant influence within the new organization. Some outsiders — former resistant association supporters and some administrators — referred in our interviews to the change in leadership as a "union take-over." This criticism, however, was at no time offered by any respondents from within the new organization. Both organizational activists and rank-and-file members pointed out that the leaders had been democratically elected with overwhelming teacher support. Respondents also indicated that the strength of teacher support for these leaders reflected the esteem in which colleagues held the union officers.

THE STRIKE PERIOD

The 1973 Contract Negotiations

Negotiations for the next teacher contract began in January 1973. (The existing contract was due to expire on August 31.) CFC leaders were determined to obtain the best possible contract, in part, because former union activists now representing the CFC had been outspoken in their criticism of previous association contracts and, in part, because they felt their new organizational solidarity mandated a show of teacher strength. CFC leaders were also optimistic about the new organization's potential for protecting and enhancing the professional lives of rank-and-file teachers, and they perceived the contract as the vehicle for achieving these ends.

After soliciting suggestions from its membership, the CFC negotiating team compiled a 30-page document detailing proposals for changes in virtually every article of the existing contract. Major proposed changes were geared essentially toward strengthening contract provisions in the following areas:

improved financial benefits, including substantial increases in salaries and fringe benefits to bring these to a level commensurate with surrounding districts,

strengthening provisions for due process in areas of teacher grievances, teacher evaluation, and granting tenure,

assurance of job protection for all teachers, specifically through a "no reduction in force" clause,

clarifying job requirements and reducing workloads, including setting limits to class sizes, eliminating nonteaching duties (for example, playground duty, hall duty), setting limits to the number and length of required after-school meetings, and clarifying duties of nonteaching personnel (for example, guidance counselors, department heads),

professional involvement of teachers in decision making in a number of areas, including selection and evaluation of administrators, development of curriculum, determination of criteria for teacher evaluation, and programs for new teachers, and

a "Matters Not Covered" clause, in which the CFC sought school board agreement that it would make no changes in existing practices in areas not covered by the contract without previous negotiations with union representatives.

The Cedarton School Board, however, was under both external and internal pressures to take a firm stand. Recent budget defeats and criticism of the school system from conservative community sectors put pressure on the board not only to curtail school expenditures, but also to seek greater staff accountability to school managers. An administrator in close contact with the board during this period explained:

> Teachers had made tremendous strides with the beginning of the Taylor Law. Now . . . five years later, it was time to balance those gains and to take a strong position. . . . There was a good deal of that sentiment in the community, and it was represented . . . on the board.

A majority on the board at this time could be described as pro-education but conservative and business oriented in their philosophies of education and school administration. According to school board respondents, most members at that time believed strongly in maintaining management prerogatives in the hands of the board — a view strongly supported by Wilson.

The school board presented the CFC negotiating team with a series of counterproposals before even considering the teachers' demands. The board's proposals were less extensive than the CFC's, but were hard hitting in that they aimed not only to limit spending, but also to tighten controls over several areas of teachers' professional lives. Key board proposals included the following:

limiting existing teacher benefits — providing no across-the-board salary raises, eliminating automatic increments, reducing personal leave, and reducing sabbatical leaves,
a "merit pay" proposal — wherein previously automatic annual salary increments would become dependent upon the quality of teaching performance as determined by administrative evaluations,
making teachers accountable for preparation periods — requiring them to report to building principals regarding their utilization of time during what were currently free periods and empowering principals to assign extra professional duties during these periods,
more required meetings — specifying more frequent and longer after-school faculty meetings.

During negotiations the union was represented by a seven-member negotiating team, including most major officers of the CFC and a representative from New York State United Teachers. The NYSUT representative served mainly in an advisory capacity to the CFC, taking a back-seat role during negotiating sessions. Board members seldom met directly with the CFC team, and Wilson did not meet with them at all. In most negotiating sessions, the board was represented by two intermediaries: a New York State attorney specializing in labor relations and a member of the district's central administrative staff. Dealing largely through these intermediaries, the board rejected most of the union's proposals as falling outside the scope of mandatory negotiations under the Taylor Law, stating that it would not negotiate anything it was not compelled to. The Taylor Law specified that employees' wages, hours, and other conditions of employment were areas subject to negotiations between public employees and employee organizations. However, questions about what constituted "other conditions of employment" and where negotiations over these conditions intruded on powers granted to the board under other state laws left specific negotiating areas open to interpretation. (Court decisions and further legislation somewhat clarified these ambiguities in later years.)

The board proposals both angered teachers and put them in a defensive position, at a time when they had hoped to negotiate a contract which extended teacher benefits and rights. They were particularly upset with the merit pay recommendation, for they felt that it could not be administered fairly, given the limitations generally inherent in evaluating teacher competence and, especially, given the district's existing evaluation procedures that they had already suggested revamping. They also believed merit pay would introduce an undesirable element of competition into their ranks.

The board's refusal to negotiate many key teacher demands further angered them. Finally, lack of direct access to board members was frustrating to members of the CFC negotiating team, who reported they felt board members neither heard nor acknowledged their demands. A teacher respondent offered this perception: "It was really a refusal to deal with the union as a legitimate force, representative of teachers in the district, with legitimate concerns." Teacher respondents often expressed the belief that the board took a deliberately uncompromising position during the 1973 negotiations because it did not want to deal with a union affiliated with organized labor. A member of the CFC negotiating team described his view of the board's position as follows:

> The union had just gotten in and the board believed . . . that we didn't really represent teachers . . . because in the collective bargaining election, the union had lost. . . . They felt the union was a bad element they wanted to keep out of the county and out of Cedarton. I believe they pushed us because they believed if push came to shove, the teachers would not support the union.

Several respondents who had been on the 1973 school board admitted the board at that time held an antiunion bias. This was influenced in part by the business and managerial perspectives board members brought from their own occupational backgrounds. The 1973 board president explained:

> Because of the work I do in dealing with management and seeing labor able to exert strong pressures on management, I suspect I brought to the board an antilabor prejudice. . . . I think I view it more philosophically today, in that I recognize no rights and wrongs in the situation.

From school board respondents' viewpoint, the central issue, however, appears to have been more the protection of management prerogatives than a desire to break the union. One 1973 school board respondent articulated his position as follows:

> A school should not be run as a democracy or by consensus. . . . It's more akin to a business where you have an authoritative management and employees who perform according to the dictates of that management. . . . Our superintendent described to us some of the demands by the union as interfering with the authority — taking away management prerogatives. . . . At that point I thought he was right.

In February, the CFC withdrew some demands from the negotiating table, but none were items the board regarded as significant. The board did not withdraw any of its own demands. It asked the CFC to join in a request for outside mediation. The CFC refused on the grounds that a satisfactory agreement depended upon cooperation between the two parties, and that intervention by a third party would only delay this necessary cooperation. The board then unilaterally requested the state Public Employee Relations Board (PERB) to provide mediation. Two negotiating sessions were held in March with a PERB mediator who determined mediation could not be fruitful and referred the dispute to a PERB-appointed "fact-finder," who was empowered under the Taylor Law to inquire into the causes of disputes and to recommend bases for settlement. The Taylor Law grants the fact-finder authority to recommend contract settlements, but the recommendations are not binding upon either party in a dispute.

During March and early April, while fact-finding was still pending, the board clearly antagonized the union. It publicly announced, first, a decision to reorganize certain staff positions in the high school and, shortly after that, a decision to eliminate 17 teaching positions and certain supplementary positions from the budget for the 1973-74 school year. Both announcements were made without consulting either union representatives or teachers at large. These decisions angered both union leaders and rank-and-file teachers. For the board to have made such decisions unilaterally was a clear departure from the way in which things had been handled under Long's administration. More important, as the announced changes affected terms and conditions of employment and, therefore, were subject to negotiations, they undercut specific union proposals for the 1973 contract. Teachers, therefore, viewed the board announcements as a clear indication of its unwillingness to negotiate in good faith.

The board had the legal authority to make these changes unilaterally, for school boards may, but are not obligated to, negotiate questions of reduction in staff. The antagonizing factor to teachers was that the board made these announcements without consultation, in the face of the union's proposal that a no reduction in force clause be included in the contract under negotiation. The board's unwillingness even to explain its position to teachers seemed to them a clear indication of disrespect.

The fact-finder held hearings in April. He recommended the scope of negotiations be limited to only a few issues and recommended a compromise position on salary, teacher evaluation, and merit pay. Neither side, however, found the fact-finder's recommendations satisfactory as a basis for settlement.

Following the release of the fact-finder's report, the board conducted hearings for the purpose of legislating a contract — a right granted school boards under the Taylor Law at that time. At this point, the CFC withdrew a substantial number of their demands, eliminating almost one-third of their proposals, because it had become clear to the CFC that the board would not negotiate anything that it was not compelled to by law and that the board was determined to make inroads upon the existing contract. Now it became clear to them that they would have to defend not only their existing contract rights, but their right to negotiate at all. They, thus, focused upon only those demands that were clearly negotiable under the law. At this stage, therefore, they dropped their demands related to professional involvement along with a number of other items the board had insisted were nonnegotiable.

After hearing revised proposals from both the union and the district superintendent, the board stopped trying to legislate a contract and determined simply to extend the existing contract for one year without changes. The union found this extension unacceptable, for once again the board had failed to negotiate. The school board then issued a memorandum stating it would be willing to extend the current contract to three years, if the union would accept merit pay as a condition of the new contract. Even though this was clearly unacceptable, the CFC saw it as an opportunity to reopen negotiations — board and CFC representatives had not met in a negotiating session since they had sat down with the mediator in March. The CFC requested the board to have its representatives meet with theirs. The board, however, did not respond to the CFC's request until the middle of September, by which time the current contract had already expired. The board now withdrew its demand for merit pay, but on the condition that the union drop its demands for strengthening grievance procedures; the board continued to insist that teachers be made accountable to administrators for their use of preparation periods. On the matter of salary, the board now agreed to an across-the-board increase of 3½ percent, but this was well below 1973 contract settlements in surrounding districts and below the fact-finder's recommendation, which had been 5½ percent. Thus, the union found the board's offer still unacceptable.

Shortly after the opening of school in September 1973, the CFC held a membership meeting in which the Cedarton teachers determined to strike. The vote was overwhelmingly in favor of the strike action. While some teachers abstained, over 95 percent of those voting supported a strike.

The Strike

Some respondents thought the board had deliberately provoked the strike. Others thought union leaders wanted a strike as a means of strengthening their organization. What seems more likely is that the strike occurred as an outcome of the determination of both groups to dig in and assert their respective positions — that is, the board's desire to establish its authority over the school district clashed with teachers' desire for recognition of their right to negotiate. The following comment by the president of the 1973 school board supports this interpretation:

> Most of the board members were strong personalities who felt confident in their own abilities. . . . Most had the strength to follow through on their conclusions, despite the fact that it would generate controversy. . . . We took specific issues, and we said, "Will we take a strike if the union doesn't agree to this issue?" And on certain issues, we decided yes, we would take a strike.

Teachers were angry — over the board's refusal to negotiate in good faith, the merit pay proposal, the tone of its contract demands, and the arrogance board members exhibited at public meetings and in the press. A rank-and-file union member explained, "The spirit was, we're going to band together and not take this kind of treatment." For the first time, the teachers' organization had a unified membership to support a strong stand.

Over 90 percent of the teaching staff actually stayed away from work, and most also walked the picket line. A former association president commented:

> The board was putting us under tremendous pressure at that time. It had been such a frustration, for so many years, to see ourselves so divided. . . . To me, the most significant thing was to see teachers work collectively. We saw people who were part of the old guard, who never would have embraced the merger, support the strike.

Once the strike was under way, the issues changed on both sides. Taking full advantage of the Taylor Law's prohibition against strikes, the board acted quickly to halt it. They not only imposed the law's two-for-one salary penalties (a fine of two days' pay for every day on strike), but also served 22 teachers (including many rank-and-file members along with CFC leaders) with injunctions to appear in court. Ten days later, all 22 were sentenced to jail, with terms ranging from 15 to 30 days. Teachers were escorted from the courtroom by armed guards, fingerprinted, and taken away in paddy wagons to the county jail. This was the harshest treatment ever given rank-and-file teachers for striking within New York State. A New York *Times* report on the Cedarton case, dated October 4, 1973, notes that until this occasion, school boards had been reluctant to utilize the courts in their disputes with teachers. The school board declined the opportunity to make a plea to the court for leniency, as it might have done. A 1973 school board member commented:

We were asked by the judge if we wanted to make a statement to him before sentence was imposed. We went around the room and we considered the possibility of jail sentences. It was surprising to me — people that were on the board elected on proeducation platforms . . . — some of them felt that if jail sentence was a possibility, the board should strive for the harshest possible sentence. . . . The final decision taken was that we shouldn't ask for a jail sentence, but that we should not do anything to weaken our position.

NYSUT attorneys providing legal assistance to the 22 teachers appealed the sentences as imposing excessive penalties and had them substantially reduced. But the initial jailing served to dramatize the board's punitive stance, and rather than having the intended effect of cutting the strike short, the board's action heightened teachers' anger and boosted their determination to hold when financial and other pressures might otherwise have induced many to return to work.

In addition to invoking the penalties available under the law, board members publicly denounced the union at meetings and in the press. A rank-and-file teacher explained:

They accused us of having the union heavies running the show. . . . We tried to get some of the board members to meet, to talk, but . . . it was always "the Union, the Union, the Union," as if it were some kind of five-headed monster. It turned out the board president was going to save the district from the . . . unionization that was going to ruin public education. That's really what the issue came to. It didn't matter about us. Instead of trying to negotiate, what they did was to see what they could do to wreck us.

Far from its leaders being union heavies, almost all teacher and administrator respondents commented on the quality of leadership exercised by CFC as exceptionally responsible. The union president, James Nelson, was described as a strong, level-headed leader who communicated very well with the membership. One rank-and-file union member explained:

You couldn't get a more clear-cut individual. You knew exactly where he was, exactly what he was doing. He involved his organization every step of the way. . . . You know, in any organization, there are hotheads and people who will be unreasonable. . . . So you had people suggesting crazy things. But Jim was always clear. He was intelligent and very articulate. So we knew we were in good hands.

Nelson's leadership appears to have enhanced union solidarity and a sense of clarity about the issues; there is no evidence at all that he encouraged teachers into taking more militant positions than they themselves were willing to undertake.

Nor was there evidence that NYSUT representatives encouraged or prolonged the strike, as some board and administrator respondents charged. In contrast to board claims regarding outside union influence, union respondents indicated that the decisions to strike and to continue the strike were strictly internal. Some union member respondents were actually indignant at the suggestion that NYSUT influenced the strike. One said:

> Maybe there were people up in Albany who hoped we would go on strike, but no way were they in that room. No one from the state [union] even spoke to us, and Jim Nelson made no reference to them. . . . Jim stood up and said, "This is what they have offered us. What do you want to do about it?" It was the merit pay thing. . . . He said, "How do you want to deal with it?" It was our decision, our vote. We didn't have to go on strike.

During the strike, the district superintendent, Andrew Wilson, kept a low profile. He spoke neither with teachers nor at board meetings. Teachers took his silence to mean approval of the board's position. Other administrators appear to have been divided in their loyalties during the strike. Some actually handed out subpoenas to picketing teachers, and several testified against strike activists in court. Only a few were genuinely supportive of teachers or made efforts to mediate between parties. Most, like Wilson, played passive roles. Many teachers were embittered by administrators' passivity and instances of outright compliance with the school board's position. Teacher respondents reported they believed administrators, especially Wilson, could have done far more to promote dialogue between teachers and the board during the strike and to help bring about an earlier settlement. This bitterness became an important factor affecting teacher-administrator relations after the strike was over.

Early in the strike community residents were mainly in support of the board. As the strike progressed, however, community support shifted toward teachers. Several factors accounted for this change. First of all, union leaders deliberately sought channels for informing people in the community about the issues and CFC positions during the strike. They released statements to the press regularly, and a local paper gave them favorable coverage. In addition, the union held numerous community meetings and coffee-klatches — sometimes more than five such meetings a day — so that residents could directly meet with and talk to teachers. Rank-and-file members even canvassed residents on a door-to-door basis. All of this exposure to teachers' views strongly influenced community attitudes toward the strike. According to several respondents from the community, who later became school board members, the board's position began, increasingly, to strike community people as unreasonable and arrogant. The jail sentences, especially, aroused their sympathy.

The teachers' strike activities now had the effect of heightening community awareness of school affairs. According to the same community respondents, during the strike many people began for the first time to sit up and take notice of what took place in the school system. People began attending official school board meetings and reading school news more regularly. Parents and other residents for the first time became aware of aspects of the school system that went beyond budgetary concerns or the immediate types of school activities that children reported to them.

Toward the end of the strike, therefore, attitudes in the Cedarton community shifted conspicuously to a point where respondents estimated at least 50 percent to have been proteacher and where residents were far more cognizant of problems and issues within the school system than they had been before the strike.

The strike lasted for 28 days — far longer than either side expected. Teachers had fully expected the board would quickly come to terms when confronted with their own determination, and board members had not expected teachers would hold out for long. However, intense feelings, mounting on both sides, lent fire to issues on which one side or the other might earlier have been ready to yield. A member of the 1973 union negotiating team explained:

> You can be close to a settlement, and the minute you have a strike, all of a sudden the teachers are saying, "No way. We're not going to give an inch. Boy, they're going to give us this, and this...." You can be very close together and suddenly you're miles apart. It takes a long

time to get back together again. We had gotten closer together [at one point], and all of a sudden the board of ed jailed teachers. Then we flew apart again.

The jailing of teachers also gave rise to new teacher demands. Following the jailing incident, a "no reprisals" clause became a key union demand; teachers feared many could lose their jobs as a consequence of strike activities because the Taylor Law provided the board the right to fire tenured teachers for participating in a strike. Teachers could also lose tenure. Such action was unprecedented in the state, but in view of the board's vindictiveness, further penalties seemed plausible.

As the strike continued, however, pressures mounted on both sides to settle — pressures on union leaders from rank-and-file teachers and pressures on the board from parents. The same union respondent quoted above explained how time and pressure affected the negotiating climate:

> Time had to go by and pressure had to be applied until finally the settlement was easy. . . . Pressure had been applied. We knew we had to give on some dear items; the board of ed had to give on dear items, and we got a settlement that wasn't outstanding. We got pretty much the kinds of things we should have gotten without a strike.

According to a local newspaper report dated October 6, 1973, a parents' group petitioned the State Commissioner of Education to intervene in the strike and to use his influence to end it. Both the board and the CFC were called to a meeting in New York City, and a settlement was reached in hours. A contract agreement between the CFC and the Cedarton School Board was ratified on October 13. To that time, the Cedarton teachers' strike had lasted longer than any in the state outside New York City.

The Strike Settlement

Based on teachers' initial demands, the strike settlement provided them no significant gains. A small across-the-board salary increase was far below the Consumer Price Index that year and did not nearly make up for the heavy financial penalties imposed on striking teachers. (Teacher respondents reported having lost an average of several thousand dollars apiece.) Playground duty was eliminated as a regular obligation for elementary teachers, and there were slight improvements in fringe benefits. On the issue of teacher evaluation, the settlement stipulated the establishment of a joint CFC-administration committee to review existing evaluation procedures and to recommend revisions. On the matter of strike penalties, the settlement agreement stipulated that no teacher be dismissed or lose tenure for having participated in the strike. The board insisted, however, on imposing the two-for-one salary penalties provided by the Taylor Law. This meant that in addition to salary lost during the strike itself, teachers who stayed out were to have large amounts deducted from future paychecks. (The average strike penalty amounted to a loss of several thousand dollars for each teacher.)

In spite of the penalties, teachers felt it was the best agreement they could obtain at that time. They had made their point in striking. None of the regressive measures originally sought by the board were included in the settlement, and salary increases, while minimal, were increases, across the board, and not tied to any merit plan.

Impact of the Strike

As indicated earlier, the events associated with the strike had two major effects: they enhanced teacher solidarity, and they woke up the community. Both these effects had important long-range implications for the district in that they positively influenced later negotiations and better relations between community, school board, administrators, and the teaching staff.

In the period immediately following the strike, however, the effects were negative. Many teachers were embittered. They were embittered by the severity of penalties imposed upon them, by the administrators who cooperated with the board during the strike, and by those colleagues who had crossed their picket lines. A rank-and-file elementary teacher explained:

> The district sunk, and it was in pretty sad shape for a hell of a long time. . . . Under the Taylor Law, we didn't receive our regular paychecks until February or March, so . . . you're trying to pick the pieces

up, and you're not getting paid. . . . You saw a board of education and an administration that really didn't value what we'd been doing. That was crushing. . . . The teachers had a wonderful sense of being together and of being pitted against this board. A lot of crazy humor went on, it kept you going. But in terms of the business of the day, well, you taught the kids, because that's what you were there for — I never felt the kids were penalized. . . . Teachers picked up for their kids and went back to teaching. But when it came time for committees, there were no volunteers. That district was on strike for years afterward, in spirit, and that broke it.

Administrators were unable to deal effectively with that bitterness, that resentment, for most were afraid to take any initiative to turn things around. A school board member explained the situation at the time she came on the board in 1974:

We found . . . the administrators were afraid to do anything. They were afraid to get in trouble with the superintendent . . . and they were afraid of the board. They were always looking over their shoulders, which made them almost impotent.

In summary, for some time, tensions between teachers and administrators were high, communication poor, and important details frequently neglected.

But teacher solidarity shown during the strike had important long-range effects in that it gave the union clout. An administrator commented:

Materially, they didn't gain a lot, but they gained a lot of power . . . almost, if you will, a psychological type of power. . . . I think teachers had the feeling, "Look, we showed our strength," and it gave them a cohesiveness that wasn't there before. I'm not saying power where they feel they can run the district, but [that] they realize they have a lot of strength.

And a former association officer remarked:

Prior to that [the strike] every time we got to a crisis situation, we didn't deal from power. . . . We felt so . . . frustrated by anything we wanted to accomplish. The point was we finally could deal from a unified position. It was remarkable . . . what we were all looking for, the solidity. The strike was bitter, tough, but it was like a very healing situation. That unity, strength is still there — can be depended upon, called upon.

This evidence of having strong teacher support for the union influenced the board and the administration in later negotiations. Henceforth, the board took the union seriously.

The strike's sensitizing community residents to teachers' concerns also had long-range implications. During the spring following the strike, a group of residents launched a campaign to oust every school board member up for reelection — three of the seven members. They ran an opposition slate on a strong proeducation platform in which school board nonresponsiveness and poor staff relations were key campaign issues. All incumbents, who emphasized budgetary issues, were soundly defeated — an outcome that teachers interpreted as a moral victory and a vindication. A few months later, a member of the strike board resigned for personal reasons, and a fourth, new, strongly proeducation person, strongly sympathetic to teachers, took his place. Thus, the new school board had a majority highly sensitized to issues involving staff relations.

Their spirit appears to have carried over to remaining incumbents as well. Although the new board was far from unified, being subject to many internal tensions, its members did share common concerns for improving relations with teachers and for the need to listen to teachers.

THE POSTSTRIKE PERIOD

Respondents who served on the 1974 school board were struck by the intensity of tensions within the staff at the time they took over. One of these respondents reported:

> We felt we needed to take a deep look at the district — where we were and where we could go. . . . We decided that the undercurrent of feeling in the district had to be turned around if we were going to do anything toward improving the [school system] . . . . We laid down a policy of communication. . . . We called people to come to us. We went out into the schools. We talked to teachers. We listened to people, we did a lot of listening, and we learned a lot of things.

Another said:

What we tried to do was first sit down with everybody. We used to meet three days a week until two or three in the morning, talking to everybody, just to listen.... It wasn't a stroke of genius on our part. It was simply a matter of learning what precipitated the strike. The teachers felt isolated; they felt that nobody was listening to them.

A third commented: "The board went over backward to being open and communicating with everybody. Interestingly enough, we may have overreacted." In later years, the frequency of board meetings and hearings was greatly reduced, and direct contacts between teachers and board members were less frequent. But now that the board had accepted the union and that lines of communication had been established, there was less need for frequent contacts.

The board's openness to communication and its responsiveness to teacher concerns encouraged teachers and seemed to them to have further vindicated their strike. But for administrators, this was an uncomfortable time, especially because criticism of administrative policies and practices headed the list of teacher complaints at board hearings. During this period, the board often by-passed administrators, approaching teachers directly and encouraging teachers to seek them out. Several respondents felt that some board members were "out to get" certain administrators, especially Wilson; they claimed board members were openly disrespectful of Wilson at public meetings. This situation added to existing tensions between administrators and teachers. Administrators now felt they were treated as second-class citizens; issues of respect and job security became their issues. In 1975, Cedarton administrators formed their own union chapter — affiliated with the AFT, but independent of the CFC.

In spite of the board's sensitivity to teacher concerns, it now found itself faced in the community by two factors that, combined, severely limited its capability to finance the schools, to offer wage increases, and even to retain all its teachers. The first was an unexpected, rather sudden decline in the school-age population. Projections made in the 1960s for future district growth were very different from actual developments in the 1970s. As residential expansion slowed and housing costs rose, new young families were no longer moving into the district; those who had moved in during the 1960s now had children in high school. As a result, numbers of children enrolling in the elementary grades dropped dramatically. By the mid-1970s, an elementary school had been closed, and a second was closed shortly thereafter. These closings were accompanied by heavy cuts in teaching positions.† At the time this research was conducted, additional closings and staff cuts were anticipated.

A second factor influencing school financing was inflation and the accompanying public resistance to increased school taxes. This resistance was less extreme than in some neighboring districts and elsewhere in the county — Cedarton residents, for example, never voted down a school budget after the year of the strike. Nevertheless, district tax rates were already high relative to the county, and both the working class groups and some middle class residents were becoming more vocal taxpayers. The school board was under considerable pressure to hold expenses down. Because of inflation, the only way to accomplish this was to cut services, and cuts in services could be most broadly applied by increasing class size, thereby further reducing the teaching staff.

In a period of less than five years, between 1974 and 1978, over 20 percent of the elementary teaching staff lost their positions for budgetary reasons.

Issues during the Poststrike Period

Naturally, teachers were distressed by the extensive cuts and the prospect of these continuing indefinitely. The union, however, was powerless to prevent them. It could not challenge cuts based on declining enrollments, and, because the union had been unsuccessful in negotiating limitations to class size for the 1973 contract, there were no grounds in the contract for a legal challenge to cuts based on increasing class size. The most the union could do was to ensure fair, predictable procedures for how cuts

---

†Because state aid to a school district is based on per-pupil costs and because district financing is heavily dependent upon state aid, losses in enrollment literally forced most of these cuts upon the district. State law permits boards of education to eliminate unnecessary teaching, administrative, and other staff positions, even though incumbents may be tenured. Boards have wide latitude in determining whether a position is necessary or unnecessary, although provisions negotiated in a local teacher contract may impose restrictions. Such provisions include board commitments to limit class sizes and agreements to maintain a staff of a certain size — along the lines of what the CFC sought but failed to achieve in 1973.

were to be exercised, insisting on administrative adherence to a strict seniority system.

The new school board had been reluctant to increase class sizes, and it had anguished over having to dismiss additional teachers, but because it was accountable to the community and because school budgets rose annually in spite of staff cuts, it was under pressure to demonstrate its fiscal responsibility to taxpayers. And, as a post-strike board president explained:

> What it comes down to . . . is a class size of, say, 20 . . . justified in terms of education? Does a teacher teach differently with 20 in a class instead of 23? . . . From a community point of view — and this is not a wealthy community — taxes are quite high, so we try to consider the fact that . . . if [maintaining a low] class size doesn't do anything educationally — and there's no strong evidence that it does — then we'll make the cuts.

Board members and administrators during interviews often repeated the argument that research on class size did not indicate smaller classes made much difference educationally and that increases were therefore justified.

Class size had already been an important issue to teachers, even before the strike, and continued to be a teacher concern on its own merits, apart from its implications regarding staff cuts. Class sizes had been increased by one or two pupils each year, and some elementary and many high school grades now had enrollments of more than 30 students. Some first grade sections had as many as 28 pupils in the late 1970s, in contrast to 22 or 23 in the late 1960s. Before the strike, the class size issue focused on teachers' concern for maintaining an optimum teaching-learning environment. In the poststrike period, these concerns continued to be significant, as teachers actually witnessed their former standards eroding, but, in addition, their original concerns were compounded by a further concern for protecting job security. Both these related issues continued to be of primary importance to the union through the 1970s, although the union was virtually powerless to protect either class size or job security.

A third important issue during the poststrike period was that of teacher evaluation. Like class size, this had been a strike issue — in this case, related to the board's merit pay proposal. Agreement to establish satisfactory evaluation procedures had been a part of the strike settlement. The 1973 board had wanted tenured teachers, as well as probationary teachers, routinely evaluated, with rewards and penalties linked to quality of teaching performances. Members of the poststrike board also wanted tenured teachers evaluated, although they were more sensitive than their predecessors to teacher resistance to merit pay. Several board respondents remarked on having been shocked to learn that few Cedarton teachers had been formally observed by administrators since the time of their receiving tenure and that most teachers' files contained no records of their teaching performance for periods of 10 to 15 years. The board took the position that more routine evaluations were necessary for all teachers, in order to improve instruction.

The concerns of the teachers focused upon how evaluations would be conducted and how written evaluations would be utilized. A major concern, dating back many years, was that evaluation procedures were so poorly defined that they could be arbitrarily manipulated by administrators to single out teachers unjustly for differential treatment; such treatment had occurred earlier, they believed, in respect to the dismissal of some nontenured teachers. In the poststrike period, teachers feared the possibility of arbitrary application of evaluations in the dismissal or harassment of tenured teachers.

Within the union, there was extensive discussion about how the issue of teacher evaluation ought to be handled. Members agreed about the importance of developing clearer, more specific and objectively based evaluation procedures but did not agree what these procedures ought to be, who ought to do the evaluating, and how often they were to be applied.

A further issue was teacher participation in school planning and policy making. This, too, had been an issue before the strike — stressed by the early union before merger with the association and included in the CFC's original 1973 contract demands. It was an issue that appears to have concerned high school teachers considerably more than teachers in the lower grades, for reasons that I have discussed elsewhere.†

---

†See Jessup, "The New Unionism" (1971). Reasons offered for greater interest of high school teachers in school policy are as follows: (1) the departmental structure of the high school made for more complex institutional arrangements affecting teachers' daily work lives over which they had relatively

High school teachers' desire for more influence in school decisions came about in part because teachers felt that the school was not being well run. Teachers, both in and out of the high school, and administrators confirmed that severe problems had existed in the high school; key problems were student discipline, ineffective administration, and high turnover among administrative staff. Moreover, there had been frequent changes in administrative policies with little faculty consultation. Teachers wanted changes that would assure greater teacher participation in decisions pertaining to the operation of that school — for example, changes in the basis of departmental governance and greater administrator accountability to teachers.

Changes in Administration

Administrative leadership continued to be a teacher and community concern during the poststrike period. Wilson was an especially controversial figure because of his passivity during and immediately following the strike. Some respondents defended Wilson on the grounds that he had been forced into a difficult position by the board's stance during the strike, but others saw his passivity as reflecting sympathy with the board. Although he was personally liked by teachers, union leaders faulted Wilson for both weak administrative leadership and his failure to consult them before making a number of important decisions, and they demanded Wilson's resignation.

The new board found that Wilson exercised little direction over the district; many decisions were being made and carried out almost exclusively by the board in consultation with union leaders. To neither board nor union was this a desirable situation, and the board soon concluded that the superintendent ought to be replaced. Union

---

little control, in contrast to the more self-contained classroom situation of elementary teachers; (2) student problems, especially discipline, took on greater magnitude at the high school level because students were older, became involved in more serious trouble, and were less easily controlled than elementary school students; (3) differences in the characteristics of teachers themselves, as documented by survey results that show high school teachers to be more ideologically oriented toward professional autonomy (apparently based on their higher levels of advanced training).

leaders also asked for the resignation of the high school principal on grounds of ineffective administration, which they had carefully documented. Within the next two years, the board replaced first the superintendent and then the high school principal.

Many teachers wanted to elect the new high school principal — an early union concept. School board members, however, were less receptive to this idea, for they viewed the principal, as they did the superintendent, as their own administrative representative. They did, however, permit teacher representatives to serve with administration and community representatives on screening committees established to select the new administrators. Among the criteria set by the board for both the new superintendent and the new principal were a demonstrated ability to work in consultation with teachers and an acceptance of teacher unionism.

A new superintendent, Matthew Crane,* was hired in September 1976. Crane was a strong administrator — a capable manager and a man with firm convictions regarding educational goals and the running of the district. To many rank-and-file teachers Crane was too impersonal and management oriented. Complaints about his and other administrators' management mentality and depersonalized attitudes were common during the teacher interviews. Many rank-and-file teachers regretfully contrasted both Wilson and Crane to Long, whose more personal, informal style they missed. For union leaders, however, the district's changes precluded its successful operation in Long's style.

School district administration by this time was clearly larger, more complex, more bureaucratic than under Long — in part because of the district's earlier growth and in part for other reasons. For example, state and federal regulations tied to funds allocated for special programs mandated local district accountability, limited flexibility, and increased record keeping. Innovations in curriculum and specialized programs required greater administrative coordination. Factors related to the union — for example, the contract and grievance procedures — forced administrators to be more systematic and, therefore, more formal in their dealings with teachers. Union leaders were more likely than rank-and-file teachers to acknowledge this complexity and to recognize the nature of constraints upon central administration. They were, therefore, more appreciative than the rank-and-file of Crane's skill as an administrator and of his reasonable, direct treatment of them. They established a good working relationship with him. They insisted on a policy of routine administrative consultation with teacher representatives about any changes the superintendent or building principals considered making, and they found Crane generally supportive (although some building principals were still resistant to consulting them). Gradually, as union leaders and top district administrators were able to define more clearly the necessary differences in their positions, much of the poststrike bitterness and tension between administrators and teaching staff subsided.

THE UNION IN THE 1970S

Organizational Structure and Leadership

The formal structure of the CFC differed only slightly from the old association. As in the association, the major officers were the elected officers (president, vice presidents, secretary, and treasurer) and appointed committee chairpersons (for grievance committee, negotiating committee, welfare, and other committees). These elected and appointed officers together formed the Executive Council — a body of about nine members — which was the organization's top decision-making body. The only significant difference between the CFC Executive Council and the association's executive body was the former's expansion (in 1975) to include division vice presidents, each representing one of the major school divisions — secondary, middle, and elementary. These positions were devised to improve liaison between top union leaders and the rank-and-file.

Another carry-over from the association was the position of building representative, with the difference that instead of a single representative for each building, the CFC constitution provided for one representative for every ten teachers (about 30 representatives altogether) and for a Representative Council that met bimonthly, alternating with full membership meetings, to discuss and act upon presidential and Executive Council recommendations. These formal structural changes paralleled developments in teacher union locals elsewhere in the state and in other districts studied.

A third, major structural difference from the association was the inclusion in the CFC of nonteacher groups (aides, clerical, and service workers). This change, in keeping with practices in local teacher unions throughout the state, was reportedly instituted by the CFC for the purpose of providing unified union representation for all groups within the staff (with exception of administrators), thereby reducing potential competition among them. There is no evidence that inclusion of these groups in the organization significantly altered its activities or direction. Nonteacher groups were represented on the Representative Council but operated under separate contracts, separately negotiated. By virtue of their greater numbers, teachers continued to dominate the organization.

These organizational changes were far less important than changes in the nature of organizational leadership. Important informal differences in the nature of leadership were evident in respect to the degree of continuity or stability in top leadership positions, the type of teacher who tended to be active, and the style of leadership.

Continuity in Office

Under the association, officers had changed virtually every year. By contrast, most top officers in the CFC in 1979 had been active since 1973, and several, including the president, had been active members of the early union during the late 1960s.† Although officers were duly elected and reelected by democratic procedures, CFC leaders made a deliberate effort to maintain continuity in key positions such as president, division vice presidents, and chairpersons of the negotiations and grievance committees. The leaders assumed that experience gained by an individual continuing for many years in the same office was too valuable an asset to the organization to be sacrificed for the sake of circulating offices more. Nelson commented on his own situation, as president:

> I can say — and all the others say it, it isn't a question of egotism — right now I'm too . . . valuable not to run. I have too many state contacts, I've been through bargaining, I've been through arbitrations,

---

†Among the most active core of union officers in 1979, a majority were former members of the Cedarton Teachers' Federation, rather than the association. Few officers from the old association continued to be active after the merger, in spite of deliberate efforts at the time of the merger to recruit candidates equally from both former organizations. Interest in serving in the organization appeared to be the major factor accounting for differences in activism.

I've been to court.... My experience is invaluable.... I've worked with Michael Crane and the assistant superintendent week by week, for years. It's taken me years to develop all those contacts, to have the experience. When I go into a meeting and Bob [another union officer] comes with me, Crane [the new superintendent] can say something, and we say, "No, that's not true, because we agreed in 1975 to this." And he'll say, "Well, I'll have to go check...." And he'll come right back and say, "Yup, you were right."

A former association officer had this to say in comparing conditions in the association to the current situation:

Every year you had a new series of faces, and this worked to our discredit. I see the strength of the new organization as far superior..., but you have to have some very dedicated people. There's no question that experience and continuity are a tremendous asset. When you go in and start to negotiate and you've had the same negotiator for six to seven years, there isn't a line he hasn't heard, there isn't a game he hasn't played, there isn't any nonsense he hasn't experienced. And he can, like a good card player, read the cards so much ... more effectively.

Type of Teacher Assuming Leadership

Under the association, top leadership positions had been concentrated mainly among elementary teachers. The caliber of people serving varied from year to year, with some presidents commanding considerably more respect from both staff and administrators than others.

In the new organization, leaders came mainly from the high school staff. A deliberate effort was made to recruit candidates who were highly respected by their colleagues. The CFC was successful in sustaining a stable, active core of about 15 teachers regarded by one another and by most rank-and-file teachers as an unusually competent and principled group. To compensate for the difficulty of sustaining activism among so many, some lesser leadership positions were rotated among a cadre of people who served for a few years, took time off, and then resumed an active role.

Respondents from among all categories interviewed generally spoke very highly of CFC leaders. Those few who were more critical fit into no special pattern and appeared to have no special information, but rather seemed to be random individuals having their own axes to grind. Some typical comments by union members were:

> I think we've got some . . . good people. . . . That's always going to be the real strength — the people we have that are running that show. We have very effective leadership. . . . Jim [Nelson] is a very effective person.

> Very bright, very sharp on his feet, very logical. He won a great deal of support because of his whole manner, the way he handled himself.

> The people who are the leaders are people who are respected. . . . They are good teachers. People realize this, and it helps to get the union's point across. They're not people who take days off and so on. They're there. They're hardworking, they're interested in kids.

> A lot of it is the people . . . people like Jim Nelson and Joe* [an early union president, still active] who, when they talk, make a great deal of sense and, therefore, people follow them.

Administrators commented:

> The union officers . . . are strong teachers, good teachers concerned about their classes, concerned about their kids. . . . They are some of the best teachers we have in this building. It's not the way you find in some school districts, where the . . . union officers are not the best teachers. . . . I think that's a major thing.

> I've always felt the union leaders in this district have been the hardest working and most dedicated teachers. I know in some other districts, the leadership tends to be indifferent to goofing off and absenteeism — a lot of rhetoric. But here, people in the union leadership are really professionals.

> In think it's the most responsible union I've worked with. . . . In comparison to the group I worked with in Soundview* [another New York school district where respondent previously served as principal], this group is head and shoulders above them, in integrity and honesty and also in effectiveness.

And school board members remarked,

> In Cedarton, we're particularly fortunate. The (union) leadership has been good. (Current member)

> We have very responsible union leadership. A lot of other districts around don't. The whole group of them, not just Nelson. (Current member)

> I certainly had a great deal of respect for . . . Jim Nelson and many of the other people on the Executive Board. . . . I felt these were among our best teachers, and when they spoke, . . . I felt I really had to listen. (Former member)

Leadership Style

Continuity in office allowed top leaders to develop expertise and a leadership style not possible when there had been continual turnover. Top union officers in Cedarton played active, strong leadership roles.

The stable, active core of officers provided Nelson with a cadre of people whom he could trust, consult, and rely upon. Members of this group (fluctuating in size from the four most active to about 15, depending upon the situation) met almost daily in informal consultation. Nelson commented:

> We'll hash things out, develop positions. You see, most of the clarity in our thinking comes informally. I have a pretty good group of people I can talk things over with. . . . [We] mutually criticize each other. . . . We make a decision as to where the union should go, then it's my job to sell it. I've never gone into a meeting not knowing what to do.

An official from the state organization, NYSUT, commented upon the CFC leadership style:

> They are without question the greatest joint decision-making body around. It is done jointly. I'm talking about the top leadership. . . . Generally, it works this way: the officers will talk over a proposal or problem and make a recommendation. . . . They make sure their building reps are well aware of what's going on. . . . Their competency as leaders, and their ability to analyze a situation [are unusual]. It's one of the few organizations I know of that takes hard positions that the teachers would oppose, saying, "Hey, we did it for a reason. . . ." There is a real honesty, trust that the top officers have carefully evaluated the situation, and so they [the membership] will generally support.

This style of leadership, in which a small group actively led the rank-and-file in developing union positions, represented a change from both the old association, in which leaders were generally weaker (largely because of leaders' lack of expertise) and the early union, in which decision-making processes were more fully democratic. Some members of the early union were critical of the current style, contrasting it to the premerger union philosophy, which had emphasized more internal democracy. In the early union, there had been greater circulation in offices and more extensive, open discussion of the issues among members. Important decisions were, therefore, based upon fuller member participation. In the premerger period, however, the small size of the union permitted fuller membership involvement, and because the union did not at that time officially represent the entire Cedarton staff, issues could be considered on a more theoretical plane, less subject to the pressures associated with the need for immediate, practical application.

During the course of an interview with Nelson, I commented on the resemblance of CFC (1979) leadership patterns to oligarchy. Nelson replied:

> Yes, but it's elected. . . . The democratic process requires professionals, I believe that. . . . I believe most strongly in representative democracy. I don't believe in pure democracy. . . . Then you have ignorant people making rash judgments, at the moment. That may be callous, but I think it's the truth. We've talked about this with all the representatives.†

Other activist respondents commented on the difficulty of sustaining rank-and-file involvement in the organization as a factor contributing to the CFC leadership style. A union officer commented:

> It's easy to say, "Run a democratic union." But you can't get people. . . . That's the biggest difficulty, just getting people involved. The major portion of the work is done by a few people, and it's becoming less democratic for that reason.

---

†Note the contrast in this organizational philosophy to that of the Middlebury Teachers Federation (Chapter 3). In Middlebury, union leaders strongly emphasized grass roots union democracy.

Membership Participation and Support

Activists commented almost unanimously upon the difficulty of sustaining rank-and-file involvement in the organization. One remarked:

> It's a lot of work, and it's hard. . . . You have to . . . get everyone involved. That's a difficult problem. We have meetings, and [people don't show]. We try, because we have to make sure everyone is involved who wants to be.

Another commented:

> This is our biggest problem right now, I think . . . just getting people involved. They're not showing up at meetings, and there are few issues now to make them show up. . . . The major portion of the work is done by a few people, and . . . if you do a good job, people tend to think, "Fine, let them do it."

A third observed:

> They're happy that you do the work. They feel that things are running pretty smoothly, somebody must be doing the work. As long as it's not them, they're happy. . . . They'll occasionally stop me in the hall, and ask, "What's happening? How should I vote? Should I get upset?"

Both activists and rank-and-file members commented that in spite of low membership participation, rank-and-file teachers were generally very supportive of their leaders. One rank-and-file respondent explained:

> The leadership always feels they're not getting quite the support they need from everybody. But [they] know that the whole group out there is responsive and that if there's a problem, they can call upon them, and they'll be available, ready. So it's more relaxed support, but the base is there.

Leaders used a variety of techniques to maintain lines of communication with the rank-and-file. A major line was through the vice presidents and the building representatives, who disseminated information at the division and building levels. Another was through ad hoc meetings on issues of particular, widespread concern; these were generally better attended than regular membership meetings. An activist respondent gave the following example:

> Take, for example, our idea of teacher coordinators. We had an awful lot of teacher involvement in that.... The first thing I remember is that we called a meeting of the entire high school faculty.... The administration, typically, had come out with a bulletin saying, "This is what we're going to do." We went down to the faculty room and everybody was in an uproar. They wanted to know all the details. So we had a meeting of the whole faculty. We presented what our solution to the problem would be, but we didn't have any idea whether the administration would accept it. I can't remember exactly — but we spent a lot of time on it. We had a variety of meetings. When we finally got to the point where there was a certain number of teachers interested ... in this position, we met with them a lot. Then we would meet with the whole high school staff, tell them how far we'd gotten, and would involve them in the middle of the fight.... We'd call meetings to give progress reports.

Degree of Organizational Solidarity

Solidarity within the union was strong. While disagreements occurred, these were not severe enough to cause rifts among members or within the activist core. There were no real factions within the CFC. The only reported major divisions were between secondary versus elementary teachers. These differences appear to have derived mainly from the inability of each group to understand the other's problems, but they did not weaken the union.

When, however, the NEA and AFT, which had merged on a statewide basis in New York in 1972, announced their decision to again separate in 1976, a small group, following a dispute about affiliation with the larger organizations, pulled out of the CFC to form a separate, competing organization affiliated with the NEA. To gain representation rights, this group challenged the CFC in a collective bargaining election during the winter of 1979. Motivation for the challenge arose in part over an issue in which CFC leaders took a stand unpopular with some rank-and-file teachers.† The challenge,

---

†See the discussion of the retroactive pay issue, on pages 75-77. Officers in the new NEA affiliate in 1979 tended also to be critical of CFC leaders

however, was overwhelmingly defeated by a vote of 210 to 30, leaving the CFC as bargaining agent. This solid victory confirms other findings regarding the strength of rank-and-file teacher support for CFC leaders.

Relationships of the CFC to the Statewide Organization

The CFC maintained loose ties to their statewide affiliate, the New York State United Teachers. During the strike NYSUT provided the CFC with invaluable legal and financial assistance. In later years, it continued to provide information and advice on contract negotiations, and it served also as a central base from which teachers across the state organized politically. Legislative lobbying and support for selected political candidates during statewide elections now became important NYSUT activities, in which some CFC members participated.

Access to NYSUT was maintained both through a well-staffed county headquarters and a local field representative. The Cedarton field representative, an experienced labor negotiator, was available to the local organization for consultation on a continuing basis, but, both by his own testimony and according to CFC respondents, he played a "back-seat" role. On contract negotiations — the area in which the field representative was most strongly involved — he provided helpful suggestions about phrasing of contract demands and strategy, but final decisions were always made by the local leadership and/or membership. A CFC officer explained, "Ben* [the NYSUT field rep] doesn't pressure us. He gives us his opinion and his advice, and then we weigh it and go the way we want. . . . We may disagree. It's always ultimately our decision."

A few administrators and school board members from the strike period charged NYSUT with having influenced the local union to take certain positions and to have ultimately caused the 1973 strike, but there is no evidence to bear out such a charge. A member of the 1973 CFC negotiating team commented:

---

in respect to their lack of success in negotiating better job protection, salaries, and fringe benefits. Note, however, that such issues did not draw wide rank-and-file support for the new organization.

The first year, the board thought we were going to have a strike because of the NYSUT [representative] we were given. . . . They thought Al Shanker was telling us what positions to take. . . . But . . . the only input we get from the state is stuff we request. . . . Our NYSUT rep . . . doesn't tell us what to do. He's invaluable, will give suggestions, but it's never that he'll tell us what to negotiate or how.

THE LATE 1970S

Negotiations: 1976 and 1979

In February 1976, negotiations began for the next contract that would take effect in September 1976. The board and CFC representatives met many times over several months. The CFC contract proposals fell essentially into the same categories as those of 1973: increased salary and benefits, strengthened provisions for due process in grievance and teacher evaluation, job protection, limited workloads (especially in respect to class size and extra duties), and professional involvement of teachers in school decisions.

The 1976 board differed little in its response from the 1973 board. It, too, for example, emphasized management prerogatives. But it differed from the 1973 board in the way it conducted its negotiations with the union and in its attitude toward it. It made no demands as provoking as the merit pay proposal of 1973. Board representatives met frequently, face to face, with the CFC negotiating team. The negotiating sessions, although difficult and often tense, went on in an atmosphere of trust, with a desire to resolve all issues.

The negotiations continued through June of 1976 — longer than either side had anticipated — and, when a number of issues were still left unresolved, by mutual agreement the outstanding issues were referred, in late June, to fact-finding. These, too, were resolved, however, before the intervention of a fact-finder.

The 1976 settlement pleased neither union leaders nor rank-and-file members. The union succeeded only in protecting gains made in previous years, and across-the-board salary increases were below the inflation level. Union leaders explained they were not in a position to press for more. Given current economic conditions, declining enrollment, and taxpayer resistance to spending, union leaders were unable to gain more, for it was clear that any further gains would have required concessions in other areas.

The 1979 negotiations went more smoothly and far more quickly. Essentially, the settlement was an extension of the existing, 1976, contract with a small salary increase. But the union, for the first time, gave up some benefits included in previous contracts, the most significant being sabbatical leaves. These they exchanged to protect some faculty positions, in view of the continuing decline in enrollment.

In both 1976 and 1979 contract negotiations, the major issues were job protection and class size. The board would not include class size limitations in the contract, fearing it would "handcuff" future boards. It did, however, agree (in a side letter of agreement) that a committee composed of teachers and administrators be formed to determine guidelines for class sizes, establishing maximums and taking into account special classroom situations (for example, primary grades, shop, or labs) and special types of students (for example, learning disabled). Teachers were not given contractual guarantees absolutely limiting class sizes, but they were given informal assurances that the board would take these guidelines seriously.

In order to help preserve teachers' jobs, the union offered the board a proposal for creating retirement incentives; because many older teachers were at salary levels of more than double that of the lowest ranking teachers, this plan could potentially save the jobs of two teachers for every one who retired early. Union leaders also noted they knew of many middle-aged teachers who would have liked to leave teaching for other jobs, but could not afford to do so because of difficulties in finding new employment. They reasoned that incentives equivalent to a year's salary would provide such teachers with some financial security while they sought new employment or perhaps retraining and that such a plan could provide the district with considerable savings after the first year. Such a plan would permit the retention of other, younger teachers who wanted to remain in teaching.

The board agreed, in principle, to the advantages of such a plan, but board members feared public criticism if they offered too generous retirement incentives. ("People would be upset if we used tax dollars to pay people not to teach," claimed a board member.) The board, therefore, agreed to offer a retirement incentive of $12,000 to teachers close to retirement (over 55) and having over 20 years of service in the district. However, the cash sum proved too small and the age limits too high to induce more than eight teachers to retire.† Thus, between 1973 and 1979, although faced by a far more sympathetic board, the union made no significant contract gains, and there were some losses. Economic circumstances and political pressures on the board imposed powerful limitations.

Negotiations went quickly in 1979 because they were more direct than in earlier years. A board representative participating in the negotiations explained:

> They came in with proposals they felt were realistic, could be accepted, and we went to them with things we felt were reasonable and acceptable. . . . So, essentially, what we did was to take the game playing out of it. There was still compromising to be done and there were a couple of issues we [questioned], but you didn't have all this back and forth game playing . . . each side coming in with 172 proposals, bargaining off things that really don't matter. We said, "Let's skip this whole thing. We trust each other. Let's get to the issues." So that's what happened.

Union leaders pointed to the poststrike board members' greater acceptance of the legitimacy of the negotiations process and to the board members' realization of the union's strong teacher support in accounting for the greater ease and speed with which negotiations took place. The union's chief negotiator explained:

> Now they know we're talking with a united voice. They accept that, and it makes all the difference in the world. I suspect our next negotiations are going to be just as easy. . . . It's completely different. It's a friendly coexistence now, whereas before . . . we were always fighting.

---

†However, union activists reported they had counted another 16 mid-career teachers who told them they would have accepted the opportunity to retire early in order to seek other employment had the age and longevity requirements been less stringent and the salary incentives higher. A year later (in 1980) the board made a more generous, flexible proposal which induced a larger number to retire early.

Noncontractual Gains

While the CFC was unsuccessful in negotiating any significant contract gains after 1973 and actually incurred some contract losses in 1979, it made several important noncontractual gains between 1973 and 1979. These included establishment of alternate guidelines delineating teacher rights and obligations and working conditions, smoother operation of both formal and informal teacher grievance procedures, and more regular consultation between union leaders and district administration on all matters of concern or potential concern to teachers. These gains came about through the trust and respect that developed, first, between board members and union leaders and, later, between union leaders and central district administrators.

Alternate Guidelines

Before the strike, both association and union activists had regarded the contract as the only vehicle for specifying guidelines regarding teacher rights and obligations or working conditions. On issues the board had been unwilling to negotiate (for example, class size and teacher evaluation, which board members claimed as their prerogatives), there had been no possibility of establishing even a common basis of agreement about their handling. Board members simply maintained they would make the decisions in these areas, passing instructions downward to teachers, through administrators. Over the years following the strike, however, the board indicated increased willingness to develop some guidelines (for example, on detailed procedures for teacher evaluation and on class size) in written memoranda of agreement outside the contract. Such memoranda, even though not subject to outside arbitration if violated (as with violations of the contract), served to formalize and clarify district policies in many areas previously left undefined and, therefore, subject to administrators' personal discretion. (Such undefined areas had, in the past, allowed arbitrary treatment of teachers.) Once clarified, the new policies had the effect of being morally binding.

Memoranda specifying guidelines pertaining, at first, to teacher evaluation and discipline policy and, later, to class size and retirement incentives were developed by committees having both administrator and teacher representation in consultation with both the board and the union. These extracontractual agreements greatly improved the flexibility of the contract, for they allowed ongoing discussion of particular issues, as they arose, rather than discussion only during formal negotiations.

For the union, such memoranda also enhanced its meager contract gains, for the board committed itself in writing on some issues it would not include in the contract — for example, class size. Although that memo was not legally binding, the board did not violate its memorandum of agreement specifying limits. In 1979, union respondents still complained that class size limits were too high. Nevertheless, the formal assurance that they would not be increased further had some positive value.

Smoother Operation of Grievance Procedures

Grievance procedures had been developed before 1973 by the association and in accordance with developments elsewhere in the state. Some of the procedures were mandated by law. As far back as 1971 the Cedarton teachers' contract had a detailed grievance procedure providing for binding arbitration on all matters relating to violations of the contract. The union had wanted to include violations of board policy and administrative regulations in the 1973 contract, and this had been a strike issue. The 1973 settlement included a clause permitting teachers to grieve violations of policy and regulations, but such grievances were specifically excluded from binding arbitration, with the district superintendent assigned the power to make the final decision in such matters. In 1976, the union again demanded that violations of board policy and administrative regulations be grievable, subject to binding arbitration, and the board again, while agreeing in principle that such violations were grievable, refused to make them subject to outside arbitration. The 1976 board was, however, willing to allow grievances based on policy or regulations to be appealed beyond the superintendent, to the board itself.

Contractually, therefore, the union did not achieve what it sought in this area. Noncontractually, however, the provision for bringing grievances to the board had two important effects. First, it served to increase board members' awareness of teachers' problems and concerns. Even in cases where teachers lost a specific grievance, the act of having brought it before the board could have the effect of influencing later changes in policy that were in the long run beneficial to teachers, as in the following illustration provided by the CFC grievance chairman:

> That grievance had to do with teacher aides. [The CFC also represents aides.] It had to do with seniority problems. The principal had a neighbor whom he wanted to work — he gave her a special job, ahead of all the other aides. . . . They [the board] listened, and they rejected the grievance, because they said there was nothing specifically in the contract that said an administrator couldn't do that. But then they said they thought it was unfair, and directed the principal to come up with a policy that guaranteed that sort of thing didn't happen in the future.

Second, this provision put moral pressure on both administrators and the board to be responsible in their treatment of teachers. The grievance chairman explained further:

> If the board takes a position which is adamantly against us and we lose [the grievance], we actually win, because we involve a lot of teachers in this. . . . It gets people to our meetings. At the end, people say, "Those damn jerks. . . ." They're completely behind us, then. So the board loses on a thing like that. . . . They're beginning to realize this. So now, the position they follow is, "All right, we're going to listen, to try to be reasonable with these people."

By 1979, most teacher grievances were settled easily and amicably at the informal level. Before the strike, few had been settled without resorting to outside arbitration, and a large number of unresolved grievances were pending at the time poststrike board members took office. Between 1974 and 1979, only one grievance was taken to arbitration.

To board and administrators this greater ease in the settlement of grievances reflected their own increased sensitivity to teacher concerns (in contrast to previous boards and administrators), but to the union it was clear that the level of cooperation finally achieved had not come without a struggle: it was only after union leaders had applied considerable moral pressure and after administrators or board members had suffered embarrassment from having lost grievances taken to outside arbitration, or after having been exposed to the faculty or community as seeming unreasonable or unfair, that these groups appeared motivated to settle grievances amicably.

Consultation

The extent to which teachers were consulted by administrators and the board on matters of school district policy and planning, and the extent to which administrators and the board were responsive to teacher suggestions pertaining to such matters, had been union issues before the merger, as well as strike issues. The union had been unsuccessful in negotiating any contract changes pertaining to this issue in 1973, 1976, or 1979. As in prestrike contracts negotiated by the association, later contracts simply acknowledged the value of board and administrator consultation with teachers in regard to the development of educational policy and provided for regular meetings between district administrators (the superintendent and building principals) and representatives of the CFC.

Yet, union respondents claimed that by 1979, in actual practice, teachers had considerably more say in school district policy and planning decisions than they had had in the past, their voice being channeled primarily through union leaders in consultation with top district administrators and building principals. Although few claimed they had as much effect as they would like, union respondents were virtually unanimous in maintaining that their say had improved, especially with the district superintendent and in the high school.

Some administrator respondents at both elementary and high school levels denied consultation was a legitimate issue, maintaining teachers had always been consulted and listened to in Cedarton. Other administrators, at both levels, however, pointed to differences in individual administrator styles and to the difference between an administrator consulting with a few individual teachers and consulting more generally. As one administrator explained:

> Principals always had individual teachers whom they respected and listened to, but I think . . . teachers' impact as a group is certainly greater than it was 10, 15 years ago†. . . . The people in central administration, the building principals, and certainly the board are listening more. . . . Also, with a strong union, you have a more defined

---

†Even under Long, administrators consulted with individual teachers. But under Long, in the early years, teachers felt less need for organized consultation than they did later, after district expansion.

channel of information and opinion, and if the people who are in leadership are people you respect, and you know they're speaking for a large group, then the result is that it has more impact.

A union building representative commented:

> The old ideal was . . . arbitrary and at the whim of individuals. . . . In a large institution, there have to be [ways] of formalizing the input. . . . You just can't depend on good will. You have to have a more formal channel and a recognition that there are legitimate concerns — a necessity for input. It's very different now. . . . For example, last year a new discipline policy was devised — not by the administration, it was a cooperative effort. It's a new ball game.

Some respondents attributed improvement in the level of consultation mainly to a more responsive central administration and school board. Although this interpretation may be partially valid, data provided by this research, from both interviews and the survey, suggest that the union played a key role in bringing about this improvement. First, survey data indicated that rank-and-file teachers in Cedarton perceived their union to have given more emphasis to the goal of strengthening teacher participation in educational policy than was the case in other districts studied.† Survey data also indicated rank-and-file teachers perceived their union to have been more effective in meeting this goal than was the case in the other two districts.‡

---

†See Appendix, Tables 5 and 6. In all three districts, activists tended to report their unions as giving "much emphasis" to teacher voice in policy in greater percentages than members. This is consistent with the pattern in other tables, wherein activists generally reported stronger union emphasis and effectiveness than did members, on a variety of issues. The tables also show larger interdistrict differences among members than among activists. The reason for this inconsistency is not clear. Perhaps the phrase "voice in policy" carries different connotations to different teacher groups; or, perhaps activists in all three districts actually do give more emphasis to this issue than members realize. Information from the interviews, however, supports the members' perception that Cedarton activists gave considerably more emphasis to strengthening teacher voice in various policy areas than did either Middlebury or Oakville activists.

‡See Appendix, Tables 7 and 8. On the question of union effectiveness in strengthening teacher voice, between district differences between activists and members were more consistent than in the case of union emphasis. In Cedarton, significantly higher percentages of both activists and members indicated their union to be "effective" in strengthening teacher voice than in the other two

Furthermore, consultation at both building and at districtwide levels was usually either channeled directly through union representatives or granted in response to union pressure. A union activist explained:

> It isn't done without a struggle. . . . Once in a while, the best administrators will revert back to the good old-fashioned dictatorial self. . . . Like, the superintendent had this pet idea regarding two-hour faculty meetings where we were going to discuss "real issues," . . . claiming he had the right to do it and he was going to do it [without having consulted teachers]. He said, "We are going to have after school meetings of two hours each, four of them per month." . . . Well, we had one hell of a fight on that! . . . There was this big reaction on the part of faculty, and we all got together and told him exactly what we thought of the idea and where it was going to lead him. We said, "Did you [propose] these meetings because you wanted to discuss things that are bothering you, or did you want to have this meeting to prove that you're the boss and we're the peons? Because if you did, you succeeded, because now we're going to discuss whether or not you have the right to do this. We're going to go back and find something in the contract that will snag you, and we're going to fight you on this. But we're not going to discuss what you really wanted to call these meetings for — the problems of the school." We hit him like this. He didn't give up; he still wanted these meetings, but as a result, we came up with something that was mutually agreeable.

Improvement in the level of consultation was greatest in the high school, where teacher participation in policy formation had been a union issue since the late 1960s. Teacher respondents from the high school claimed that by 1979, teachers had considerable voice in almost every area of school policy and planning: curriculum decisions, for example, were handled mainly through the departments; the scheduling of hall duty and other nonteaching assignments were handled chiefly through union representatives in conference with building administrators. Decisions concerned with overall building policies, such as changes in departmental structure, discipline policy, and even the selection of new administrators were determined by committees having administrator, faculty, and union representation.

---

districts. Note also that for Cedarton, there is a percentage improvement in the comparisons of respondents' reports of organizational effectiveness in teacher voice between 1969 and 1979, while the other two districts show a percentage decline in activists' ratings of their organizations of effectiveness in this area.

Union representatives acted as "watchdogs" to ensure that committee recommendations did not violate the contract, that administrators fully attended to and responded to these recommendations, and that administrators brought their own ideas to the faculty for discussion before any enactment. A union leader in the high school offered the following example to illustrate how the union informally exerted influence over administrators in the latter case:

> The principal had worked with us on a committee to work up a grievance program [in the high school]. He had worked with us; everyone was pretty well satisfied. But at the faculty meeting, the principal came up with six additional things he was going to lay upon us. There had been no prior discussion of any of them. One of the good things about the union is that teachers are now amazed if anybody does that. . . . His position was extremely rigid, and when we attacked him, the guy was upset. . . . But he did react. He called me after the meeting and apologized for the position he had taken. Formerly, when administrators came in and said something — for example, "You know, there aren't enough contacts between students and teachers outside the classroom. I'm going to institute a program" — people would have said, "Okay, try it. I'm not going to bother debating it." The program would have failed . . . because you can't force things like this. But the administrator would have felt good, that he had authority. With the union, they can't get by with this anymore. People say, "You've had no previous discussion. You haven't shown the need for this kind of program." So I think the union forces administrators to be less sloppy about things like that.

This improvement in consultation had little to do with the contract — contract provisions in this area were too vague to have a binding impact. It reflected, rather, a change in teachers' expectations for administrators, sanctioned by informal pressures exerted on the administrators by union leaders. The respondent cited above explained further:

> It's really an attitudinal thing, on the part of teachers and administrators both. . . . It has to do with the feeling of unity that we have. If he makes a statement like that [referring to statement cited above] and somebody from the union gets up and starts attacking him, he has the feeling that the entire faculty is behind that person, and he can't take it lightly. This feeling of unity has been built up slowly and painfully by all kinds of things . . . we have done.

Respondents attributed the greater degree of consultation achieved in the high school, as compared to the lower grades, mainly to differences in teacher characteristics, with teachers at the elementary level less prone to questioning the legitimacy of strong administrative authority. As indicated in the example offered above, the union's ability to enforce administrator consultation in the high school was dependent on leaders' ability to demonstrate strong rank-and-file support for their position.

Discussion and Analysis of the CFC Position in the Late 1970s

Because the economy created pressures for budgetary cuts, the union was forced to emphasize protective concerns (related job protection, teacher welfare, and the protection of teachers' rights). Such concerns, however, came at times into conflict with other teacher interests — especially those related to maintaining professional standards and good relations with administrators and the community. Such conflicts arose, for example, in respect to teacher evaluation, grievances, and faculty participation in school decisions. Union leaders, for years, had thrashed out the issues surrounding these conflicts among themselves, raising questions, for example, about how far the union should go in protecting teachers who did not adequately fill their professional obligations or to what extent it should press for teacher benefits without regard to cost (at the risk of antagonizing the community). By the late 1970s, leaders had arrived at a clear, consistent view of their position — a position in which the union's protective functions were carefully balanced with leaders' desire to foster high professional standards and good external relationships. The three following cases illustrate how union leaders handled issues where concerns for teacher protection came into conflict with such other considerations.

Grievances and the Retroactive Pay Issue

The union had pressed for improvements in grievance procedures since its inception. Yet, because union leaders were sensitive to the dangers of stressing teacher protection without regard to other concerns (professional standards and community relations), the CFC placed moderate, qualified emphasis upon the pursuit of individual teacher grievances. Thus, although its emphasis upon sustaining machinery for protection was strong, its handling of individual cases varied depending on the merits of the case.

The grievance chairman defined his role as one which emphasized a sense of what was fair or reasonable, rather than as blind teacher advocate. He was, by reputation, a "fighter with a strong sense of justice" — he had pursued and won important cases on behalf of teacher grievants. Yet, though obliged to file any legitimate grievance a teacher wished to pursue, this man frequently dissuaded grievants from filing ones that seemed unreasonable or trivial, even when they involved technical violations of the contract. The most conspicuous example of such a grievance involved a claim for retroactive pay for longevity on behalf of a group within the Cedarton staff.

The Cedarton teachers' contract provided that after 15 years of teaching — ten of which were to have been in Cedarton — a teacher was entitled to additional compensation for longevity. During the mid-1970s, a teacher elsewhere in New York State, working under a similar contract clause, sued his board of education for full longevity credit, challenging the requirement that ten of the 15 years served be in the local district. The teacher won, opening the door for teachers in other districts having this contract clause to demand retroactive longevity pay for teaching experience outside their districts. Because many Cedarton teachers had extensive previous teaching experience, a good many were qualified to make such a demand. Some chose to file grievances demanding retroactive longevity pay based on this previous experience.

The union took the grievance as far as Level 3 (the superintendent), at which point union leaders learned the amount of money potentially involved. If teachers won, this grievance would cost the district as much as $750,000, at a time when the budget was already strained. At this point, union leaders discussed among themselves what course to pursue. The grievance chairperson explained:

> Besides thinking the grievance was not totally legitimate, we wondered what it would do to the negotiating atmosphere and what we have in the district. . . . It became obvious to us that if we won all that money, the district would get the money out of our hides in getting rid of younger teachers. The administration has a lot of power — for example, if we come up with an idea for using a new teacher [who would otherwise have been cut] they will sometimes go along with it, so we save

a job that way, and we work very hard on things like that. We didn't want to ruin all that by demanding this money for the old timers who have been here and will stay here. . . . So we did not go ahead with that grievance. I would have resigned rather than go ahead with the grievance.

Union leaders met first with the building representatives and then the general membership to explain their position and to ask for membership authorization to seek a settlement. The grievance chairperson went on to explain:

We had a lot of meetings on this, argued pro and con. We encouraged people who disagreed to present their arguments, and they did. We explained our position. We took a vote, and then went by the vote. . . . We were successful in getting . . . a settlement . . . a difficult settlement. . . . In order to get this agreement, we had to supply the board with waivers. People signed away their right to sue — for $6,000, $5,000. We got 72 percent of those involved to sign waivers. But there are a number who didn't sign and are quite aggravated.† But . . . we made a decision we thought was right. To pursue [this grievance] would be very harmful to our relationships in the district.

In this case union leaders placed other priorities above grievants' technical rights. They took a hard position with the membership, pursuing what they deemed to be reasonable and fair, because they saw this course as better serving long-range teacher interests by maintaining good relations with the school board and community.

Teacher Evaluation

In the use of evaluations, union leaders again balanced the union's protective function with other, professional considerations. Teachers had been concerned in the early 1970s about how administrative evaluations would be conducted and how written evaluations would be utilized. The union itself had not been sure of what

---

†A fraction of those who did not sign waivers did sue independently and won retroactive pay through the courts. The union's failure to support this grievance lost it some members to the rival NEA-affiliated teachers' organization and was, thus, also a factor in that organization's growth and in its collective bargaining challenge of 1979.

procedures to advocate. Some unfair dismissals on the basis of arbitrary application of such evaluations made them suspicious of board proposals. Many teachers, including most union leaders, however, felt that improved procedures could be an important aid to professional development and, moreover, that it should not be the union's role to protect teachers from honest professional criticism.

Discussion of this issue had been taking place within the union even before the organizational merger. Questions had arisen within the union about the extent to which leaders could protect members and enhance membership solidarity without violating their own professional integrity. Many felt strongly that the union should not protect members who were demonstrably poor teachers, especially because many capable young teachers were being "excessed" on the basis of seniority.† Questions had also been raised about whether poor teachers could be helped to improve teaching skills through the use of evaluations. Lack of administrator support for new, inexperienced teachers had been an issue in the late 1960s. By the mid-1970s, many teachers had been teaching over a decade with virtually no feedback about teaching problems or guidance in correcting them.

Internal discussions of these questions again enabled union leaders to clarify the issues and to develop a position in which their protective obligations were clearly balanced with professional considerations. On an interview question asking whether the union's protective functions conflicted with professional standards for teaching, CFC leaders responded, without exception, that it did not. The following two statements illustrate their positions:

> None [no conflict] whatever in my mind. I think an incompetent teacher should certainly be fired, and I think an incompetent teacher should have due process of law, just as I think a criminal should be punished, but a criminal should have the protection of due process of law.

---

†Some even wanted to go so far as to have colleagues evaluate one another, thus providing a basis for determining which teachers deserved protection, because administrators' evaluations were not generally trusted. This position was rejected by the larger group on the grounds that for teachers to evaluate one another would introduce a competitive note that should be avoided in interests of maintaining solidarity.

I don't think so in our district. We've talked about it, among the leaders. We feel that if the administrators do their job and they can prove that a teacher is incompetent, then that teacher should be let go.

Key components in their position were clear separation of administrative functions (in this case, conducting evaluations) from union functions (ensuring due process) and clear conceptual separation between guarantees to due process and outright protection. Based on these distinctions, the union leadership developed the following guidelines:

1. That teachers should not themselves formally evaluate colleagues, but that the union should support and encourage more extensive, careful administrator evaluation of all (including tenured) teachers.
2. That the union should play an active role in developing procedures and guidelines for administrators' evaluations and should act as watchdog to ensure that administrators adhered to these.
3. That guidelines should emphasize specific, objective criteria for basing evaluations and that written evaluative reports should adhere to these.
4. That where teachers' weaknesses were identified, administrators should be held accountable to provide the teachers with direction and assistance in correcting them.
5. That the union's role was to protect teachers' right to due process — but not to protect incompetent teachers; that, in fact, if administrators could document that a teacher was performing ineffectively and if that teacher failed to respond to genuine administrator efforts to correct his/her performance, that teacher should be dismissed.

Because union leaders had clearly thought through the ramifications of their position on evaluation, they were able to easily convince the rank-and-file to support their position. In their dealings with administrators and the school board, they were able to present solid reasoning and a united front. As a result, when members of the poststrike school board approached union leaders for the purpose of formulating evaluation procedures, as specified in the 1973 contract, the union was in a strong position to offer criticisms of existing evaluation procedures and suggestions for their revision. Development of a set of procedures that satisfied all concerned parties — the union, administrators, and the school board — took over a year. The end result, however, was a carefully prepared, workable plan that all parties found acceptable.

Thus, union leaders' ability to recognize potential conflicts between their protective and professional concerns enabled them to develop a plan that acknowledged both sets of concerns, separating them in such a way that the union's ultimate position did not jeopardize one set of goals at the expense of the other.

Departmental Governance in the High School

A third case illustrating how the union resolved contradictions between protective and professional concerns focused upon the structure of department governance in the high school. Teachers perceived this as key to their gaining more influence in ongoing school decision making: they had been highly dissatisfied with existing arrangements.

The position of department chairman had been abolished by the central administration in 1973, just before the strike; an alternate plan for administering departments under a more centralized system had been imposed, then modified and decentralized, without faculty consultation. Neither the alternate plan nor the modifications had operated well, and by 1975 the superintendent wanted to reinstitute the department chairmen.

At this point, many teachers, including those designated to be chairmen, opposed the plan on several grounds. A major basis for opposition was that the chairman's role had never been clearly defined. It was a quasi-administrative role in which the chairmen stood in authority over teachers in the departments and yet had very little autonomy in exercising decisions affecting the departments, being accountable mainly to central administration. Many teachers were interested in creating greater departmental autonomy and wanted to establish more collegial relationships with the chairmen, to make them accountable to the faculty within their departments, and to permit them to represent department concerns to central administration rather than merely convey administrators' instructions downward to faculty.

Like other issues, these ideas had been discussed within the union for several years before the organizational merger. In the late 1970s, however, union leaders also had a further concern, which was to avoid confusion within the staff concerning the identification of personnel in respect to administrative versus teaching positions. This concern became important in view of the union's protective role. Because administrators made decisions affecting staff assignments that teachers might find objectionable or that might threaten job security, administrators were at times in a clearly adversarial relationship to the union. Union leaders did not want any members of the teaching staff placed in a position where they formulated decisions in conjunction with administration, but not with colleagues, because such decisions could be divisive to the staff and, therefore, threaten union solidarity. Furthermore, they did not want department heads evaluating colleagues, for reasons discussed earlier. The problem, therefore, was to devise a system whereby teachers could achieve better professional leadership within their departments without introducing adversarial relationships into the departments.

After extensive consultation with the entire high school teaching staff, union leaders developed a proposal for departmental governance that met both union concerns and teachers' professional concerns. The proposal was to provide a professional leader for each department by creating a position called Teacher Coordinator: an elected position, with the faculty within each department electing their own coordinator for two-year terms. Election by faculty was intended to make the coordinators accountable mainly to colleagues (rather than to administrators), thus enhancing teachers' voice at the department level. The coordinators' role was carefully defined so as to separate those types of administrative duties that could lead to adversarial or competitive relations (such as staff assignments and evaluations) from more strictly collegial types of responsibilities. The proposal suggested, for example, that only administrators conduct formal teacher evaluations, but that once evaluations had been completed, those teachers the administration designated in need of help would be referred to the coordinator, who would provide the help. It was believed that within such a framework, the coordinator could work with colleagues in a more supportive fashion than would be possible under circumstances in which he/she made any formal judgment of colleagues. A high school union activist explained:

> We felt very strongly ... that in order to improve instruction, we would have to have someone who was in a nonevaluative capacity. So we said

that the teacher who was in need of improvement would be identified by administration. . . . The administration would then call in the teacher coordinator and say, "Look, this person is in need of improvement in instruction, and I'd like you to work with him." The teacher coordinator would then work with that person. There would be no evaluations, no notes, no communication — I should say, no evaluative communication — between the teacher coordinator and administration. The teacher would be fully aware it was not evaluative. In that case, the teacher is more likely to communicate with the coordinator and say, "These are my weaknesses; I'll work with you." Because it's an elected position, they [the teacher coordinators] have to be respected . . . trusted people.

This proposal also took well over a year to formulate. It followed extensive consultation with both administration and the teaching staff and was, therefore, broadly acceptable to both, and to the board that had been aware since the strike of these teacher concerns. (Board members were less receptive to a companion plan for administrative reorganization involving an elected principal.) The plan was instituted along lines developed by teachers, under union leadership, and proved effective. It was especially satisfactory to teachers in that it provided a structure within which they could administer internal department affairs (including, for example, curriculum planning and classroom organization). As such, it enhanced teacher voice in school decision making.

In this case, again, careful consideration of conflicting teacher interests permitted their resolution by the union through a balancing, yet separating, of teacher and administrator functions. Thus, teachers' interest in administering their own affairs did not conflict directly with the union's protective concerns, as it did in Middlebury — our next case study.

To avoid potential conflicts between professional and protective concerns relating to other kinds of issues — for example, the development of discipline policy — union leaders openly employed a practice of having union representatives nominated (as teachers) to serve on all school committees. The respect union leaders commanded ensured acceptance of their candidates by colleagues. This tactic enabled the union to keep abreast of issues developing within the district so that any issue bearing potential relevance to union concerns could be openly addressed from the outset.

CEDARTON IN 1979

In 1979, Cedarton was clearly a better school district than it had been ten years earlier. Although pressures to limit school spending continued, community-school relations were considerably more harmonious. Parent complaints had dropped substantially, and taxpayer groups were quieter. In spite of the negative effects of budgetary cutbacks (increased class sizes, building closings, and loss of teachers), the school board, administrators, and teachers were proud of their school system in 1979. There was far greater stability in both administration and teaching staff, and relations between the two were basically good. Student achievement levels had improved, and discipline problems had been reduced. In spite of substantial faculty retrenchment in the late 1970s, with more cuts predicted for the 1980s, teacher morale appeared to be generally high.

In all this, the union had been an important contributing force. The CFC was a strong organization in 1979 — a power within the district, respected both locally and outside Cedarton as a responsible and unique teachers' union. Its effectiveness as a protective, welfare organization was limited, on the one hand, by economic constraints and a declining student population and, on the other hand, by union leaders' desire to weigh professional, educational, and community considerations against its protective concerns. The latter, self-imposed restraints had roused some opposition to the union from within teacher ranks and had been a factor contributing to the growth of an opposing (NEA-affiliated) teachers' organization. Yet the opposing organization failed to win substantial membership away from the union.

Union relations with both administrators and the school board were far better in 1979 than in 1973, when the CFC was first recognized as the collective bargaining agent. In 1979, the three groups had developed good, working relationships. Recognition by all parties of teachers' need for economic and personal protection led to a greater acceptance (among board members, administrators, and teaching staff) of teachers' right to formal representation by a union, of collective bargaining, and of the teacher contract. The board and central administration no longer perceived union challenges to their authority as threatening; they came to understand and accept the inevitability of some conflict with their staff, based

84 / Teachers, Unions, and Change

on differences in their interests and perspectives. Moreover, they came to view the union and its machinery as helpful in resolving such conflicts. In short, the union was accepted. Far from destroying the school district, it had enhanced it. An administrator who had served in an advisory capacity to Cedarton school boards since before 1973 had this to say in 1979:

> I believe that the union has . . . become more sophisticated. . . . As we have, too. . . . Not only in bargaining, but in employee relationships and in relating to a union. If you always resist the idea of a union and it's an anathema to you, you're hardly going to relate well to the spokesmen for the majority of the teachers. . . . If you've learned over the years that the union serves its purpose, that its leadership is not irresponsible — and I think it's very responsible in this district [breaks off]. . . . They're more sophisticated, . . . we're more sophisticated as an administration, and . . . the boards have grown — even though you have turnover in board membership, the boards, collectively, have become more aware of the need for compromise, conciliation, consultation, sensitivity, and so forth. . . . There appears to be better communication.

A teacher moderately active in the union also commented positively on the quality of union-administrator-school board relationships:

> There's no question that they [union leaders] feel that they are able to communicate with these people now. They may have legitimate disagreements, but they don't have the kind of arrogance — they don't have to deal with this entrenched suspicion, or entrenched annoyance and anger that a union exists. They've accepted us, and they deal with us. . . .
>
> We can disagree, and we can argue, but at least there is an ability to talk and a respect for one another. The union respects what the administration must do, what its obligations are; it respects the fact that the school board has to reflect community views and has to have a concern for money. But they also have respect for teachers' legitimate concerns and input.

A 1979 school board member commented: "In talking to people from other school boards, I get the impression our relations with teachers are better — there's a better give and take." A union activist, commenting on the change in relationships between the union and administrators had this to say:

It's completely different now. There's trust on both sides, openness. We feel we can go to them with all kinds of questions. The CFC president meets with the superintendent regularly. Many times, administrators speak to representatives of the union before they try new things. . . . It's completely different, a friendly coexistence now, where before it was always an adversary position.

In 1979, the union was important in promoting teacher participation in a wide range of school decisions. It served as spokesman for teacher welfare interests, and it facilitated consultation between administrators and teacher groups in respect to professional and educational interests. With union influence, exercised through informal channels, often behind the scenes, teachers were able to contribute substantially to important district decisions in areas of program, discipline, department structure, and appointment of administrators.

The union drew its strength from high quality, experienced leadership, a spirit of unity among membership ranks, and a realistic recognition of the reciprocal nature of the union's relationship to administrators and the community. Union recognition of community and administrative constraints and concerns contributed to a spirit of informal cooperation between these three groups, in spite of their formal adversary roles. The cooperative atmosphere so engendered, coupled with an unwavering insistence by union leaders on teacher rights to due process, enabled the union to contribute effectively to ensuring fairness and predictability in teacher evaluation and retrenchment. Thus, in spite of its powerlessness to protect objective job security, it was able to mitigate teachers' subjective sense of insecurity.

In 1979, the CFC, therefore, appeared as a significant, stabilizing force in the school district, contributing to teachers' sense of well-being in spite of threatening, external pressures. A union member and informal leader, on the teaching staff in Cedarton for over 20 years, observed:

There are many things . . . today that are making it [teaching] not an easy and relaxed place to be. The classroom is tougher. . . . External things . . . [like] attrition [breaks off]. . . . It's a tougher time for everybody. But our situation makes us more ready for this new era. I think the [teachers] . . . here are able to cope, to handle, able to survive, better than in some other districts, where there is a lot of confusion and chaos. . . . The reason I say that is not because of the boards. It's because of our own make-up . . . as a faculty, in terms of [our] organization. . . . We have an awful lot going for us that the rest . . . out there can't match.

3

MIDDLEBURY

The story of the Middlebury union is the story of a teachers' group concerned at the outset primarily with obtaining a voice in formulating school policy and, only secondarily, with issues of teacher protection and salary. This union — formed in the 1960s — was unique in terms of its leaders' vision of an organization blending professional, social, and teacher welfare concerns. By the end of the 1970s, however, it had reversed its priorities, coming to place far greater emphasis on teacher protection and welfare. This transformation was a result of a complex combination of circumstances.

Middlebury is a racially mixed school district, having a strong liberal and proeducation tradition. As in Cedarton, the union emerged in the mid-1960s as a result of changes due to school district expansion and a lowering of public commitment to education, but this union developed more rapidly than the one in Cedarton. Strains caused by changes in the school system motivated teachers to seek more formal, organized participation in school decision making through negotiations, even before the enactment of state laws mandating collective bargaining for teachers. The Middlebury School Board's refusal to recognize teachers' right to formal participation, through negotiations or in any other form, led these teachers to change their organizational affiliation from the NEA to the more militant AFT. Widespread rank-and-file acceptance of unionization at this early stage reflects Middlebury's highly liberal, socially aware teaching staff.

The story of the Middlebury union is in some ways disillusioning. On the one hand, a highly supportive school board, committed to both educational improvement and liberal, social integrationist goals, became increasingly fragmented by changing economic conditions, racial tensions, and community pressures. On the other hand, a teachers' group initially unified by common ideals and professional concerns became similarly fragmented as a consequence of both external changes and internal organizational pressures. In addition, mounting tensions between teachers, administrators, and the school board led to a strike that, rather than resolving tensions, further polarized these groups.

We shall see how early leaders' inability to find avenues for sustaining their professional goals in a changing, less supportive environment led to their own disenchantment and withdrawal from union activism and, furthermore, how the union's emphasis on democratic, grass roots staff participation appears to have undermined its ability to sustain strong leadership. In contrast to Cedarton, Middlebury's leaders' inability to recognize certain inherent contradictions between teachers' professional goals and welfare goals led to the union's inability to resolve these contradictions, resulting in greater factionalism within the union than might otherwise have occurred and, eventually, in diminished teacher involvement with professional and educational issues.

In the 1970s, the local union's increased reliance on New York State United Teachers (NYSUT), the statewide subsidiary of the American Federation of Teachers, helped to strengthen the local in terms of bargaining power and political clout. This alliance, coupled with the union's strong defensive posture, appears to have reduced its sensitivity to professional issues, however, and to have further contributed to its alienation from the community. By 1979, the Middlebury Federation of Teachers had become a strong, traditional labor union, respected as a power in the district, but having a diminished role in educational decision making.

BACKGROUND

Middlebury is an amorphous, suburban district lying in the region between several "older" suburban towns in the New York City metropolitan area. As in Cedarton, the district underwent considerable population growth following World War II, with accompanying expansion of the school system during the 1950s and 1960s. But in Middlebury, the expansion was less extreme, occurring at a slower rate over a longer period of time. Until the early 1960s, Middlebury was an elementary school district only. Grades K through 8 were housed in three school buildings that predated the war. Students attended high school in a nearby town.

Historically, the district had a diverse population − racially, ethnically, and socioeconomically. Dating back to the 1920s and 1930s, Middlebury had a sizeable black population, including middle class professional, working class and poor black groups. Altogether, blacks comprised about one-third of the school population from the 1950s through the 1960s and 1970s. Also historically, the district contained a large Jewish population − mainly middle class professionals. Jews constituted another third of the school population from the 1950s through the 1970s. The balance was composed of a mixture of various white ethnic working and middle class groups, including a large number of Catholic families who utilized parochial, rather than public, schools.

Middle class, liberal blacks and Jews were the only groups especially vocal in school affairs until the mid-1960s. These were people who placed high priority on educational values; they could be counted on to provide solid support for school budgets, staffing, and expanding programs. These two groups also tended to be in the vanguard of those concerned about the race problem. Starting in the early 1950s, they formed a prointegrationist, educationally progressive coalition that dominated the Middlebury schools and school boards until the late 1960s, when mounting racial tensions in the nation and population changes in the district began to undermine local support for their positions.

From the mid-1950s through the mid-1960s, the district operated under unusually supportive school boards − supportive of the teaching staff, of educational programs, and of a social philosophy of racial integration. During the 1950s, Middlebury earned a reputation as a model school system for its approach to racial issues. Long before de facto segregation was widely recognized as a problem in northern schools, the Middlebury School Board abandoned the neighborhood school concept and traditional grouping practices, moving to a plan that through busing and heterogeneous grouping provided for extensive interracial contact among students in all grades. The grouping policy appealed to liberal parents and teachers on two counts: one, the social ideal of racial integration; the other, a progressive educational ideal of teaching the whole child in order to achieve his or her full potential.

During this same period, staff morale was high. Teachers felt they were part of a school system moving toward finding solutions to problems plaguing educators everywhere. A teacher who came to Middlebury in the late 1950s described the excitement teachers felt in that period:

> There was a creative ferment and an atmosphere that went with it. . . . We were there to change America — to solve America's social problems through education, to prove that all children could learn in more or less the same way, that racial differences and socioeconomic differences could be overcome — And, I think, we did damn well . . . before the black movement overtook us and outside pressures started polarizing people.

Teachers did not perceive their task as easy: heterogeneous grouping accentuated the academic and social problems associated with economic and racial disadvantage such as the enormous achievement gaps between upper middle class children (mainly white) and lower class children (mainly black). They were optimistic, however, because they felt supported by their administrators and school board. When it became evident that heterogeneous grouping and attention to the whole child were not enough to close these gaps in academic achievement, the Middlebury School Board did not blame teachers (as happened elsewhere). Rather, it was among the first to apply for funds from outside sources to initiate special compensatory education programs, such as Head Start and Project Able. It brought in university consultants to lead workshops on new approaches in teaching and curriculum. Teachers, administrators, and school board members felt they were a team working together to meet a common challenge.

No particular administrators were especially important or charismatic figures in the history of the district (as was the case in both Cedarton and Oakville). The optimistic school atmosphere in Middlebury was attributed instead to admirable school boards and to the spirit of mutual supportiveness that derived from meeting a common challenge. So even without a charismatic administrator, teachers' relations with the administration were good during the 1950s and early 1960s. And before the construction of the high school in 1961, teachers had easy, informal access to administrators, who not only were responsive to teachers' ideas and concerns, but also shared these ideas and concerns.

Because of its reputation, Middlebury attracted many highly qualified, strongly committed teachers during the 1950s and 1960s — teachers liberal in both social and educational philosophy. But also, the district had its old guard — teachers hired in an earlier era (as one respondent called them, "stiff-necked teachers, who didn't smile until Christmas"). And, of course, some hired during the period of district expansion were less highly committed, capable, and liberal in philosophy, because of teacher shortages at that time.

During district expansion, including the opening of its own high school in 1962, the district began to be affected by a number of problems, internal and external. As in Cedarton, rapid increase in district size brought about tensions and instability within the staff. Administrator-teacher contacts were reduced, school management became more formal, less flexible and less responsive to teachers, and, as the staff expanded, there was greater turnover among both teachers and administrators.

Moreover, the addition of an older student population in the high school brought about a host of student-related problems the district had not previously handled and for which it was, therefore, not prepared. Older students presented far more complex needs and problems than elementary students — academic problems, discipline problems, social problems. Policies reflecting the district's social and educational philosophy developed and applied at the elementary level were often unsuited at the secondary level, and there was no appropriate model outside the district that offered better ways of meeting the problems presented. Questions that arose about the suitability of tracking, for example, were less easily resolved at the secondary level.

Only two years after the opening of the high school, the supervising principal left the district for another position. This man had served simultaneously as chief district administrator and as high school principal, but because of growth in the district's size, the school board replaced him with two new administrators — one for the high school, the other to serve as superintendent. Both new administrators said they supported the district philosophy, but, for reasons that are not clear, neither appears to have been as fully committed to enacting this philosophy as the man who left. The high school principal lasted two years, and then left. (The superintendent — a man more politically talented — lasted longer.) Substantial turnover in the high school principalship continued after that, throughout the 1960s. Thus, the high school lacked stable, effective leadership in developing programs, policies, and staff relations during its initial period of establishment. This lack appears to have been an important factor leading to rising dissatisfaction among high school faculty during the mid-1960s. No respondent was able to explain why the district was not more successful in recruiting outstanding administrators.

Changes taking place in the larger community were also beginning to have their effect on the schools, although their full impact was not to be felt until the 1970s. New, upwardly mobile families, both black and white, in predominantly blue-collar or lower white-collar occupations, were moving into new housing developments in the district in large numbers. These were people who came to Middlebury primarily because housing was less expensive there than in neighboring towns, not because of any awareness of the school district's integrationist philosophy. This population expansion was costly to the school district. The new families brought children to the schools disproportionately to the revenues added by their property taxes. Property taxes on a modest single family dwelling provided little more than what it cost to educate one child in the schools. Most families, however, brought two to three children. Only those utilizing private schools were not costly to the district. The district, almost exclusively residential, was caught in a severe financial bind. Had it contained more commercial property (which contributed taxes without children), perhaps it could have weathered expansion more smoothly.

In 1966, the school board proposed merger with an adjoining, wealthier district as the solution. This other district contained extensive commercial property and some apartment complexes having few children, thus having a far more substantial tax base than Middlebury. The school board of the other district was also interested in merger, for it badly needed high school facilities. Support for merger was divided among residents of both districts. Conservatives in the wealthier district opposed merger because they opposed racial integration. Some liberal whites, most blacks, and most teachers in

Middlebury opposed merger because they feared residents in the wealthier district would not support integrationist and other socially progressive programs. But most Middlebury residents supported merger on the grounds it would bring needed revenues to the school district. Those liberals who supported merger believed (short-sightedly) that their coalition would be strong enough to outweigh any conservative opposition that might come from the second district, because Middlebury was much larger. Merger supporters won, in a hotly contested referendum held during the summer of 1966.†

Merger did bring added revenues to the district, but it also seriously diluted support for a liberal school board, at a time when the new, more conservative lower middle and working class residents within Middlebury were starting to become vocal and critical of school policies and programs. These various new, more conservative groups were far from unified. Some (especially those utilizing parochial schools) were primarily interested in reducing taxes; others were concerned with bringing school programs back to basics; and a third group wanted a more sophisticated academic curriculum (for example, with tracking for talented students). Neither did they coalesce along racial or religious lines: black and Italian lower middle class parents, for example, shared similar educational values (back to basics, with reduced spending) while conservative upper middle class parents, whether Jewish, Catholic, or Protestant, tended to support more elaborate programs, but wanted a return to academic tracking throughout the school system. What all of them had in common, however, was a dislike for the progressive education and social philosophy that until then had dominated and unified the school district.

While the liberal black-white coalition continued to maintain a majority on the school board for some time, more conservative candidates of both races began to gain seats. In response to increased pressures from conservative members and their constituencies, the board began to take a more moderate approach toward resolving school problems. In spite of the merger, the district continued to suffer problems related to school financing because of inflation and

---

†A majority of votes cast was based on the total number voting in both districts. Because Middlebury had twice the population of the second district, favorable votes from its residents determined the outcome.

more organized opposition to high taxes. In response, the board began to initiate cuts in school programs and personnel.

Merger also brought changes in the teaching staff, because faculties from the two districts were combined. Many teachers from the wealthier district were unprepared to deal with the academic and behavioral problems presented by lower class children. Some also showed signs of racial prejudice. Differences in social and educational philosophies became a new source of tension among teachers, especially because the new teachers were not offered the kinds of institutional support that had been provided earlier to the Middlebury staff. Staff differences were of less immediate concern to teachers, however, than other problems they faced at this time.

By 1966, obvious school needs were not being met; there were shortages of specialized personnel (for example, reading specialists) and building facilities were overcrowded. Also, many teachers felt that the school district lacked direction, that adequate programs were not being developed to meet student needs, and that their own suggestions for improvements were not being heard. While administrators and school board members continued to advocate faculty participation in decisions affecting the district and frequently established faculty committees to make recommendations on such matters as curriculum or in-service programs, teachers complained that by the late 1960s, such committees seemed little more than forums for discussion, an "outlet for faculty feelings." A 1969 teacher respondent commented:

> We used to make up lengthy reports. They [administrators] would take the reports, read them, then write up their own report with a few things that we had mentioned — you know, never consult us on this kind of thing — and then come up with a beautiful document stating "This is a summary of the faculty and administrative [opinions]."
>
> I remember they did this on in-service programs, and we would do a complete flip. We'd go in and say, "But look, this is a half of what we said." They would say, "Well, we're compromising." But we didn't have a chance to say that's where we wanted to compromise. Then they would say, "Well, we felt that that's fair enough. Now don't you think that's fair enough?" What were you to do?

Some blamed these problems on changes in the people occupying top administrative or school board positions, but most saw the problems as reflecting new pressures on the board and administration from outside sources, resulting in a slackening of their commitment to earlier educational goals. In both cases, teachers' perception that their own ideas were being ignored in the face of multiple problems and ineffective administrative leadership was central to their frustration.

By 1966, teachers found themselves at odds with both administrators and the board, in contrast to their earlier feelings of unity in a common cause. Feeling estranged and threatened, they sought the influence they once had through unity with school board and administration in a new source of unity of their own — a stronger teachers' organization. But, as we shall see, even within their own organization, unity became difficult to sustain.

TEACHERS' ORGANIZATIONS

Changes in the Teachers' Organization

The first teachers' organization in Middlebury was a teachers' association formed in the late 1930s, affiliated with the NEA and the New York State Teachers' Association (NYSTA), the statewide education association, a subsidiary of the NEA. As in Cedarton, respondents recalled the old association as a kind of social club, to which both teachers and administrators belonged. Although the association made annual recommendations regarding salary and fringe benefits to the school board, it did not, as an organization, engage in or press other issues, and it did not conduct negotiations with the administration or school board in any formal way.

In the mid-1960s, as teacher dissatisfaction began to mount, several association leaders began to suggest that the organization play a stronger role in representing other kinds of teacher interests and in influencing school policy. As a first step, they attempted to reorganize their association chapter because they thought the current structure neither provided adequate communication among teachers nor adequately represented teacher concerns. As in Cedarton, it eliminated administrators from the organization, in recognition of a growing dichotomy between administrator and teacher interests and in the belief that the presence of administrators at meetings hindered open discussion of certain issues. Reorganization also broadened teacher participation in the association through a more complex structure, wherein the faculty of each building was treated as a unit, holding meetings of its own and communicating through a system of delegates to a central assembly. The membership strongly supported these changes.

These changes improved staff participation and communication between buildings, but they did not substantially increase teacher power in the school district. Teachers continued to perceive their role in school decision making as weak, and were further frustrated by the accompanying perception that administrators were not making progress toward resolving educational problems.

Attempts toward Professional Negotiations

The rise of organized teacher militancy elsewhere in the state and nation sensitized Middlebury teachers to the possibilities of collective action as a means of coping with their dissatisfactions. The civil rights and peace movements also served as models for collective action to this highly liberal staff, lending legitimacy to their own, new militancy. Middlebury teachers, who already expected more of their school board than did teachers in most other school districts at that time, were inspired by these national movements to demand fuller recognition as professionals and as equals.

In the fall of 1966, the teachers' association decided to ask the school board for a Professional Negotiations Agreement. This was before the enactment of the Taylor Law, which later mandated collective bargaining for public employees within New York State. Middlebury teachers were well aware, however, that teachers in some school districts had achieved bargaining rights.† A new literature associated with the teacher movement served to further legitimize these desires by advocating increased professional participation in school affairs. Professional negotiations were now being advocated among an educational avant-garde, within both the AFT and NEA, as an avenue for increasing teacher participation. Based on leaders' perception of their school board as still having a liberal majority, friendly to teachers and sharing common concerns, they hoped to

---

†New York City teachers won the right to collective bargaining in matters of salary and working conditions in 1962. A few other school districts, mostly urban, both in and out of New York, had also granted teachers bargaining rights.

persuade the board that formal negotiations would be mutually advantageous. They thought the board needed only to be impressed with how strongly teachers felt — that a well-meaning majority on the board, now bending to community pressures, would be at least as responsive to teacher pressures.

Association leaders drew up a proposal for the negotiations agreement to present to the board (the membership endorsed the proposal by a vote of 142 to 17). Central to their proposal was the concept of establishing a structure that would ensure greater teacher participation in all areas of school decision making. A voice in educational policy was especially important. An early activist explained: "The teachers' demand for a voice in curriculum probably represents the main key. But you can't negotiate complex problems. You can negotiate procedures."

The essence, therefore, of what they were seeking through negotiations was the establishment of a set of procedures through which participation of teachers in formulating school policy could be sustained. Teachers wanted, also, to establish mechanisms that would make their own participation more than merely advisory. They were becoming more aware, not only of political pressures on the board, but that school board members, however well meaning, tended to interpret school problems from a perspective quite different from their own. Because teachers were in far closer contact with both schools and students, they felt it especially important that their own insights be taken into account in considering solutions. They wanted to ensure, therefore, that teacher recommendations at least be given serious consideration.

The set of procedures or structure that the teachers' association proposed was based on principles advocated at that time by the American Federation of Teachers:† recognition of the teachers' organization as the official representative of the teaching staff, regular negotiating sessions, and some form of mediation to be adopted in the event of impasse. All these had been won by New York City teachers in their earlier (1962) struggle for collective bargaining. In addition, they wanted to establish the relevance of both teacher welfare and educational policy items as legitimate

---

†The AFT advocated collective bargaining for teachers long before the NEA began to do so. Some NEA chapters (such as this one) adopted AFT guidelines before their adoption by their parent organization.

negotiating areas. At this time, Middlebury association leaders were far more aggressive in insisting on negotiating in areas other than teacher welfare than were leaders in either of the other districts studied.

The school board was willing to meet with teachers' association representatives to discuss the proposal, and several meetings (one tape recorded) were held over the next few months.† Both parties appear to have met together in a spirit of good faith — a clear contrast to teacher-board relations in both Cedarton and Oakville. From the teachers' viewpoint, however, good faith was not enough. They wanted a commitment from the board that a "new seriousness" would be attached to teacher proposals — some kind of guarantee that their role in decision making would be extended beyond that of mere consultation. For this reason, they viewed the principle of outside mediation as crucial. A member of the committee elected to meet with the board in 1966 explained in a 1969 interview:

> We wanted some recourse beyond the board, so that if total disagreement should develop, it [teachers' proposals] wouldn't just die. . . . And that's where the major hang-up came with the board. We wanted recourse to outside mediation — and we used the word advisedly; that somebody versed in education would come in and listen to both sides and at least offer an objective viewpoint as to the possibility of implementing what we were suggesting.

In retrospect, several association leaders involved in pressing for the Professional Negotiations Agreement recognized their approach as having been naive. In effect, they were asking the school board to voluntarily agree to submit its decisions to outside review. Their appeal to the board was based overtly on the argument that such action would improve teacher participation and teacher morale, thus benefiting the operation of the school district. Because of both their training and their direct contact with students in the classroom, many teachers felt that they were better equipped than board

---

†Evidence of the nature and content of discussions between the two parties is contained in a tape recording of their first session dealing with the Professional Negotiations Proposal in 1966. The taped discussion and copies of documents exchanged between the two parties provide the basis for the ensuing account and serve to support respondents' later assessments of the situation.

members to make certain types of decisions and that a negotiations situation, with recourse to mediation, would help to strengthen faculty influence. Mediation, while not legally binding, might have the effect of exerting pressure upon the board to give more serious consideration to teacher proposals than had been given in the past.

Board members were unable to accept the desirability of creating a negotiating situation between themselves and the faculty, and they could not see any need for outside mediation. Why, they argued, should it ever be necessary, if all parties were equally committed to educational goals and if they met in good faith? Teachers tried to explain. The association president told the board during the first meeting in 1966 to discuss professional negotiations:

> We've asked [that] ourselves: if all parties are acting in good faith, why [should there ever be] impasse? But it is . . . possible that after the board and teachers have attempted an honest, objective answer to a problem that the personal positions we have may lead to divergent views, even though the overall objective we [both] have is to benefit the child.

A second teacher argued more heatedly:

> There have been discussions in the past between the board and teachers which have reached impasses. And when these positions have been reached, there has been a tendency . . . for the board to say, "Thank you very much for your recommendations; we'll consider them very seriously," and then, at that point, the teacher representatives are finished. . . . The board decides — I don't know whether you prefer to call it unilaterally or arbitrarily — but it decides essentially on its own . . . whether the policy will be implemented, whether the teachers' recommendations will be taken into account or whether they will be ignored. And I think this is at the very heart of what 142 teachers in the district are upset about. . . .
>
> It's not a question of good faith. We assume good faith. But [our feeling is that] it's no longer possible to just come up with recommendations to the board and, granting all the good faith, to then walk away and say, "Well, that's it. I've done my bit. They have to decide. . . ." We feel that if we consider an issue important enough to spend hours and weeks researching material to present recommendations, that there should be something more than merely the process of recommendation. . . . If the board doesn't agree, . . . [but] recognizes the staff as professionals, as serious, and concerned with the basic welfare of the district,

the board should be willing to at least allow an impartial observer to evaluate and comment on the situation.

It is clear from the taped session that liberal board members, on whom teachers had especially counted for support, were hurt by implications that they did not fully consider teacher recommendations. They failed to see that legitimate differences might arise from their differing perspectives or that they, as a board, might at times be susceptible to political pressures. They could, therefore, see no reason for discontinuing the old system wherein faculty recommendations were subject to the board's final decision. In short, liberal and conservative board members alike were simply not prepared to relinquish their own authority as trustees of the school system. Such resistance to voluntary acceptance of professional negotiations by school boards was a common pattern throughout the nation during this period (see Wollet 1967).

Discussions between teacher representatives and board members ultimately collapsed over these two issues — the establishment of mediation procedures and the degree to which teachers were to be accorded a voice in policy on any educational matters beyond what could be strictly defined as welfare items, that is, salary, fringe benefits, and physical working conditions.

The Move toward Unionization

Activists interviewed in 1969 expressed little doubt that had the school board accepted their proposal for a Professional Negotiations Agreement, with mediation provisions, the move to unionize Middlebury teachers would not have occurred. According to their reports, the desire to establish mechanisms for strengthening teacher voice in policy was the primary, immediate motive. That the impasse between teachers and the board did not occur over welfare items supports this argument. Undoubtedly, there were discrepancies between what teachers sought and what the board was willing to grant on bread-and-butter items, and undoubtedly many teachers saw advantages of establishing a negotiations setup vis-à-vis those items. Nevertheless, the school board did grant teachers the right to participate more fully, with collective representation, in decisions related to teacher welfare — specifically, salary and fringe benefits — before the formation of the union.

In the early spring of 1967, the first step toward forming a union chapter was taken. An officer of the teachers' association, who had been active on the committee that met with the school board, began on his own to circulate a petition, gathering names of teachers who would be willing to join with him in obtaining a charter for an AFT local. His success in obtaining signatures was unexpectedly dramatic, with over one-third of the faculty signing in a few days' time. Other officers of the association, many of whom were sympathetic to his move, feared that the formation of a second teachers' organization would have the effect of splitting teachers down the middle and ultimately weaken their position in relation to administration and the school board. The officer who had initiated the petition was persuaded to withdraw it, in favor of an alternative plan to hold a referendum among members of the teachers' association on the question of whether the organization should change its affiliation with NYSTA and NEA and join AFT. Notices were sent out, and teachers were given three weeks to debate the matter. When the vote was held, affiliation with the union was supported by almost two to one, and the teachers' association became the Middlebury Teachers' Federation (MTF).

But why was joining the union (that is, the AFT) considered a relevant response in terms of the concerns identified in the preceding analysis as prevalent among Middlebury teachers at that particular time? The following statement, made by one of the original proponents of unionization, helps to clarify the relevance:

> Affiliating with the union would in effect be telling the board of education that not only do we represent the feeling of the faculty in these discussions — that a negotiations situation should exist — but the faculty feels strongly enough to affiliate with a group allying itself with an approach that stresses collective bargaining.

Some teachers also felt that alliance with the union would have the effect of bolstering membership morale, in the sense that their new identification would be with a more militant organization. Furthermore, they hoped it would bring some outside support to their demands, in terms of organizational and legal assistance available from the state affiliate of the AFT (then known as Empire State Federation of Teachers), although desire for such support was of only secondary importance. In contrast to Oakville (the third case study) teachers in Middlebury perceived the strength of their union as dependent mainly on their own activity.

A factor of crucial importance in accounting for the success of the move toward unionization in Middlebury is that it was strongly supported at the elementary level as well as at the junior and senior high school levels. This pattern deviated noticeably from that observed by others, elsewhere, and from the pattern in Cedarton, where early union members were concentrated almost entirely in the high school.†

This greater support from the elementary staff for the early union in Middlebury can be attributed in part to these elementary teachers' greater sense of involvement with their schools and, hence, their greater dissatisfaction as the schools changed. It can also be partially attributed to their greater political liberalism, which predisposed them to be more favorable toward labor militancy. Their sympathies with labor influenced them not so much in moving them to affiliate with the union as in not deterring them from affiliation. In other words, unionization was more generally perceived as an appropriate means for expressing teacher dissatisfactions earlier in Middlebury than it was in Cedarton or Oakville.

Union Leadership and Factionalism

Although elementary teacher support for the union was strong, its top leadership was initially concentrated in the high school. The presidency circulated among several highly respected high school teachers until the 1970s. The active high school core who dominated the union during the late 1960s had a strongly idealistic vision of

---

†Respondents claim that the vote in favor of union affiliation was as strong at the elementary level as at the junior and senior high school levels. Questionnaire results tended to confirm this observation. Out of my entire 1969 Middlebury sample, 63 percent of elementary teachers (N = 40) and 67 percent of secondary teachers (N = 60) were union members. Findings reported from other studies indicate that the common pattern in the 1960s was for union membership to be far more heavily concentrated in secondary schools than in elementary schools (see Cole 1969 and Rosenthal 1969).

the organization's purpose. These leaders viewed the union as a mechanism for changing not only their relationship to the board, but also the structure of administrator-staff relations. They sought to increase teachers' professional autonomy and participation in all decision-making areas — program, selection and retention of staff and administration, as well as decisions affecting teacher welfare and working conditions. They viewed professional autonomy and teacher welfare as inseparable, complementary goals ultimately related, on the one hand, to enhancing teacher dignity and morale and, on the other, to benefiting the schools through improved staff participation.

This view of the union was most clearly articulated by a high school social studies teacher named Seth Landau.* Landau had been active in founding the union, and many considered him its spiritual leader through the 1960s. He served as president for only two years, between 1969 and 1971, but he was an active member of both the union Executive Council and negotiating team from the time the union was founded. Landau was a controversial figure, viewed as too ideological by some union respondents, but highly respected by a large segment of the teaching staff and by those school board members who knew him through negotiations. His supporters described him as a highly intelligent, sensitive, and principled person, with a strong commitment to improving education. A respondent who had been on the school board while Landau was union president described him as follows: "I have great respect for him . . . Seth is very professional. He is interested in schools and teachers doing a better job — always. He's very competent . . . and . . . he remains true to his inner self." Another school board respondent commented:

> Seth is my ideal of what a teacher . . . should be. [But he] is more than just a teacher . . . he's an ideologist, . . . an institution unto himself. . . . Seth is a charismatic leader . . . who excites strong feelings in other people — of admiration, and of dislike.

Landau and others in the leadership core might be characterized as professional-idealists. In addition to having professional goals for the union, they believed strongly in the district's social philosophy. They also espoused principles of grass roots participation and democracy for their organization. They were ideologically pro-labor but critical of the U.S. labor establishment, abhorring trends toward oligarchy in labor organizations. As in the early Cedarton union, and in contrast to the later CFC philosophy of leadership, they envisioned their own organization as needing to operate completely according to democratic principles, and they advocated cooperation — rather than competition — with community groups.

Landau and the other professional-idealists recognized that most rank-and-file members did not fully share their own vision of the union. Rank-and-file support had been motivated by more immediate, simpler concerns (such as teacher dissatisfaction with administrative leadership and cuts in funding for support services). Although most union members enthusiastically supported the demand for greater teacher voice and were eager for the board to know the strength of their dissatisfaction, a majority appear to have only partially understood the more complex, professional issues and goals (such as professional autonomy) articulated by Landau and other leaders. Only later did leaders come to understand that limitations to rank-and-file understanding of the issues meant that grass roots participation would dilute the organization's capacity to achieve some of their more elusive professional goals.

The Middlebury Teachers' Federation was more prone to factionalism than either of the other unions studied. While professional-idealists dominated the Executive Council through 1971, there was also a vocal group on the council who espoused a more traditional and labor-oriented view of the union's purposes — believing that it should limit its goals to welfare functions, that is, improving salaries, benefits, working conditions, and protecting teachers' personal rights. A member of the union's executive Council in 1969 made this observation:

> There is a split. . . . We haven't allowed it to become a divisive split, but there is a faction [on the council]. And it's the old-type union people against the new-type union people. . . . You see, we (the new type) are not primarily union people per se. We're primarily school people who are looking for the best mode whereas the others are primarily union people.

Also contributing to the factionalism was the presence of a group of teachers whose loyalties still remained with the NEA. Right after the union's formation in 1967, some association members who openly opposed affiliation with the AFT (as unprofessional) split away from the new organization to form their own organization — a new association chapter. But the new association was unsuccessful in gaining substantial membership, and it soon disbanded. By 1970, most of this group had joined the union, and some gained representation on the Executive Council. This group tended to be more conservative and more accepting of administrative and school board authority than the professional-idealists, while less bread-and-butter oriented than the traditional unionists.

Early leaders' more far reaching, idealistic vision of their union seems to have been another important factor contributing to factionalism, for leaders' idealism caused them at times to take controversial positions within the organization — positions some members were unwilling to support. A further factor may have been the rapidity with which the majority organization was transformed into a militant union: early union leaders did not have an extended period in which to develop and clarify their positions on various issues before assuming the formal responsibilities associated with running the majority organization. Had the union developed more gradually before assuming these responsibilities and before absorbing the dissident NEA teachers, internal differences might have been more satisfactorily resolved, as in Cedarton. Finally, early leaders' commitment to grass roots membership participation, while leading to more open expression of opinion, also encouraged the development of divergent views within the membership; and because leaders' belief in democratic processes made them reluctant to exert strong leadership and direction, these divergent views more easily solidified into distinct camps or factions.

Although the professional-idealists successfully dominated the union for several years, factions within the union and the tensions these generated were important factors contributing to later changes in leadership and union goals. Meanwhile, the ideal of democratic, grass roots participation contributed to a diffusion of the union's initial focus.

THE LATE 1960S AND EARLY 1970S

Negotiations in the Late 1960s

The public Employees Fair Employment Act (the Taylor Law) enacted by the New York State Legislature in the spring of 1967, only months after the formation of the union chapter, settled the conflict between the Middlebury Teachers' Federation and the school board over negotiations by mandating collective negotiations between public employers and duly elected employee representatives. The law specified wages, hours, and "terms and conditions of employment" as the areas subject to negotiations. Differences in interpretation of "terms and conditions of employment," however, left some ambiguity on the types of issues to be negotiated.

Representatives of the MTF and the Middlebury School Board held their first formal negotiating sessions under the Taylor Law in the spring of 1967. Interpreting "conditions of employment" as including a broad range of conditions in the occupational setting, the MTF presented the board with a list of 128 contract proposals compiled from rank-and-file teacher suggestions. The list ranged from salary, fringe benefits, and working hours to class size and involvement of teachers in curriculum, program development, teacher evaluation, and the hiring of administrators. Board members adamantly refused, however, to negotiate in areas other than those strictly pertaining to teacher welfare or benefits. A respondent active on the 1967 MTF negotiating committee explained:

> Within the proposal there was as much dealing with policy and curriculum and larger teaching conditions — there's probably as much of that, if not more, than bread-and-butter issues. But the bread-and-butter issues may seem more important because that is what the board of education wanted to talk about. . . . What happened was that whenever they came to anything vaguely concerned with policy, they said "Not negotiable. This is not a condition that has been defined by the Taylor Law — salary, fringe benefits, and working conditions."

School board respondents clearly confirmed the board's opposition to discussing policy issues. A board member active in negotiations during the late 1960s said:

> As a board member, I started out very much with the feeling — and I think this was common for most board members — that really we did have the power and the right to decide what was done in regard to the teachers. . . . On certain items, we just responded that they were not negotiable, and they would argue some about it, but we, for the most part, just stuck to our position, saying they were not negotiable.

Although the school board refused to yield on any of the broad, policy-related demands, they were quite generous in this first negotiating period regarding salaries, fringe benefits, and other items pertaining to teacher welfare. Ironically, teacher appeals based upon their own economic interests appear to have struck a sympathetic chord with liberal school board members while their appeals for participation in larger programs that would affect students did not. A school board member active in negotiations during that period explained:

> Teachers said that they worked very hard and they didn't get enough money and they should have more benefits. . . . I always felt, being liberal, you know, that the teachers were not paid as much as they should be paid, and it was very responsible work, and so on.

In contrast to negotiations held by the old teachers' association before the Taylor Law, respondents report these sessions to have been more businesslike, although still informal by comparison to what they were to later become. Negotiations were conducted between school board and teacher representatives, without intermediaries. Landau and other professional-idealists among the union leadership played a prominent role in negotiations during this period. A representative from NYSUT attended some sessions, at their invitation, but he remained largely in the background. The school board employed no outside negotiators and relied upon those among their own members who were attorneys to provide legal counsel. After the opening sessions, the superintendent of schools was not involved in negotiations.

Both board and union respondents report informal relations between the two sides to have been good during this period, in spite of differences over the content of negotiations. Formal negotiations took many long hours, but generally went smoothly because participants on both sides of the table treated one another with respect. Difficult issues tended to be hashed out in informal discussions away from the negotiating table and were frequently resolved informally. Respondents from both sides reported having learned a great deal about the perspectives and problems of the other during this period. A board member explained:

> In the course of collective bargaining, over many hours, many things are discussed, there's a lot of give-and-take. School board members are bound to get a lot of information . . . that they would otherwise not get and not solicit. . . . It [give-and-take] cannot effectively take place in the course of a formal school board meeting, and it doesn't have official sanction where a faculty member just calls up a school board member. . . . In the course of bargaining, it has the sanction of state law. If, for example, teachers are demanding fewer supervisory periods, as a matter of collective bargaining, you are bound to get into the question in negotiations of how students are supervised. What happens in the lunch periods? What happens in hall duty? . . . There's always discussion of these subjects and one subject leads to another. School board members were given a great deal of insight into how schools were being run.

The establishment of this avenue of communication informally accomplished one of the major purposes of the professional-idealists, even though the school board turned down their demands for more formal participation in decision making. The same school board member cited above stated:

> It was important from their point of view to have access to the decision makers — direct access, without being accused of being insubordinate, disloyal, or unprofessional. . . . Collective bargaining gave them that context. It was very important to them to maintain that relationship and have that avenue of communication.

The major contractual gains made by the union in 1967 negotiations included the following: improvements in salary and fringe benefits, a grievance procedure with binding arbitration, teacher aides for cafeteria duty (releasing teachers from supervision), and the right of appeal to the school board for probationary teachers denied reappointment.

The next negotiating period was in 1970, when the contract negotiated in 1967 expired. In the 1970 negotiations, the union was able to obtain further reductions in teachers' workload through eliminating other supervisory assignments and winning for teachers the right to a free preparation period during the school day. In addition, in 1970 the union made its first gains in areas not strictly limited to teacher welfare. Most noteworthy among these was the teachers' right, written into the contract, to have advisory input in selection of future administrators.

Union leaders interviewed in 1969 were far from discouraged regarding issues they had wanted to negotiate but that had been left pending. Relative to other school districts, they were doing well; they had reached further and attained more than most other teachers' organizations in the state. And so they regarded each new contract as a step in which they made important gains, believing they would continue to make further gains in future negotiations. Their optimism was soon to be undermined, however, by circumstances beyond their control.

Changing External Conditions

Additional external circumstances developing during the late 1960s began to affect teacher-community relations and, by 1972, to further alter the school board. Changing racial attitudes in the nation were especially important. The rising tide of black separatism and an accompanying distrust of liberals and liberal causes had already begun to influence local black residents in the late 1960s. Discouraged by a lack of clear progress in improving black student achievement (in spite of the district's philosophy), disheartened by the merger, and now lacking in strong national leadership for integration, those local blacks who had once been active supporters of integrationist goals began to lose faith in the school system and to withdraw from participation in it. Middle class blacks were less willing to run for the school board, and some even withdrew their children from district schools. Others became openly critical of Middlebury's schools, programs, and teachers. As the calming influence of pro-integrationist black leaders waned, open expressions of hostility coming from other sectors of the black community began to increase. Less well-educated blacks, having more simplistic expectations for the schools, now began to run for school board seats.

Another external event that influenced teacher-community relations was the 1968 teachers' strike in New York City. This bitter strike intensified black antagonisms toward teachers, and these antagonisms spilled over into Middlebury. Two earlier strikes in New York had elicited sympathies for city teachers among liberal

Middlebury residents, both black and white, but the issues in 1968 were more divisive. In brief, the New York strike involved two groups — each struggling to increase its own power — unexpectedly forced into a mutual confrontation. Blacks' battle for community control over their schools clashed with city teachers' struggle to increase their own influence in the schools. Blacks, perceiving the teachers' union as central to the school establishment, challenged it directly, forcing the still relatively new union into a defensive battle to protect teachers' rights.† A long, bitter strike followed. Issues were oversimplified on both sides. Anti-Semitic slurs used by some black community leaders in criticizing the teachers' union angered and alienated the union's predominantly Jewish, liberal leaders who had themselves been strong supporters of black civil rights.

This hostile confrontation between black community leaders and white, liberal, mainly Jewish teachers in New York City — so close to suburban Middlebury — further threatened the cooperative, integrationist spirit which had earlier pervaded staff-community relations in Middlebury. The frustrations New York blacks suffered in their struggles to gain greater control over the schools in New York City appear to have encouraged Middlebury blacks to express their own rising anger toward liberals and teachers more openly.‡

White, liberal, Jewish residents were shocked and offended by the open expression of black antagonism in New York City, and even more so when they heard this antagonism repeated in Middlebury. Middlebury teachers, most of whom were liberal and many also Jewish, found themselves in an ideological bind. On the one hand, they were sympathetic to the black community control movement as a struggle for power that in many ways paralleled their own; on the

---

†When black residents in the experimental, community-controlled Ocean Hill-Brownsville district decided to evaluate local teachers themselves, transferring those they found wanting out of the district, they violated basic union principles of due process. The city's central board of education, in allowing these transfers, incurred the wrath of the union (New York's United Federation of Teachers), thus prompting the strike. For further details and an excellent analysis of issues in the 1968 school strike in New York, see Ravitch 1974.

‡That their anger was directed more toward liberals and teachers than toward conservative whites and taxpayer groups appears to stem from their feeling that the former let them down. In the late 1950s blacks placed much faith in liberal causes and in education — neither of which, however, satisfactorily fulfilled what it appeared to have promised. Thus, many blacks perceived that liberals were not to be trusted.

other, however, they felt loyalty to union brothers under an attack having strong anti-Semitic and antiprofessional overtones. The New York union had also, in its early days, served as an important model for their teachers' organization.

Some Middlebury teachers, including Landau and his followers, were openly critical of the New York union's handling of that strike; they felt the leadership ought to have shown more sensitivity to community concerns and community relations. Under Landau's leadership, therefore, the Middlebury union attempted to communicate to local black residents its concerns about the New York strike and the local union's interest in working cooperatively with residents toward common educational goals. But antiliberal and antiunion sentiments were already so high among local blacks that many mistrusted the union leaders, and, rather than responding positively to their overtures, the blacks attacked Landau's motives for expressing interest in cooperation. The New York strike had so heightened public awareness of potential conflicts of interest between teachers and community groups that the image of a union pursuing goals for the common good of teachers, students, and community ceased being credible to many local residents, especially blacks. The teachers' union, they believed, was interested in only one thing: improving benefits for teachers.

Antagonisms roused by the New York City strike polarized blacks from white liberals in Middlebury, even within the teaching staff. Following the New York strike, many black teachers (close to 25 percent of the staff were black in the late 1960s) withdrew from the Middlebury Teachers' Federation because of a negative symbolism they had come to associate with teacher unionism. Similar antagonisms also polarized teachers from the community, especially the black community, destroying what remained of the liberal black-white coalition on the board. Respondents on the school board during this period noted a marked change in the attitudes of black board members. One former school board member, herself a liberal, made this comparison:

> In 1967 [when she first came on the board] I felt there were people of differing points of view, more liberal and less liberal, but in general, they all basically wanted Middlebury to be something special.... Then it became factionalized. In time, there was no longer a black spokesman for integration. When it became no longer feasible [to have] a

coalition of blacks and whites who cared about integrated schools, then everything, attitudinally, fell apart.

Coinciding with that time, the white, Jewish liberal teachers and the union . . . were blamed by the blacks for a lot of the problems — reading, . . . discipline . . . and, what is saddest, this played into the hands of [conservative] whites. . . .

Executive sessions got to be — I couldn't bear it. You would hear it [black criticism of teachers] in the executive sessions. Then you would begin to hear it outside of executive sessions. . . . And then you would hear it in the public meetings. They were so angry. . . . And teachers were very much the victims.

By the early 1970s, black antagonists had gained support from an unexpected quarter — those conservative whites who had been moving into the district since the late 1960s, and who were gradually becoming politically active. These two groups, both hostile to the district philosophy but otherwise having little social interchange, now joined in opposing rising school taxes and liberal board candidates. They succeeded in defeating school budgets in several consecutive years, forcing the school board to become still more cautious in district spending.† While the new, conservative coalition was not successful in defeating all liberal candidates for the board, liberals could no longer retain their majority. By 1972, it was a clearly divided board — divided not along racial lines, but according to educational and political philosophies. The board now contained a few liberals, a few moderates, and several members sharply critical of earlier district policies. This was a board at odds with itself, and even less inclined than its predecessors toward cooperating with teachers or their union.

---

†New York school districts (other than cities) are required by law to hold an annual referendum in which taxpayers vote whether to approve proposed school budgets. When voters defeat a budget, school boards have the option of revising and resubmitting it for another referendum or adopting an austerity budget, based on a state-determined expense floor. Austerity budgets allow only for expenses essential to maintaining safety and a modest educational program. Budget defeats, therefore, considerably hamper a district's flexibility in program and staffing.

Changes in Union Goals and Leadership

Increased public criticism, greater budget austerity, and a more divided board forced union leaders into a more defensive position in the early 1970s than they had held in the late 1960s. There was increased pressure, both from without and from within the union, to emphasize protection of teachers over the broader, more idealistic professional goals that interested Landau and his supporters (such as changing the structure of administrator-staff relations and increasing teacher participation in educational decisions). Furthermore, lack of success in negotiating any substantial teacher gains in the professional and policy-making areas made it difficult for the professional-idealists to persuade a divided Executive Council and membership that energies expended on such goals were worthwhile.

Protection fell into three main areas: protection of contract gains in negotiations — especially of gains in salary and fringe benefits; protection of jobs; and protection of individual teacher rights (through grievance procedures). Traditionally a primary function of labor unions, worker protection had never been a goal union leaders could afford to ignore. The professional-idealists, however, were not prepared for the extent to which teacher protection now began to dominate organizational attention.

A more hostile community and budget cuts, both forcing greater emphasis upon teacher protection, led local union leaders to turn more frequently to the statewide teachers' union for advice and support.† In addition to providing advisory services pertinent to particular local problems, the state union had, by this time, established itself as a strong, centralized political action group acting on behalf of teacher interests on a statewide level. Establishment of stronger ties to the state union was distasteful to the professional-idealists, because such ties were inconsistent with their conception of their union as a grass roots, locally based organization and because they felt such an alliance would contribute to widening the gap between teachers and community. Pressures on leaders to protect teacher

---

†At that time, the statewide union was still the Empire State Federation of Teachers, a subsidiary of the American Federation of Teachers (AFT). When the state affiliates of NEA and AFT merged, in 1973, the state teachers' organization became the New York State United Teachers (NYSUT).

interests, however, made them feel they must utilize available resources for strengthening the organization.

The needs for increased emphasis on teacher protection and strengthening the organization led to disenchantment with the union among the idealists — not because they disagreed with the importance of protection, but because opportunities to pursue the more far-reaching goals, which interested them more, were now diminished. Professional-idealists began to drop out of active leadership roles, and by 1971, when Landau's presidency expired, no one from the idealist group was willing to serve in his place. The leadership fell, more by default than design, to an elementary teacher not strongly identified with any faction. While the welfare-oriented faction never actually gained control over the organization, it was able to make its influence more strongly felt on the Executive Council and in the negotiating committee as professional-idealists withdrew from leadership positions.

From the early 1970s on, the presidency and top union leadership stayed with a group composed mainly of elementary teachers not strongly identified with either the professional-idealists or the welfare-oriented faction. While this new group continued to support some professional goals, their energies were concentrated mainly on building organizational solidarity, in fulfilling the union's protective functions, and in building and sustaining ties with the state teachers' organization (for example, attending statewide meetings and conferences and being involved in statewide political activity). These pursuits arose more out of leaders' needs to satisfy a diverse membership and in response to immediate pressures than from any clear leadership philosophy.

THE STRIKE PERIOD

Contract Negotiations in 1972 and 1973: Underlying Issues

Negotiations for the next contract were conducted in the spring and summer of 1972, under the new union leadership and with a largely new school board. The board was under pressure to resist teacher demands in areas where it had previously been lenient. Many members on this new, more conservative board felt that earlier boards had "given away the shop" and that it was now time for belt tightening. In addition, the district's budget defeats in 1971 and again in 1972 clearly indicated public sentiment against increasing school taxes. In this atmosphere, union leaders reluctantly agreed to an eleventh-hour settlement, in August 1972, for a one-year contract they considered unsatisfactory, making a promise to themselves and their membership that they would do better in 1973.

The district had been having problems with administration during this period. Administrative turnover had been high, especially in the high school, and in the superintendent's position. Teachers had complained, also, about inadequate supervision in the high school. In September 1972 the board appointed a man named Milton Avery* as new superintendent. Avery had been serving as assistant superintendent for business affairs in the district and had a reputation as a business management man in contrast to the more humanistic orientation of his predecessors. This appointment was made in spite of strong objections by the teachers' union — a clear indication that teachers' advisory role in selecting administrators, won in 1970 contract negotiations and repeated in their 1972 contract, not only had no binding power, but was not even taken seriously by the new board. Board members themselves were divided over Avery's appointment, but a close majority supported him on the grounds that he would be a strong administrator who could enforce board policies and control the staff. His appointment aroused great animosity among teachers, both because of his administrative orientation and because their own recommendations had been disregarded. Furthermore, teachers did not trust Avery. In his position as assistant superintendent he had reportedly been inconsistent in his treatment of teachers, inclined to show favoritism, and undependable.

Teachers' anger over Avery's appointment, combined with their dissatisfaction with their 1972 contract, were important background factors underlying 1973 negotiations. Issues teachers wished to press focused especially upon job protection this time, though salary was also an important issue, district salaries having slipped considerably relative to others in the county after 1972. The basic, underlying issue for teachers, however, was trust.

Assurances of job protection became especially important to teachers because of their lower trust in both administration and the school board. Job protection issues were included in their 1973 contract demands in the following forms:

No reduction in force — meaning that no position would be cut during the life of the contract

A just cause provision to protect probationary teachers, meaning that no teacher could be denied tenure or reappointment except where unsatisfactory teaching performance and/or conduct had been documented

Limits to class size — meaning that the total number of teaching positions, as well as teaching conditions, would be protected

Reductions in staff positions had not been a threat until the early 1970s, with the first budget defeats, for before that, positions had expanded. Neither had job security for nontenured teachers been a widespread issue before 1973, for until then most probationary teachers had received tenure and, unlike Cedarton, Middlebury respondents did not report dramatic cases where teachers felt colleagues had been unfairly dismissed. However, the threat of possible reductions in staff positions because of economic tightening, combined with teachers' lowered trust of both superintendent and school board, sensitized them to the precarious position of the probationary teacher at this time.

Furthermore, the just cause provision reflected broader teacher concerns about teacher evaluation in respect to tenured as well as nontenured teachers throughout the state. Middlebury teachers had become more sensitive now to unfair treatment of teachers in other school districts, partly because of increased union contacts between school districts and partly because of changes in the character of local district leadership. Now, they felt the need for assurances that had seemed less important in the past. Therefore, they wanted to establish more systematic procedures for the conduct and use of evaluations as protection against all types of arbitrary judgments of their professional lives.

Class size had always been an issue for teachers in contract negotiations. Before 1973, the union's rationale for maintaining low class sizes had been that smaller classes provided more desirable teaching and learning environments; now, class size was becoming a job protection issue, for larger classes meant fewer teachers. Furthermore, inclusion of class size limitations in earlier contracts had had little urgency because previous school boards had shared teachers' belief in the importance of small class sizes and, in practice, had maintained them. Now, with a less supportive school board, one concerned with economizing, the threat of increased class size became real.

Staff cuts projected by the board in 1973 were, in fact, very limited. Neither the union nor the board had any conception at that time of the drastic cuts that were to take place later in the 1970s. Teachers' concern for job security in 1973 was based more upon a decline of faith in their administration and school board than on a perception of significant change in external conditions.

The Conduct of Negotiations in 1973

Teachers' anxiety and anger over changes in the school board and administration, together with their dissatisfaction with the 1972 contract, put the union negotiating team under pressure to take a tough stance in the 1973 negotiations. Board members, on the other hand, continued to be subject to pressures from the community groups previously identified and were ready to demonstrate that they, not teachers, were in charge.

The school board in 1973, we have noted, was clearly less supportive of teachers than earlier boards — less oriented toward progressive educational and social programs and more budget oriented. It was a divided board, with some elements hostile toward teachers. But at no time were Middlebury School Boards dominated by people as hostile toward teachers as those board members who dominated Cedarton and Oakville boards in the late 1960s and early 1970s. Middlebury's 1973 board was dominated, rather, by moderates. There was still, in Middlebury, the potential for cooperation between board and teachers, for the trouble between them was not so much a matter of disagreement over specific issues as one of underlying attitudes toward negotiations themselves.

However, according to respondents from both sides, the 1973 board was, while not hostile, exceptionally resistant to meeting any teacher demands. A member of the 1973 union negotiating team commented: "The board of education had taken a position, 'We beat them down once [in 1972]. We can beat them down again.' They were not trying to negotiate in good faith." A school board respondent who came onto the 1973 board a few months after the start of negotiations observed:

> It seems ridiculous, but they [board members] really were not interested in negotiating. They felt they were in a position to say "take it or leave it"; and attempted to do just that. . . . They had not really looked at the demands of the teachers, had not developed a list of demands or even alternatives, had not even talked to one another in terms of what they were willing . . . to address. . . . It was as if the board members didn't want to deal with it. It was a thorn in their side, it was taking a lot of their time, . . . a pain in the neck.

Teacher negotiators, determined as they were to take a strong stand with the board, were angered and frustrated by board members' apparent refusal to negotiate in good faith. And these feelings further heightened tensions between the negotiating parties.

Added to this situation was the fact that 1973 representatives of both the union and the school board were relatively new to the negotiating process. The union was operating under another new president — a second elementary teacher who had assumed office only a few months earlier — while the 1972 president (who had little negotiating experience) now served as chief negotiator. Only a few members on the union negotiating team had participated in any previous negotiations. The board also had a new president, with a former president serving as its new chief negotiator. The presence of these inexperienced negotiators on both sides further aggravated existing tensions between the parties.

Because of their desire to take a firm stand and because of their own lack of experience, the MTF negotiating team began to rely more heavily upon the state organization (now NYSUT) for advice during negotiations; the local NYSUT field representative participated more extensively in actual negotiating sessions than had been the case in previous years. This change, which benefited the union, antagonized some members of the board. Old board members resented this intrusion by an outsider into the personal relationship that had existed when board members and teachers negotiated directly. They also correctly read the union's greater utilization of the field representative as an indication that teachers had little faith in the school board.

Thus, the 1973 contract negotiations were pervaded by far more tension, hostility, and polarization than had existed during any previous negotiations. Negotiations took on a more formal character than in the past, for informal channels of communication had been disrupted both by changes in leadership on both sides and by the loss of trust between them. Across the bargaining table, little real communication took place. A teacher respondent on the 1973 union negotiating team commented: "It was a feeling that everybody was playing games. . . . There was a lot of posturing, a lot of fist shaking." A 1973 board member reported:

> Neither side was making any kind of offer at all. . . . It wasn't, "Let us make a proposal to you" or "Let us give you two or three proposals and . . . talk about whichever one you're interested in." . . . It was just a stating of, "We don't want this, we don't want that," and waiting [for the other side to respond]. And, of course, nobody was responding.

In the spring of 1973, both parties agreed to request outside mediation under the auspices of the state's Public Employee Relations Board (PERB), an agency created under the Taylor Law to facilitate public employee negotiations. When the mediator was unable to bring about a resolution, the case was referred to a second procedural level provided within the PERB structure, fact-finding, a process in which an appointed fact-finder investigates factors in the dispute and makes a nonbinding recommendation for settlement. The fact-finder's recommendations, however, were not acceptable to either party.

In June, just before the close of school, the union membership met to determine whether the negotiating committee should be authorized to call a strike at the opening of school in September in the event a contract had not been obtained by that time. The meeting was heavily attended. Members, already angry with the board and with the superintendent, Miller, were now further angered by the board's resistance to negotiations. Because striking was an option more easily acceptable to them than to the more conservative faculties of Cedarton and Oakville, membership sentiments were already strongly prostrike. In fact, over 90 percent of the members attending that meeting voted for strike authorization.

Even with the threat of a September strike, negotiations continued as before, with little progress during the first part of the summer. Not until August did both parties begin seriously to focus their demands and identify essential differences. By the end of

August, they did succeed in substantially narrowing their differences. In fact, the board and union were close to resolution. But the atmosphere of distrust and recrimination had become so intense that they were still unable to reach a settlement.

Board members found union negotiators hostile and aggressive; union negotiators found board members unreasonable. The degree to which any remaining spirit of good faith had deteriorated during the 1973 negotiations is illustrated in the following incident, reported by a board member who was not part of the 1973 negotiating team, but who attended some sessions:

> At the last point after an all-night session, after they thought they'd worked everything out, one of the union representatives came charging into the room where a couple of board members were, and he said something . . . absolutely had to be changed, that it was different from what they had agreed to. One of the board members immediately said that that was the way it was going to be and there was not going to be any change, no matter what. That was it. The person responding had not even looked or considered or heard anything other than, "It's got to be changed. . . ." When finally the union member left, I discussed it with the board member, and I said, "Whatever was agreed to, what he wants to do to change it seems better for the board. What are you objecting for?" And the response was, "He just gets me so angry."

Issues that both sides claim in retrospect ought to have been easily resolved, had a better negotiating climate prevailed, were not resolved before the opening of school. Thus, in September 1973, the MTF leaders called a strike.

The Strike

Rank-and-file support for the strike appears to have been strong among union members. But not all teachers were union members, and some nonunion teachers refused to join the strike on the grounds that it would be harmful both to children and to teacher-community relations.† Activists estimated from 70 to 90 percent of the teachers

---

†Such sentiments were reportedly strongest among those black teachers who had resigned from the MTF following the 1968 strike in New York City.

supported the strike. Survey data indicated 79 percent of respondents supported the strike; 64 percent were active supporters (see Appendix, Table 3). By all counts, however, a strong majority within the teaching staff were active strike supporters, and this included all union factions.

Reasons for rank-and-file support were not clear. An open-ended questionnaire item asking rank-and-file teachers their reasons for supporting the 1973 strike yielded a wide variety of answers, ranging from specific issues like salary, job security, and class size to general statements about the arrogance of the school board, a feeling the school board wanted to dictate the contract, and a feeling that teachers were not being given humanistic treatment by Miller. Interviews helped to explain this apparent variety of reasons for the strike by clarifying common undercurrents. A teacher respondent, active during the strike period, pointed out:

> Actually the strike had nothing to do with what was on the negotiating table. Money, job security, things like that were so-called strike issues, but had the tone been different at the time, we might have gone through those issues without getting into a strike.... Underlying everything was attitude.

Another teacher activist from the strike period explained:

> I don't think you can say that any one issue was the issue that caused the teachers to go out. Everyone had their own reason. I think what happened, essentially, was that the entire package — the things that were important to me, the money that was important to other people — kind of coalesced into a total package the staff as a whole found unacceptable.... And I think the climate was ripe for everyone putting their foot down and saying, "It's time to take a stand."

Negotiations continued during the strike, but they were tense. Three or four days into the strike, the board's chief negotiator resigned because of exhaustion. Only a few days later, the union president announced that he would resign as soon as the strike was over because he had "had it." These resignations further indicate the emotional intensity of the strike atmosphere in Middlebury. They also appear, however, to have reflected the existence of strains within both the union and school board, because there is no evidence that the objective conflict between parties placed unusual pressures on those in top leadership positions.†

Union respondents from Middlebury made few comments during interviews that directly indicated tension or divisiveness within the union during the strike period. In fact, most recalled the strike as a time of strong organizational unity — a period when internal factions pulled together in the face of external conflict. Yet there were subtle indications of continuing internal division, which respondents may have either forgotten because of more vivid recollections of member solidarity in most areas or which they chose not to reveal in their desire to protect the image of organizational unity during the strike. For example, several school board respondents reported the union negotiating team to have taken unusually lengthy breaks for internal deliberation during negotiations. In contrast to Cedarton activists, who spoke candidly and without hesitation about internal union deliberations during the strike, Middlebury union activists disclosed undercurrents of dissension by their hesitation in responding to questions about internal union issues during that period. A few others, however, were more openly critical of certain aspects of their leaders' positions during the strike. This last point will be addressed in more detail below.

School board respondents were generally more open about their internal disagreements. Some felt others were not sufficiently understanding of teachers' concerns. Others objected not so much to the substance of the board's position as to members' tones and postures during negotiations (for example, colleagues taking moralistic, patronizing, or inflexible attitudes that antagonized teachers). Thus, there were, within the board, pressures by some members to be more conciliatory while others exerted pressures toward taking an unyielding stance.

After the union president announced his intention to resign, the vice president assumed a more active leadership role. The vice president was another elementary teacher, a woman named Jenny Abrams,* who at that time had had little experience in either union

---

†In fact, in Cedarton, where the polarization between negotiating parties was far more extreme than in Middlebury, there were no indications that pressures on top leaders were unmanageable, although members of both the school board and union negotiating teams were as inexperienced in contract negotiations as in Middlebury. Nelson and his negotiating team had assumed office only months before the start of 1973 negotiations in Cedarton.

leadership or negotiations. By her own admission, she wouldn't have become active in the union had others not pushed her to do so, and she certainly had not anticipated assuming the presidency. In her words: "When he announced that [he would resign] I nearly fainted. . . . My choice was to call for a new election, or — But, I guess I'm not one to run away." Thus, the top union leadership was determined virtually by default — another indication that the union lacked cohesiveness during this period.

The board negotiator was replaced by an attorney, a former board president who had negotiated an earlier union contract in 1969 during Seth Landau's presidency, when the board and union had had better informal relations. The new board negotiator attempted to utilize his old connections to broach a settlement, approaching Landau informally with a tentative proposal. Because Landau was no longer a union officer, he could do no more than pass the proposal on to the current officers, on the assumption that they would take it into consideration. However, union officers rejected the informal proposal, apparently more for tactical than substantive reasons. In fact, substantially, both Landau and a board respondent reported that this proposal had been not only reasonable, but more favorable to the union than the settlement the officers later accepted. On the one hand, in their mistrust of the board, union leaders had difficulty in accepting an informal, behind-the-scenes proposition; they wanted everything open and on the table. On the other, because of their inexperience, they had difficulty carrying a response to the board proposal into open negotiations without seeming to have yielded in their own position. Thus, in the next negotiating session, the union's chief negotiator ignored cues offered by the board negotiator to move in the direction of the proposed settlement, laying out instead substantially the same position the union had taken in the previous session. At that point, the new board negotiator, surprised and annoyed, walked out of the session. This development, therefore, further polarized the two parties, and negotiations remained at an impasse.

Administrators' Reactions during the Strike

Administrators' sympathies appear to have been divided, as in Cedarton. Most kept a low profile during the strike. The district superintendent remained in the background, occupied with keeping the schools open without adequate staff. In any event, the superintendent was not in a position to play an active role in either the negotiations process or in bringing about a settlement, because of his poor relationship with the union.

Community Relations during the Strike

Community sentiments toward striking teachers were divided at the outset of the strike. Liberal white residents were reportedly predisposed to be sympathetic to teacher concerns — particularly to the just cause issue — while more conservative whites and blacks were predisposed to be more hostile. These latter groups were angry about disruptions in school programs and exerted pressure on board members to take a "hard line."

Few residents appear to have had sufficient information to fully understand the strike issues, for communication between teachers and community residents was fragmented. Both the school board and the union attended to public relations through news releases and the distribution of fliers, but the union leadership made no attempt to communicate directly with residents as had been done in Cedarton. This failure disturbed professional-idealists, such as Landau and other former union leaders, who claimed the new leaders failed to effectively utilize sympathetic community groups. By adequately informing such groups about the issues, former leaders maintained, community pressures on the board toward cooperation with teachers could have been enhanced, and dangers of long-term polarization between teachers and community reduced. In view of the racial composition of the district and racial tensions, the professional-idealists were particularly concerned that Middlebury not follow the course taken by New York City teachers in 1969, where the UFT strike antagonized both blacks and liberal whites. Landau commented:

> When New York City had the strike, we went up . . . along with a few other locals . . . and fought Al Shanker, [because] we didn't think . . . the strike . . . was run right. And here we were, in my view, being

forced to go through a similar thing, without concern about the community response.

These idealist leaders also perceived the new leaders as taking a confrontation stance in their relationship to the school board in cases where a more positive, cooperative stance would have been possible and more effective. Because the former leaders had worked directly with some board members still holding office, they were well aware that the board was not entirely antagonistic to teachers; furthermore, they noted that board members, although stubbornly resistant to teacher demands, were not expressing the kind of open arrogance and hostility toward striking teachers that had been witnessed elsewhere (for example, in Cedarton). One of the professional-idealists reported the following incident, which took place at an open school board meeting during the strike, as an illustration:

> There was one public meeting where a community member stood up and yelled that they should fire all the teachers and hire new people. The president of the board, . . . who was taking a very hard-nosed position during negotiations . . . and who was considered Enemy Number One by the teaching staff, . . . stood up and screamed at this person, "We may be having our differences now, but we have the best teaching staff in the county, and don't you dare even suggest such a thing, because this will pass." . . . A lot of people chose not to hear that, but I did.

The idealists attributed the new leaders' failure to perceive and utilize potential community support in part to their inexperience and principally to their heavy reliance on NYSUT. The idealists believed that NYSUT, as a statewide organization, lacked a community-based perspective and that NYSUT representatives, whose experience was mainly in cities or in labor-organizing activities other than teaching, failed to understand the importance of developing good teacher-community relations. Landau and other former leaders went so far as attempting to organize meeting on their own with community residents, for purposes of explaining the union position. Without the full cooperation of current leaders, however, these efforts were neither as comprehensive nor as effective as comparable union efforts in Cedarton.

The Strike Settlement

The strike lasted 13 days — longer than participants on either side had anticipated. Union respondents reported some discontent within their ranks as the strike dragged on without clear progress toward settlement. However, in spite of weaknesses in union leadership and dissension within it over tactical issues (such as the handling of negotiations and community relations), all leaders shared common convictions about their reasons for striking. This enabled them to sustain fairly strong public solidarity. The basic, unifying factor appears to have been the teachers' desire to demonstrate to the board and central administration that they wished to be taken seriously in negotiations. Supporting this was widespread teacher loyalty to the idea of a union and a feeling that striking was a legitimate response to school board resistance in negotiations. (In Cedarton and Oakville, teachers had more initial doubts about the legitimacy of unionism or striking.)

The initiative for eventual settlement of the strike came from within the board, encouraged by pressures from some community residents, despite the union's neglect of public relations. The settlement was no better than the one the board had offered the union just before the strike; it was worse than the one it had offered, informally, through Landau. Teacher respondents reported that it was, nevertheless, in many respects a good settlement. Salaries — which had not been the main issue — showed the union's major gain, because the settlement provided for salary adjustments based upon the cost of living for a three-year period. These later proved to be substantial, as the rate of inflation rose markedly during that period.† The board, unlike Cedarton's board, also agreed to a contract clause specifying limitations to class sizes. Several board respondents did not view specifying class size limitations as a concession to teachers. These board members favored such a clause as a protection for the district against possible later changes in existing policy as public resistance to school spending tightened. Thus, liberal, proeducation traditions still influenced board decisions.

---

†The Consumer Price Index rose to double-digit figures within the following year and continued at a high rate for several years thereafter. Such high increases had not, of course, been anticipated by board members, who had intended holding salaries down.

The settlement included a compromise on the issue of just cause for probationary (nontenured) teachers. Teachers had wanted a contract statement indicating that no teacher would be dismissed without just cause, with the burden of proof being upon the administration to document reasons for dismissal based on unsatisfactory performance of teaching duties. The board refused to grant such a statement but agreed instead to more detailed procedures for evaluating and recommending probationary teachers for tenure; the agreement specified that two administrators and one outside professional (selected by the teacher) would observe and evaluate the probationary teacher's performance, submit written evaluations to a Review Panel composed of teacher representatives, and to the superintendent; the Review Panel would recommend for or against tenure to the superintendent, who would then make his own recommendation. Both the Review Panel's recommendation and the superintendent's were to be only advisory, leaving the final decision to the school board.† The union accepted this compromise, hoping that the panel's recommendation would prove to be morally binding.

Even though the strike settlement did not provide the union with all that it sought, it offered Middlebury teachers considerably more than Cedarton teachers were able to obtain following their strike in the same year. In the areas of salary and class size, the MTF made important gains. Even the just cause compromise, while not providing ultimate protection against unfair teacher dismissal, did indicate the board's recognition of the problem by its inclusion in the contract. In spite of difficulties in negotiations and tensions between the board and union, this settlement indicated a greater willingness on the part of at least some board members to make concessions to teachers. Still, from the teachers' viewpoint, it was not a good settlement — not as good as the ones achieved in 1968 and 1970 under earlier boards and not good enough to override their bitterness over board members' initial refusal to negotiate and their imposition of financial penalties on striking teachers.

Under the Education Law (Section 3013), school boards must review the superintendent's recommendation before making their decision, but they need not follow it (see Hageny 1980).

Impact of the Strike

The costs of the strike to both sides were high. For teachers, the personal economic costs were enormous. Under the Taylor Law, striking public employees were subject to penalties equivalent to two days' pay for every one day on strike, and the school board refused to suspend these financial penalties in its settlement, as it had the option of doing. For the school board, the costs were not economic, but political and organizational: public embarrassment and a state of confusion within the school system. Previous antagonisms between teachers, administrators, and school board were now heightened by hostilities shown during the strike and by teacher resentment against the board for its strict imposition of penalties.

The strike improved solidarity within both union and school board for several years, blurring earlier, internal divisions, but it also polarized these two groups further from one another. A board respondent explained:

> If the strike . . . pulled teachers together, it also pulled board members together, developing new poles within the district. . . . There was a taking-off to the corners of the ring. Everybody was in his own corner. The union was in one place, the board was in another. . . . And I don't think just the teachers and the board pulled apart, but I think the principals . . . [and] top administration [also pulled apart], so you had these separate groups.

On the community, the impact was mixed. Some residents remained sympathetic to teachers and became more critical of the school board and administration; in fact, a citizens' group formed to inquire into causes of the strike. But among others, including many previously neutral residents, the strike aroused antiteacher and antiunion sentiments.

To some respondents in all three parties, the strike was unnecessary, a waste or, in the words of a member of a prestrike school board, "a symbolic battle that didn't . . . really answer anyone's needs." But to others, this symbolic battle, which in the short run yielded far greater costs than benefits, did have some long-range benefits. Most important, it brought both union and school board to a sharp realization of the costs of failing to recognize the other's point of view. This realization had an important effect in later negotiations.

THE POSTSTRIKE PERIOD

Following the strike, community antagonisms toward teachers intensified. It is not clear to what extent intensified antagonisms were a direct outcome of the strike because there appear to have been other contributing factors. Lower middle and working class residents — both black and white — had already become more vocal and more critical of the schools before the strike. Moreover, increased public criticism appears to have reflected a national trend of greater conservatism, uneasiness, and impatience with the liberal experiments of the 1960s, which had been so much more dramatic in Middlebury than in Cedarton. Some respondents, however, believed that criticisms directed specifically against teachers became more intense immediately after the strike. In content, the criticisms appear to have reflected taxpayers' resentment over improved teacher benefits in the face of their perceptions that the teachers were failing to adequately educate their children. Such perceptions were especially strong among lower middle and working class blacks, but were also increasing among working class whites. These residents' resentment focused on the union for protecting teachers from accountability for educational inadequacies. Thus, it would appear that resentment intensified more in consequence of greater community awareness of the union during the strike rather than because of any strike activities per se. Some respondents felt that the union, in neglecting efforts to rally community support through direct, personal contact, or to create a forum for dialogue with residents about teacher concerns and reasons for the strike, allowed community antagonisms to multiply.

In the poststrike period, liberal residents became less active in school district affairs because of overall changes in the district population, lowered optimism about the future of integrated education, and, for some, a sense of futility about the potential for making significant improvements in the schools. Their withdrawal from activism was significant in that this generally more educated group had earlier been better able to understand the complexities and difficult issues underlying school district problems. They had also tended to be more sympathetic to teachers and to the concept of teacher unionism than less well-educated residents, whether black or white. With the liberals less active, teachers had fewer articulate, supportive allies to assist in interpreting their concerns to others in the community. Aside from the small citizens' group formed to inquire into the causes of the strike, no concerted initiative was taken on the part of community residents to improve community-teacher relations, as was the case in Cedarton and, as we shall see, in Oakville.

Without unified community leadership, heightened public antagonisms toward teachers and schools began to manifest themselves more clearly on the school board. Respondents characterized middle and late 1970s school boards as, in the aggregate, more limited in vision and in educational commitment than in the past. While liberal professionals continued to have some representation on the board, reactionary, educationally conservative community factions of both races gained more positions. Increasing differences in philosophy among board members, combined with increased economic restrictions upon the district, led to a lack of predictability in board decision making. This lack of predictability contributed to teacher and administrator perceptions of the board as an inconsistent, often arbitrary and highly politicized body. The presence in the same period of some individuals on the board prone to making inflammatory critical comments about teachers, often in public, further contributed to teacher perceptions of the school board as a hostile adversary.

Immediately following the strike union leaders, as well as individual teachers, began, in turn, to take a more militant, aggressive stance in their relations with both administrators and the school board. Jenny Abrams, the union president in the poststrike period, commented:

> Before [the strike] there was a more relaxed kind of relationship with the board . . . and administration. . . . We were not as sharply defined. Since then, we are A UNION — in capital letters — and a power respected in the community. We began to understand that it's not a gentlemen's agreement relationship. It's definitely labor-management.

Administrators, already subject to increased pressures from both parents and the school board in this period (administrators had not yet formed their own union and were often literally insecure in their positions), report having felt especially vulnerable to the teachers' more hostile, adversarial attitude. Even before the strike, several principals had been targets of parent and teacher criticism, and two, in the high school, had been eased out of their positions as a consequence. Following the strike, therefore, principals were far more cautious in their treatment of teachers — almost, according to several respondents, to the point of immobility. A school board respondent commented:

> People . . . walked very warily. I think . . . principals, more than anybody, had the feeling . . . they were unloved by everybody. I think they feared to do very much with teachers. . . . They weren't going to do anything that was unpleasant to teachers. Therefore, they would be forced into positions that seemed to put them at odds with central administration. And, by the way, they also feared central administration.

Avery, the superintendent, had not proved popular with any groups in the district. In 1975, the board removed Avery and appointed another assistant superintendent in his place. Respondents characterized the new superintendent, Richard Roberts*, as a consensus man, conciliatory, and humanistic. Teachers liked Roberts, and he had far better relations with the staff than his predecessor, but most respondents did not perceive him as exercising strong administrative leadership.† For both of these reasons he was viewed less as an adversary by union leaders than his predecessor, and staff-administrator relations appear to have improved somewhat under him. However, whether because of personal limitations in leadership ability or because of the contradictory pressures on him, Roberts was unable to effectively insulate his staff from community or board antagonisms. Thus, teachers' insecurity and, therefore, sense of dependency on the union for protection in a volatile environment appears to have increased during his administration.

In the mid-1970s, the district began to experience declining student enrollments. Between 1974 and 1979, over 40 teacher positions were cut, including many held by tenured teachers. Some had been in the district as long as ten years. Because the union had been unsuccessful in negotiating a no reduction in force clause, the contract did not protect even tenured teachers against cuts based on

---

†Several respondents observed that given the extent of community and board factionalism, no superintendent could have exercised strong leadership, in any given direction, because of the contradictory pressures exerted by various factions from within the community, board, and teaching staff.

declining enrollments — a situation parallel to that in Cedarton. Three elementary school buildings were closed. Cuts in federal and state budgets also strongly affected Middlebury, because of its reliance on outside financing for special programs geared toward low income, minority children. These cuts meant further reductions in staff. Meanwhile, local budget defeats influenced the school board and central administration toward even greater financial caution. Class sizes were pushed to the limits specified in the contract; special programs and services eroded.

Actual teacher cuts were less extensive in Middlebury than in Cedarton, where the decline in student enrollment was sharper and the tax base smaller. Still, the antagonistic climate in which the Middlebury cuts occurred and the teachers' sense of relative deprivation, because of a lowering of school board support, appear to have influenced teacher morale and insecurity more adversely than in Cedarton.

THE UNION IN THE 1970S

Organizational Structure and Leadership

As in Cedarton, the MTF changed its formal structure very little after the old association was reorganized in 1967. Structurally, the two organizations were similar. The major officers (in Middlebury, all were elected) were the president, vice presidents, secretary, treasurer, and the chairpersons for various committees — including a grievance committee, negotiating committee, and welfare committee. These officers formed the Executive Council. Another carryover from the association was the central representative assembly in which delegates from each building met regularly to discuss and take action on presidential and Executive Council recommendations.

The major structural change from the association and early union was the inclusion of nonteacher staff members (teacher aides and clerical and service workers) in the union in the 1970s. As in Cedarton, and in keeping with similar practices elsewhere in the state, this change was instituted by the MTF for the purpose of providing unified union representation for all groups within the staff, with the exception of administrators, in order to reduce potential competition among various employee groups. Nonteacher groups were represented on the Executive Council and in the central delegate assembly but operated under separate contracts, separately negotiated. No evidence was provided to indicate that inclusion of nonteaching employees in the organization significantly altered its activities or direction, and, as in Cedarton, teachers continued to dominate the organization by virtue of their greater numbers.

In 1979, respondents were close to unanimous in reporting the union to be a far stronger, better organized group than it had been a decade earlier. Officers' formal spheres of responsibility were more clearly defined and better coordinated. Routine, procedural problems relating to teacher grievances and negotiations were more systematically managed. In discussions of organizational changes during the interviews, respondents generally gave more emphasis to changes in organizational leadership, to the union's relationship to NYSUT, and to changes in union goals than to formal structural changes, such as the inclusion of nonteaching staff.

Changes in the nature of union leadership followed a distinctly different pattern in Middlebury than in Cedarton. For comparison purposes, we shall examine patterns of difference in respect to the following aspects of leadership: degree of continuity or stability in top leadership positions, the type of teacher tending to be active in the union, and leadership styles.

Continuity in Office

Jenny Abrams, having assumed the presidency of the union on the day the strike was over, was still president six years later, in 1979. Abrams was the first in the Middlebury union to even run for this office more than once. This was in contrast to leadership patterns in the late 1960s and early 1970s, wherein the presidency was deliberately rotated. In contrast to the leadership in Cedarton, where continuity in office had been deliberately sustained, Abrams's continuity in that position was, however, more by default, even from the start. In her own words:

> My becoming president was accidental, in a sense, because I don't think I would have had the self-confidence — by myself — to say, "I'm going to run for president." But I was first vice president, and I guess I'm not one to run away.... When I got active [originally] it was ... because there was nobody on the [Executive Council] who represented the primary school. So I became involved mainly because of that.

Other respondents frequently indicated that she continued in office mainly because others abdicated. Typical comments were as follows:

> No one else has wanted to get involved in that sort of thing. . . .
>
> It's a very difficult job which requires a tremendous amount of work, and no one . . . sees how they can add it to the workload they already carry and do an adequate job. . . .
>
> No one else is willing to do the amount of work that she does. . . .

Abrams's ability to carry a heavy workload was one of her major strengths. So she continued in office and gained considerable expertise as president. Other leadership positions, however, turned over frequently. Except for Abrams, few teachers in Middlebury sustained a union leadership position for very many years after the strike. Only one teacher who had been active in the 1960s was still active in the late 1970s, and he was a traditional unionist. None of the professional-idealist group remained active in the union after 1973, although several from this group were still considered significant informal leaders in the district in 1979.

Active participation in the union dropped most substantially in the high school during the 1970s. Jenny Abrams explained:

> This has been a source of great concern to me. . . . Because the leadership had been there before, many of them now say, "I've done my bit. I'll support you, but I'm tired." And they've gone off to other interests. They're still good union members, and they'll come out for . . . [support] but it's hard to get leadership out of them.

Reference to a deliberate rotation of leadership positions and the notion that former leaders were tired were frequently offered as reasons why professional-idealists were no longer active in the union. However, although such reasons may have been valid, they do not constitute an adequate explanation of why the professional-idealists withdrew so completely from union leadership roles in Middlebury in such marked contrast to Cedarton, where many early union leaders remained active through the 1970s. A more thorough discussion of reasons for these differing leadership patterns will be offered in Chapter 5.

Type of Teacher Assuming Leadership

The leadership of both the association and early union had been concentrated in the high school in the 1960s and shifted to the elementary schools in the 1970s. This shift indicated more than a mere rotation in leadership positions. The early leaders — the teachers who had pressed for reorganization of the association, for professional negotiations, and then for affiliation with the AFT — mainly the professional-idealists — had been among the most highly educated and respected teachers in the district. In other words, the "influentials," or informal leaders within the staff, had been those elected as formal officers. When these teachers withdrew from union activism in the early 1970s, it not only became more difficult to fill major union positions, but these positions were also now more often filled by teachers who had lesser status in the eyes of their colleagues.

Teachers indicated considerable ambivalence about both Abrams and the rest of the leadership group. Most respondents characterized Abrams as a good president — hardworking, pragmatic, strongly committed to the union and to her membership. Yet further comments were often evasive, even in response to direct questions. The following excerpt from an interview with a union member was typical:

> *Question:* In another district, people often mention . . . [that] the leaders in the union are "the best people in the school." Would you say that was true of your union?
>
> *Answer:* Well, it's very difficult for me to say. . . . That's a very difficult question for me to answer.
>
> *Question:* Would you say that was true in the past?
>
> *Answer:* Yes.

Other union members commented as follows:

> It's difficult for me to criticize people who work as hard as the people in the union. They are committed people, they work long hours with pretty good results in terms of negotiating contracts. . . . But — I

> know there are people who have discussed among themselves ... alternative [candidates].
>
> Generally, I think the union leadership is respected, with one or two exceptions.
>
> Teachers who are involved with the educational concerns of the school system, teachers viewed as the intellectuals ... are [now] more on the outside of the union.

One current union activist was more direct: "The quality of our leadership in the union ... is a problem. I have to be frank."

Administrators and school board members also tended to be evasive or qualified in their comments, in marked contrast to the open praise such respondents volunteered in discussing union leaders in Cedarton. The following were typical of Middlebury administrators and school board members:

> As far as the union leadership — it's very hard for me to judge. I've had very little contact with [them] ... because we've had few problems. ... Jenny Abrams seems to be tempered, pretty middle-of-the-road. She seems to be fair. (School principal)
>
> She [Abrams] has been a reasonable person. ... I assume she satisfies the staff. From nobody do I get negative vibes. (Second principal)
>
> I think she's a strong union leader dedicated to her role. (Third principal)
>
> She's fair, and I think for a union leader to be fair requires a certain amount of courage — not to be inflammatory and not to play to the audience. She's not a firebrand, ... but she's responsible and hardworking. (Current board member)
>
> Jenny's strength is that she ... reflects the average person, for whom teaching is a living. (Former board member)

Leadership Style

In Middlebury, the union president assumed the major responsibility for carrying out union functions. Even though certain functions were delegated to others, difficulty in sustaining capable people in key union positions did not permit the extent of shared responsibility that occurred in Cedarton. Thus, Abrams herself carried out many functions that were performed by others in Cedarton — for example, composing the monthly newsletter. Furthermore, there was no evidence in Middlebury of an informal, supportive network among union activists comparable to that in Cedarton. While union officers met often in the Executive Council, these formal meetings did not permit the kind of threshing-out of union positions on difficult issues that occurred in Cedarton.

By contrast to Cedarton, where union officers exercised active, persuasive leadership roles, Abrams played more of a coordinating and sustaining role in the organization, attempting to pull together diverse points of view through compromise. A school board member commented: "I think Jenny represents somebody who can talk to all sides in the union and who can be voted for by enough union members so that she represents a consensus." In the sense that she represented membership views held in common and in the sense that she took direction from membership (rather than setting direction and persuading members to follow), Abrams's style was more democratic than the Cedarton leaders' style, more in keeping with the earlier grass roots union orientation. Her orientation toward sustaining organizational consensus, however, appears to have resulted in what some union members viewed as an avoidance of difficult, controversial issues. One commented on this as follows:

> The prevalent note is caution, always caution. Caution is important, but there are times when — [drops off] . . . Jenny's concern is, "Don't separate, don't divide. . . . Don't cause splits among the teachers." . . . Which means you have to avoid anything controversial.

Membership Participation and Factionalism

In 1979, 96 percent of the Middlebury teachers belonged to the union. But as in Cedarton, activists complained about the difficulty of sustaining rank-and-file involvement in the organization. One remarked:

> There has not been as much participation in . . . the union as there should be. . . . There are too many teachers who remain uninvolved — teachers who are dues-paying members, but don't involve themselves in union activities. . . . I think it's called, "Let George do it."

Another commented: "They join, pay their dues, but don't want to assume responsibility."

Whereas active participation on the Executive Council was more difficult to sustain in Middlebury than in Cedarton, survey data indicated Middlebury respondents to have been more likely to attend membership meetings. Their better attendance possibly reflected their stronger orientation to grass roots participation. Better attendance at meetings may also have reflected Middlebury teachers' greater freedom from responsibilities for young children after school. The Middlebury sample was, on average, about eight years older than the Cedarton sample and about ten years older than the Oakville sample.

Unlike Cedarton where a newly formed NEA chapter challenged the CFC for collective bargaining representation in the late 1970s, there were no external challenges to the Middlebury union. Nor were there any organized efforts from within the organization to challenge the top leadership in an election. Internal factions were also less clear-cut in 1979 than in the 1960s. Professional-idealists no longer debated their position strongly within the union, and external pressures — budget cuts, school closings, and cuts in staff — fostered greater unanimity on monetary and protective goals as union priorities. Still, a diffuse factionalism appears to have pervaded the union, making internal discussion of issues more difficult and less focused than in Cedarton. Respondents reported colleagues as "continually fighting," "in constant disagreement," and "always yelling at each other." Many respondents attributed internal dissension simply to the mixture of strong personalities on the staff. What seems a more plausible hypothesis is that internal dissension reflected members' general disenchantment with the union and frustration at being unable to formulate a clear organizational direction, in the face of shifts in district policy away from its earlier educational commitments.

Relationship of the MTF to the Statewide Organization

Initially because of her own inexperience and the lack of a supportive informal network within the union, Jenny Abrams relied heavily on NYSUT for guidance and advice in the early days of her presidency, immediately following the strike. Abrams explained:

> They've certainly educated me, and I've made it my business to utilize them [NYSUT advisors].... They are as close to me as the telephone.

> ... The first year, I utilized ... the local center more than I do now. ... As I become more involved on the state level, I know exactly which office to call [in Albany] and whom to speak to on whatever issue I need information.

Over time, Abrams became increasingly active within the state organization in several capacities — as did the presidents of the Cedarton and Oakville unions. As in Cedarton and Oakville, and contrary to the claims of some administrators and school board members, union respondents in Middlebury also made it clear that NYSUT representatives in no way instructed or pressured local activists concerning what positions they should take. Abrams explained: "There is no interference at all in local affairs or local negotiations. ... We get guidance. ... I can call them for advice on something, ... [but] they will never interfere." However, the frequency with which references to NYSUT came up in conversations with both activists and other respondents in Middlebury suggested the Middlebury teachers relied more heavily on NYSUT for such advice than did union leaders in the other two districts. A more stressful environment in Middlebury may have been a factor in the MTF seeking more outside support.

This closer affiliation with the state organization also represented an important change in the local union's orientation. Landau commented:

> Even in the heyday of our push for unionization, I wasn't very interested in national and state affiliation. I thought it was necessary, helpful in the bigger scheme of things, but I didn't think it meant very much to us. We put very little energy into it. Jenny and her people put a lot of energy into that. They see it as very important.

A school principal also noted a stronger affiliation with NYSUT as a significant change: "At one time I think the organization was more independent. ... Over a period of years, it got so enmeshed within the state that really they don't move now without someone from the state sitting in."

Landau and other early union activists interviewed believed the MTF's closer affiliation with NYSUT contributed to a major shift in the local organization's emphasis. Landau explained:

I'd always been very contemptuous of . . . going to conventions and [passing] resolutions. . . . That was a failing on my part, because there are larger issues. But I'd hoped there was room enough in our local organization for people who were interested in that sort of thing to deal with that. . . . I thought the leadership should concentrate on local, grass roots issues dealing with major educational programs and problems, because that would provide a base for community contacts, for a sense that we're all in the same boat. . . .

What began to happen was that it began to switch. Bread-and-butter and statewide, broad, national issues and exposure became very important to the union leadership. To be fair, I suppose they could argue that planning things on a local level is dangerous, especially in the kind of economic conditions in which we're operating, and that you have to provide statewide guarantees and support. But I think it's wrong. . . . Statewide support is not strengthening us in areas we want.

Union Issues in the Middle and Late 1970s

Economic issues took precedence within the union during the later 1970s. As in Cedarton, protection of teacher jobs became a central concern. Because of declining enrollment and budgetary cutbacks, there was little the union could do to prevent massive staff cuts.

Although there were fewer actual teacher layoffs in Middlebury than in Cedarton, these layoffs appear to have engendered more bitterness and internal dissension in Middlebury. In part, such reactions may have reflected teachers' greater sense of relative deprivation, based on comparison of their present circumstances to their earlier, better situation. Layoffs also produced more internal dissension because of the interracial character of the staff. Black teachers — most of whom had been hired in the late 1960s and early 1970s — challenged the use of a seniority system as the basis for making cuts on the grounds that the district's integrationist philosophy required preservation of black faculty. Black, and many white, residents strongly supported this claim. Liberal white teachers — torn between commitment to racial equality and anxiety to preserve their own jobs — found themselves defending a strict seniority system as the only predictable basis for determining cuts.† The seniority system

---

†Yet even the seniority system wasn't always predictable. Individual teachers' rankings changed often because of frequent revisions in state rulings, as well

was generally followed, in keeping with state regulations and union practices elsewhere, but the resulting disproportionate cutting of black teachers further raised black antagonisms to the union, within both staff and community.

Also as in Cedarton, more emphasis was placed on maintaining class size as a means of protecting teachers' jobs. Class size was a less central issue in Middlebury than in Cedarton during the 1970s because Middlebury's 1973 union contract set upper limits. Class size did become a contract issue in 1976, however — a point to be discussed shortly.

Other union issues in the 1970s dealt mainly with teacher protection and benefits. Few respondents claimed the union any longer gave emphasis to educational goals, and no evidence of such emphasis was found. Many union respondents noted the shift toward a greater preoccupation with teacher welfare goals, and away from educational goals, with regret. In Middlebury, far more than in either of the other districts, teachers made frequent reference to problems in their educational programs and practices; they were divided, however, on whether the union should or could concern itself with such problems. A rank-and-file elementary teacher complained: "Some of us . . . . . . have serious concerns about the kinds of programs that are being run. . . . What is the union doing? . . . Enough about our benefits. Where are we involved in the educational process?" A high school teacher and early union activist commented:

> Our federation has accomplished quite a few things for teachers' welfare. My disappointment — and it is a major disappointment — is that we spend no time on learning. . . . There's no time even for conversation about it. . . . It's a dilemma — perhaps it's in the nature of the beast. . . . But in being concerned so much with teacher welfare . . . [we] seem now to have moved a great deal away from what's good for kids.

But another former activist remarked:

> I feel the union [had to] narrow its focus . . . since we've been under so much attack. . . . I see the role of the union now as being largely . . .

---

as teacher retraining to obtain certification in additional subject areas to protect themselves against program cuts.

defensive, and I see that as a legitimate role — to protect the teachers, to protect their contract, and to deemphasize things not stated in the contract. . . . If teachers feel there are other things [they want to do] in terms of curriculum, development of programs, they can handle these professionally [outside the union].

THE LATE 1970S

Negotiations: 1976 and 1979

Negotiations for the 1976 contract began in January 1976 for a contract to become effective on July 1. The union hoped to maintain existing contract provisions, strengthen teacher protection, and improve salaries and benefits. The board sought to cut some contract provisions — most notably the limitation on class size.

A specialist in education law, hired by the board, represented the board in the 1976 negotiations, while a NYSUT representative and the union's chief negotiator represented the union. Some board members sat in on negotiations, but rather than involving themselves directly, as in 1973, they left actual negotiations to their hired specialist. The union reduced the size of its own negotiating team to four, and these four participated only indirectly, through their own negotiators. In part because of the hired specialist, who used a more objective, less patronizing tone than board negotiators had used in 1973, hostilities between board and union were held in check.

Even though the board continued to insist upon management prerogatives, it seemed to the union to be more accepting of the legitimacy of negotiations as a process in 1976 than in 1973. A member of the union negotiating team commented:

> The board's attempt is always to maintain board prerogatives, management prerogatives . . . to limit [negotiations] to wages and conditions of employment. . . . They still maintain that posture, more or less. But they've come to realize if we're going to live together, they'd better think in terms of other things.

The board wanted to eliminate class size guidelines from the contract, claiming it wanted more flexibility in determining class sizes because of budget constraints. Increases in salaries and fringe benefits were also in dispute. Teachers wanted substantial increases because of inflation; board members wanted to limit increases. Again, the two parties reached impasse. The dispute went first to mediation, then to fact-finding. The fact-finder supported the union position on class size on the basis of its inclusion in the previous contract, and he recommended small annual salary increases of 5 percent each year. Both sides accepted the fact-finder's report and signed the contract in mid-June 1976. Neither side made substantial gains or suffered substantial losses. But a better negotiating relationship had prevailed, and the union was able to protect existing contract provisions.

Negotiations for the 1979 contract began in the early winter of 1979. Teachers made fewer demands than in 1976, but the board made more. Town taxes had just been increased by over 20 percent, and the board felt especially pressed to keep school taxes down. Again, the board wanted to eliminate class size limitations from the contract, and now they also wanted a salary freeze and cuts in certain teacher benefits. The union was thus put on the defensive.

As in 1976, the board used an outside professional negotiator. (This contributed to maintaining a moderate negotiations atmosphere, despite some open expressions of open hostility toward teachers from board members and some dissension among union representatives — noted by board respondents.) Again, a NYSUT representative assisted the union's chief negotiator. As the two parties pared down their lists of demands over the next few months, the initially tense atmosphere improved. A member of the union negotiating team explained:

We were apprehensive, because they kept saying, "No, no, no." . . . Suddenly, it fell into line. Nobody wanted a strike, and it just got to be more of a talking kind of thing. . . . They realized we were very upset, very angry, and that we weren't planning to give in on these major issues . . . class size, a freeze on salary.

In June, a new contract was signed. The board had agreed to a small salary increase and to a continuance of the class size limitation in exchange for union concessions of some teacher benefits: loss of sabbatical leaves; loss of a tenure bonus of about $300 each year; and a modified role for the outside evaluator in tenure recommendations.

Neither board nor union was completely satisfied. The board had approved the contract by a split vote (some members wanted more union concessions), and the union had made its concessions with reluctance, giving in on some items in order to protect others having greater priority — such as class size.

Despite its concessions, the union felt that it still had an excellent contract. Except for salaries, sabbaticals, the tenure bonus, and a few minor changes in other areas, the 1979 contract was essentially the same as in 1973. Respondents called it a "strong contract" and a "thick contract." In comparison to Cedarton, terms and conditions of employment were spelled out in more detail (for example, guidelines for teacher transfers, assignments, and evaluations); salaries were substantially higher; the welfare fund was better. Middlebury had a contract superior to most other school districts in the region. Yet, in spite of its more detailed, stronger contract, Middlebury teachers lost ground during the 1970s in some important areas — areas that depended not so much upon the contract per se as upon the board's interpretation of contract provisions negotiated in earlier periods.

Noncontractual Developments

By contrast to Cedarton, where improved relations with the school board and administration during the 1970s enabled the union to exercise substantial informal influence over school decisions outside the scope of the contract, a worsening relationship with the board had the opposite effect in Middlebury. The Middlebury contract specifically provided for teacher participation in two important kinds of decisions: selection of administrators (won in 1970 negotiations) and decisions on teacher tenure (won in the 1973 strike settlement). Although teachers' participation in each of these was specified as only advisory, teachers had expected that inclusion in the contract would be morally binding on the board. But the board was continually changing, and new members did not feel morally bound to follow agreements made by their predecessors when these agreements contained loopholes. Later boards, in keeping with their less kindly attitudes toward teachers, tended to take contract loopholes literally, as developments in these two cases illustrate.

Selection of Administrators

In 1970, the union had gained a contract provision for advisory teacher participation in the selection of administrators. Initially, this participation appears to have been taken seriously by board members. Teacher representatives had participated on search committees (along with board and student representatives) in screening potential administrative candidates and in making recommendations to the board. There had been a high degree of internal consensus between teachers and representatives of other groups serving on these committees; until 1973, the school board had consistently followed committee recommendations. But in 1973 — the year of the strike — its appointment of Avery as superintendent was contrary to teacher recommendations.

From that time on, teacher recommendations on administrator appointments were often ignored. In 1979, this example was offered by a high school teacher (note the contrast between the situation in Cedarton, wherein teachers elected their own department coordinators, and this description of the process for selection of a department chairperson in Middlebury):

> We have a case in hand right now — the department chairperson for the English department. It has been going on now for a year and a half. They had some excellent people, which the board just threw away. This is the real process; they make you come up with about five choices and then they pick the one they want out of the five.

Thus, teachers appear to have had less real say in the selection of administrators in 1979 than they did in 1971.

Teacher Tenure Decisions

The settlement of the just cause issue at the end of the 1973 strike provided elaborate procedures by which a Review Panel, on which teachers were represented, made recommendations to the board for or against the granting of tenure to probationary teachers. Panel recommendations were made following its review of extensive evaluation reports, filed by two administrators and an outside evaluator, and before the superintendent made his own recommendation.

In 1975, only two years after this settlement, the board denied tenure to a teacher in spite of favorable recommendations by both the Review Panel and the superintendent. Teachers protested and, as a union, demonstrated. The board then withdrew its negative decision and granted her tenure. But in 1978, the board denied tenure to three probationary teachers, all of whom had been favorably recommended by both the Review Panel and the superintendent. This time, despite teacher protests and despite recommendations, the board did not alter its position.

While technically within board prerogatives, teachers felt this action violated the spirit of the strike settlement. Jenny Abrams reported:

> Our cry to them was, "What good is the procedure if you're not following it?" . . . It was a different board. . . . There was only one member of that board who was on during the strike, and she maintained our position, . . . because she [had been] there, and she knew what the intent of that clause was. Other board members have said to me, "I wasn't there. . . . What you did and what you said doesn't mean anything. . . . It's still within our power."

A 1978 board member said:

> Their [teachers'] memory of the strike was that they thought they got it [just cause]. I've had people tell me with tears in their eyes that this was what they had struggled for. . . . They put all their energy into something that was an illusion.

Presently, we shall be addressing the reasons for this outcome in more detail, examining, from a board viewpoint, how a lack of clarity in the evaluations — in spite of complex evaluation procedures — combined with the board's own desire to assert authority in this area led to the negative decisions.

Many respondents also reported a decline in informal teacher participation in other kinds of educational decisions (such as curriculum). Widely different respondent perceptions, apparently based on differences in individual activities and contacts with administrators or school board members, make assessment of actual changes in teacher participation difficult. Board members and administrators reported they consulted with teachers through ad hoc curriculum committees and public hearings. Teachers reported, however, that their participation on committees had declined and that, in cases where committees were active, their recommendations tended to be ignored. A high school teacher referred to:

> a tremendous number of meetings where I'm asked for my input as a member of the staff by administrators at a variety of levels. And . . . [what] we've done is essentially not used. So you become cynical, tired.

Another, referring to teacher proposals for curriculum changes, reported: "After all that work teachers put into thinking up programs on their own time, . . . not one single plan was accepted. . . . Do they listen? . . . They don't care."

Teacher, administrator, and board respondents interviewed generally agreed that teacher input in educational decision making was not channeled through, or successfully enforced, by the union (as it was in Cedarton).† A union member commented on this as follows:

> Our administration is freer to create an edict and see it be effected now, without union activity impairing. . . . It seems to me the early union was stronger [in this respect] than it is now. . . . In the late 1960s and early 1970s, the teachers' union was more . . . affirmative and action-oriented. . . . Now it seems to be in a more defensive . . . reactive posture . . . ignoring many of the issues it once addressed. So the administration has, in effect, a freer hand at ruling its own ship, for better or worse.

The union did, however, make some other important noncontractual gains parallel to those made in Cedarton. One important gain was the improvement in access of teachers to the school board through the mechanisms of collective bargaining and grievance procedures. This improvement initially began in the late 1960s when Landau was union president, negotiating with a more sympathetic board, but improved access continued also with later, less sympathetic boards in the 1970s. As in Cedarton, this improvement

---

†See Appendix, Tables 7 and 8, on teachers' perceptions of union effectiveness. Note the declines in the percentages of Middlebury teachers, indicating union effectiveness in promoting teacher participation in educational programs and educational policy, in contrast to the increases noted in Cedarton, between 1969 and 1979.

in teacher access and the board's consequent better understanding of typical school problems gave the board members information that contributed, on at least some occasions, to their making better decisions about the operation of the schools. A respondent on the school board in the early 1970s gave this example:

> In . . . collective bargaining, teachers . . . were able to explain their positions and views with respect to how schools were being run, what the curriculum was, how administrators were functioning — all of their gripes, their perspectives, their suggestions, and so forth, they could communicate directly to the school board members without going through the administration. . . . It was direct access.

Had it not been for the moderating effects of this more direct communication between board and union during the 1970s, we might expect that the tensions between them would have been even greater than they were.

Discussion and Analysis of the MFT Position in the Late 1970s

As in Cedarton, external conditions put pressures on the union to give more overt emphasis to protective concerns in the late 1970s than a decade earlier. Unlike Cedarton, Middlebury union leaders defined their organizational roles as more purely protective. They did not, as in Cedarton, deliberately moderate their protective stance in terms of other considerations — such as maintaining good relations with administrators and the community or showing concern for specific professional and educational goals. Rather, viewing their relationship to both administrators and the community as more strictly adversarial, MTF leaders took an unyielding confrontation stance. Although they did not discount professional and educational concerns, they regarded these as mainly outside the union's province. The differences in leadership orientation being noted here reflected different group definitions of the union's role in the school district — not differences in the personal characteristics of its leaders. As individuals, respondents viewed Jenny Abrams and most other MTF leaders as reasonable, fair, and professionally responsible. Reasons for differences between districts in leadership orientation are not entirely clear; these will be discussed more fully in Chapter 5. Here, we shall examine some further evidence indicating the MTF's narrower, more strictly protective approach in contrast to the broader, more balanced approach of the CFC.

In evidence of the MTF's narrower, more strictly protective approach in contrast to the more balanced approach of the CFC we will examine the Middlebury union's positions on issues arising in three specific areas where protective concerns were in potential conflict with professional and other considerations. These areas include the handling of grievances, teacher evaluation, and staff governance in the high school.

Handling of Grievances

The MTF followed a strict grievance policy, to ensure administrator and board adherence to the contract.† Jenny Abrams explained:

> We've had a lot of grievances. . . . This district knows we don't let grievances go by. . . . We will file grievances wherever we deem — it can be on the smallest issue. We watch that contract carefully. We have to, because if we allow a comma to be violated, then we might as well throw out the whole thing. And that does, unfortunately, take a lot of time.

The grievance chairperson commented, along similar lines: "Any contractual issue to me is the same, whether it's a locked desk for the teacher or a teacher being fired." According to some respondents, this policy resulted in an overemphasis upon trivial concerns. A building principal complained:

> It gets down to, "Don't make a mistake — I'm going to file a grievance." Or, "Gee, you can't do that. You haven't given me enough . . . notice. . . ." There is a lot of nit-picking, frustrating kinds of things that are thrown in your path.

---

†See Appendix, Tables 5 and 6. In comparison to Cedarton, note the higher percentages among both activists and union members reporting that the union places "much emphasis" on grievances in Middlebury. Percentage differences are 25 percent for both categories of respondents.

A rank-and-file union member said of Abrams: "She will fight for any teacher who has a grievance. She doesn't care what the grievance is, unless it's blatantly outrageous." A school board respondent claimed that during his term on the board (ending in 1978):

> Every . . . action would be contested. And the union would play a role in everyone of them. . . . The union's track record was bad, because it was taking cases it shouldn't take. From my point of view, this was bad for school relations, and bad for the union. It caused antiunion feelings on the board. It distracted from other things.

Union leaders were more cautious in their selection of cases taken outside the district to arbitration. However, the many grievances of debatable importance taken to the board were in clear contrast to the union policy in Cedarton, where union leaders were more selective in bringing grievances, and where the need, to at times confront administrators or the board was more carefully weighed against the value of maintaining good relations. The difference in approach reflects clear philosophical differences between the two unions. Middlebury union leaders assigned priority to defending the contract through grievances as the key to protecting its members. A rank-and-file member explained: "She [Abrams] feels she must emphasize the protective role of the union. . . . I've argued about that with her, and of course, . . . [she believes that] that is the job of a union." The grievance chairperson went even further, maintaining that protection of members required a strong, adversarial stance:

> People call upon you when they're in a time of conflict, looking for . . . resolution. We can [sometimes] resolve the conflict . . . [without] confrontation at the immediate building level. After that, it's total confrontation. . . . That's what a grievance is all about. That's how conflict is resolved in our district.

Teacher Evaluation

The Middlebury contract contained an elaborate procedure for teacher evaluation, including evaluation of both probationary and tenured teachers. Abrams maintained: "We probably have the most difficult [complex] evaluation procedures for probationary teachers in the state." The procedures specified that probationary teachers were to be observed 15 times each year, five times each, by three separate evaluators — two administrators, including department chairpersons in the high school, and an outside evaluator selected by the candidate. Tenured teachers were to be evaluated once each year. Each evaluation was to be written and presented to the teacher by the evaluator in individual conference. For probationary teachers, written evaluations were to be examined by a Review Panel composed of teachers and administrators, who made a recommendation — for or against reappointment — to the superintendent and school board.

In contrast to Cedarton, where evaluation procedures were developed over a period of more than a year by a committee of teachers and administrators, Middlebury procedures were hammered out in a matter of days, as part of the 1973 strike settlement, by union negotiators and school board representatives. Consequently, certain aspects of the system devised in Middlebury appear to have been less carefully thought out. Although procedurally thorough, the emphasis was upon who should evaluate and how often. Some previously existing problems in respect, for example, to substantive criteria for observation and evaluation were overlooked. Certain new problems also arose in respect to the inclusion of an outside evaluator. Because the outside evaluator was selected by the probationary teachers, some respondents (from among both teachers and board members) noted potential conflicts of interest.

Many respondents were, therefore, critical of the procedures. A teacher and early union activist commented:

> This was a patchwork system, designed to end the strike.... It was then carried forward for another three years. This system created a case where there would be votes held as to whether or not a teacher was adequate.... And the people who were really responsible for the quality of teaching — namely, the administrators — I feel that their efforts were vitiated.

Administrators were faced with having to fulfill quantitatively elaborate procedures with little direction concerning their substance. Furthermore, most administrators had never developed strong evaluative skills. During the period of district expansion, in the 1960s, when staff turnover was also high, almost all teachers who wished to remain in the district were recommended for tenure and approved by the board. Although a simple evaluation procedure had been followed *pro forma*, it had not been taken very seriously. In fact, in the late 1960s, it had been the union leadership who exerted pressure on administrators to conduct more thorough and regular evaluations. Even after the 1973 procedures were specified, the major changes were in the number of evaluations — not in their substance.

Teacher evaluation had become an increasingly important concern to school boards, however, under circumstances of budget tightening and the declining enrollments that generated teacher surpluses. Thus, during the later 1970s, they began to scrutinize tenure cases more carefully. Board respondents report having been frustrated by ambiguities in the administrative evaluations they reviewed. Referring to the evaluation for tenure in 1978, a board member explained:

> Supervisors' . . . evaluations were ambivalent. There were negative criticisms in there. What would happen was, the evaluation would say the person did blah, blah, and blah well. However, they did blah, blah, blah badly. Therefore, the recommendation is for reappointment. . . . So . . . the internal inconsistency of the document showed it to be a *pro forma* exercise . . . [indicating] the unwillingness of the supervisor to commit himself.

As indicated earlier, in 1978, the board acted on their frustration with such evaluations by reversing several administrative recommendations for tenure.

From teachers' viewpoint, this was an arbitrary action, violating their expectation of due process. From a school board viewpoint, it was an action not only within its power (according to state law) but an action exercised out of concern for improving the quality of teaching in the district. The same board member quoted above provided the following details:

> We had several people working in remediation areas. . . . These teachers were involved in education for the handicapped. They were people without proper training, who had been pulled out [of other positions] — people who were not sufficiently interested, and who didn't know how to respond to criticism. . . . We thought they were incompetent, . . . so we didn't give them tenure.

Thus, based on an inadequate system of formal teacher evaluation, the board exercised subjective judgments based upon informal sources of information (such as parents' criticisms) in determining the outcome of these cases. Failure to rely on predetermined, formal, and more objective procedures aroused teacher anxiety and anger.

The union position on teacher evaluation changed between the 1960s and the late 1970s. In the 1960s, early union activists had debated the position the union ought to take on issues of teacher competence and tenure much as early union members did in Cedarton. Many professional-idealists felt teachers ought, themselves, to exercise control over the maintenance of professional standards among their colleagues. Also as in Cedarton, questions arose concerning teachers' ability to evaluate or otherwise hold colleagues up to such standards while maintaining a sense of unity and supportiveness. Unlike Cedarton, those issues were not resolved in Middlebury in terms of solutions that recognized the validity of both sets of concerns. In 1979, some professional-idealists continued to take the position that teachers ought, as a group, to be more concerned with professional accountability; however, current union leaders maintained that in an adversarial system it was not their role to question teacher competence, but rather to protect teachers against potentially arbitrary treatment. The following segment from an interview with a 1979 union activist illustrates the current union position:

Question: Take the case of a person coming up for tenure who you know is a borderline case.

Answer: Borderline on whose part?

Question: Borderline as a teacher, in your judgment.

Answer: I don't make those kinds of judgments about teachers.

The respondent went on to say:

The person is given evaluations ... by people paid to do the job ... the principals, assistant principals, the department chairpersons. ... If they can't do their job, if they let that person squeak through year after year ... [with] good evaluations, then the person ... has a right to that job.

Union respondents claimed that they did not defend all teachers — that they could do so only where they had a basis in the law or contract. Thus, they reported they would not oppose administrators giving poor evaluations or making negative recommendations as long as they could document these and as long as they didn't harass teachers. Several administrator respondents confirmed this claim, noting that in a few cases teachers had not been retained on the basis of poor evaluations and that the union had not grieved or otherwise protested these actions. Thus, it cannot be claimed that the Middlebury union leadership took an irresponsible position in respect to teacher evaluations. The point is, rather, that they defined their role strictly in terms of their protective function, in an adversarial relationship to administration. A school board respondent explained:

> Since I've been on the board, we've had one case where the superintendent did not recommend for tenure, and [then] the union was quiet. ... But, given the slightest opportunity ... I think that the union ... would protect an incompetent teacher. ... I get the feeling that she [Abrams] feels she has no choice, that this is what they expect of her. I think she would do it on a tenure case for a person who has any leg to stand on.

(Middlebury respondents frequently referred to the MTF leadership in the singular as "she." This reference is indicative of the greater isolation of the president in Middlebury in contrast to Cedarton, where respondents usually referred to the CFT leadership as "they.")

The difference between the union position in Middlebury and the Cedarton position is a subtle one. In Cedarton, union leaders took a similar position — that it was up to school administrators to adequately evaluate and document the cases of teachers they sought to dismiss and that it was the union's role to protect teachers' rights to due process in the evaluation proceedings. However, Cedarton union leaders also assumed an active role in determining guidelines for the substantive bases of evaluations. Furthermore, in their creation of the teacher coordinator position in the high school, they built into the system a mechanism for helping to improve teacher performance in ways that did not objectively threaten teacher security. In Middlebury, union leaders took the position that all problems related to assessing and improving teachers' competence were strictly management problems.

Staff Governance in the High School

Another significant development in Middlebury, reflecting differences in union philosophy in contrast to Cedarton, was the creation of the staff council in the high school in 1977. Some detail on the council's background will be necessary before discussing its relation to the union. Student discipline problems in the high school had increased sharply — vandalism, harassment of some students by others, truancy, and defiance of school regulations and authorities. Students and parents, alike, complained that school administrators weren't effectively responding to these problems. In 1976, therefore, the school board demanded replacement of the high school principal. The principal (tenured) was promptly transferred to an administrative post; the assistant principal — a man on the verge of retirement and in poor health — temporarily assumed the position until a permanent replacement could be found, although some teachers voiced, at the time, concerns about the assistant principal's ability to manage the school. This situation therefore created what some respondents referred to as a leadership vacuum.

Martin Landau saw this leadership vacuum as presenting an opportunity to reintroduce some ideas held in the early union about staff governance. Encouraged by an initially enthusiastic teacher response, Landau convened a teacher committee to formulate a plan to present to the high school staff, central administration, and school board. Teachers active in the early union and other professional-idealists dominated this committee.

Proponents of the council envisioned it as a policy-making body within the high school to make decisions in all areas related to management of the school and its programs — including school organization, curriculum, and discipline — consistent with principles of both professional and worker self-management models. Structurally, the plan they proposed for the council included elected representatives from all groups on the staff, including administrators, paraprofessionals, secretaries, and others, as well as teachers. Representation on the council was intended to rotate among various individuals, to maximize broad-based staff participation — another carryover from the early union.

The responses of both the superintendent (Roberts) and school board to the idea of a staff council were initially lukewarm. Both groups feared it would place too much power in the hands of teachers and confuse authority relations. The high school's acting principal was clearly opposed. Over a period of months, however, as problems in the school worsened, it became apparent that someone would have to assume control, and a new principal had not yet been found. Under these circumstances, both Roberts and the school board warmed to the notion of a staff council. Martin Landau explained:

> Roberts and the board attempted to get the word "advisory" in — and, I don't remember the last time so much blood was spilled over a word. . . . Big, big conflict about this thing. The board wanted all the things we were prepared to deal with on an advisory basis. We said, "Absolutely not." . . . We finally [agreed] it was "decision making." It was very clearly spelled out — the council would make policy decisions. Decisions. If necessary, by vote.

Although it was understood that the school board would continue to have final authority, the teachers hoped that board members would tend to support council decisions in the manner they usually supported administrative ones. Landau went on to explain the teachers' understanding:

> In other words, what we've done is, through a council, upgraded the role of the staff to being at least equal to the [building] administration. The board can veto the administration or council recommendations (but is not likely to do so). . . . If a principal wanted something and could not convince the council, and it was for a policy decision, then it would not be. . . . Neither did the principal have the blocking power over policy. The principal would implement [council decisions].

Council founders claim they had envisioned the council as having a working partnership with the union, each organization focusing on different kinds of problems and issues. Union reactions to the council were initially mixed, but most union activists were favorable to it. As the council's role became clearer, however, union opposition to it rose. The opposition was based mainly on some union leaders' belief that direct teacher participation in school governance would obscure the distinction between management and employees and divide teacher loyalties. A union officer commented:

> I personally see it [the staff council] as at odds with the union, because it creates certain kinds of problems, conflict of interest. . . . They're serving an administrative purpose, and it's just not their function. . . . I like to see things in terms of categories [of responsibility]. If I know this is what this person is supposed to do, then I can deal with it. If I don't know what a person is supposed to do, then I have trouble. . . . I think there should be a division of power, clear-cut responsibilities on each party.

Another union officer explained the importance of maintaining clear distinctions between management and staff for purposes of assigning accountability and maintaining staff solidarity:

> The thing that frightened me about the whole thing was that you would have a group of people who were supposed to have a collegial . . . union relationship, who now were going to be in an evaluative, supervisory relationship to each other. Because what does a group of people who work together do when somebody doesn't show up for hall duty? Who do you go to? How does a union handle a matter like that? How do I report Jane for not showing up . . . when she's the grievance chairperson and I'm active in the union?

Council proponents acknowledged some conflict of interest between the union and staff council but claimed opponents exaggerated potential problems and maintained these could be resolved through mutual cooperation. One founding council member claimed:

> I don't think these people [union opponents to the council] really understood how this group was going to function. I think they thought we would be giving away things that were in the contract, and we couldn't do that, because a contract is a legal document. And, it just so happens that all of us [teachers on the council] were union members anyway, and . . . we weren't going to break the contract.

Council proponents assured union leaders they would instruct the council not to make any decisions that would violate the contract and invited the union to send a representative to sit on the council as union watchdog.

Union officers, however, refused to cooperate, for they viewed the council as an inappropriate investment of their energies and organizationally in competition with them. The extent of their philosophical disagreement with council proponents is indicated by the following comments by two respondents who were officers in the union at that time:

> Obviously, if we wanted to, we could work out something. . . . But we didn't see our role as that. As a matter of fact, we saw them as attempting to usurp our position.

> I don't think we need a staff council. We have the input as a union. As a union we say what teachers need. And everything beyond that is just a lot of talk, a lot of hot air, and a waste of time. I've been asked to serve [as liaison person]. I wouldn't even attend a meeting.

That early union activists — the professional-idealists — were strongly concentrated among council proponents and that later activists were concentrated among those opposed to the council is indicative of the union's major shift toward more traditional goals during the 1970s.

In spite of opposition from the union and the high school acting principal, the council operated successfully through its first year (1976-1977). Landau and another early union activist served as co-chairs. Respondents who served on the council were enthusiastic about its apparent success in that year and about its potential. A major focus of council activity in the first year had been on student discipline. Council members cited numerous instances in which discipline problems plaguing the staff for years were quickly and imaginatively resolved through interchange among members in different positions on the staff. Teacher respondents believed their greater proximity to students enabled them to provide administrators with fresh insights about both the nature of particular problems and possible solutions; they also claimed that through council participation, teacher representatives gained a greater appreciation of difficulties administrators face in running a school. Because of improved communication with the high school staff, the council was more readily able to gain staff support for changes in policy than administrators were. Landau remarked: "As far as I'm concerned, I think the council saved the school for that year."

Council members reported having invested tremendous amounts of time and emotional energy in the staff council in the first year. They assessed high school problems openly, in front of both principal and superintendent. But their discussions, often emotionally laden, appear to have threatened the administrators — especially the acting principal. The principal generally resisted cooperation with the council, making it difficult to enact decisions. As a council member put it: "The lines between policy and implementation got kind of blurred" when the principal failed to carry out council directives. In more than one case, according to teacher respondents, the acting principal openly contradicted and undermined council efforts. Council members were angry but had no recourse in enforcing their directives other than to complain to the superintendent, who tended to avoid these confrontations. A council member remarked: "On the one hand, he [the superintendent] was paying lip-service in support of the council; on the other, he was saying, 'Well, the administrator is still the administrator'." These kinds of frustrations strongly discouraged some council members from continued participation.

In the second year, Landau and his co-chairperson stepped down from leadership of the council to allow for democratic rotation of the position. At the same time, a new principal — a woman, and a stronger personality — was appointed to the high school. A condition of the principal's appointment had been that she work with the council, but respondents reported that she paid obeisance to it but did not treat it seriously, and sidestepped it. Furthermore, the new council chairperson, less assertive than Landau and his partner, was not, as a council member regretfully put it, willing to "pound the table and demand and direct and push in various areas" to ensure administrative consultation and compliance with council decisions. Thus, the council's sphere of authority, initially ambiguous, rapidly eroded in the second year.

By the end of the third year, when this research was conducted, council proponents and opponents consistently reported the council to be a weak and ineffective body, dealing with only (in a council member's words) "relatively silly, innocuous problems." A respondent active in creating the council commented on it in 1979 as follows: "The council still exists, but nobody really cares. They're just a debating society. They don't handle any matters of substance." A second remarked, "My feeling is the staff council is impotent now." Landau, himself, said, "It's still alive, but far from the healthy institution which I think it should be by now, with lots of golden opportunities . . . missed."

The case of the staff council illustrates both persistence and change in union goals in Middlebury — persistence, in that early union activists attempted to reassert early union goals in a new and far-reaching form, and change, in that later activists strongly objected to and separated themselves from realization of these goals. The polarization of these two groups on the issue of staff governance made it impossible to arrive at mutually acceptable resolutions of key issues. A divided faculty also made it virtually impossible to sustain a viable council, given administrator and school board ambivalence toward it. In contrast to Cedarton, where the union, teaching staff, and administrators worked in cooperation to resolve internal issues and to develop a more modest form of staff governance, the inability of diverse groups in Middlebury to cooperate effectively left teachers frustrated having little power over their teaching environment, and it left the high school without the benefit of systematic teacher participation in helping to resolve continuing problems.

The Teacher Center

One area in which the Middlebury union did involve itself with professional and educational concerns should be given at least brief attention. In the late 1970s, the MTF collaborated with four other local union chapters in the region to create a teacher center — an institute for in-service teacher training and professional support. The teacher center was operated by a group of teachers only marginally active in the local union, but it was established under union auspices and funding.

This venture was institutionally independent from the local school district. Thus, in the one area where the union did engage in activities of an educational, professional nature, the activities were clearly separated from the school system. This was consistent with the union's adversarial role within the district, in that it kept the organization's boundaries clear. This separation is also in contrast both to the early union philosophy in Middlebury and to the philosophy in Cedarton, where union activists sought direct involvement in educational and professional affairs within the district.

MIDDLEBURY IN 1979

Middlebury, in 1979, was a school district in conflict — conflict both within and between community and teacher groups. Program cuts, increases in class size, and retrenchment of teaching positions due to declining student enrollments occurring in the late 1970s were projected to continue in the early 1980s. Although these changes were objectively no more drastic than in Cedarton, Middlebury teachers perceived them as more threatening. Even though economic conditions in Middlebury were no worse than in Cedarton, the political climate was more controversial and stressful, for Middlebury residents and school board members had become far more openly critical of the schools in general and teachers in particular during the 1970s. Antiliberal, antiunion, and anti-Semitic themes in residents' criticisms put teachers particularly on the defensive. Problems of poor student achievement and discipline continued to plague the district. But teachers' sensitivity to public criticism and their frustrations with inconsistent board policies led many to withdraw from active participation on school committees directed toward resolving such problems and to insulate themselves more in their classrooms.

The union, by 1979, had earned a reputation in the county and state as a strong, well-organized, successful teachers' union. The MTF was by this time a part of the district establishment — an active force in the district. This, according to most respondents, proved an important advantage to its members, in that it provided them with a basic, much needed measure of stability and job security in what would otherwise be a highly precarious environment. Union leaders had developed a good, fairly stable relationship with most administrators in the district by 1979, and their relationship to the school board had improved somewhat since the mid-1970s. Union-board relations were less satisfactory, however, than in the late 1960s and early 1970s when school boards had been more supportive of teachers and programs. A key component in improved relations among the union and both administrators and the school board was the greater acceptance by the latter two groups of collective negotiations and the contract as "facts of life" in the district. A NYSUT representative commented in 1979 in respect to Middlebury:

> The chemistry between the union and the board now is basically good. There are groups and individuals on the board that we can't talk with,

but the general institutional relationship between the superintendent and the union and the union and the board of education is far better than it was in 1973. . . . The union and the superintendent can agree to disagree, and the union and the board can agree to disagree and fight one another, at least on an institutional basis, without getting shrill about it.

The union's posture in 1979, however, was still largely defensive. The MTF did not play an active role in district planning in respect to educational policies, professional arrangements, or student discipline in the way the CFC did in Cedarton. Union membership was also more divided than in Cedarton. Disagreements arose over both union goals and strategies. Many early union supporters expressed disenchantment with the organization's shift in emphasis away from educational, professional, and community-related concerns. Other members maintained the union did not go far enough in protecting teachers — as in the case of the three denied tenure in 1978 — and these advocated an even stronger, more militant protective stance.

Many union respondents, including several active in the early union, commented that, given the nature of external pressures on the organization and the diversity of staff perspectives, a narrowing of union goals and a more moderate, less militant approach were probably unavoidable. A teacher identified with the professional-idealists and moderately active in the union in the later 1970s remarked:

> I try to think of who might have done it differently, and I don't know that anybody would have. On the one hand, though we've been successful, we've had some pretty glaring defeats, and that has made everybody more reactionary. . . . [Those things] put everyone in a much more sensitive frame of mind, that they're just not going to risk — [breaks off].

Another early union activist explained in 1979 why he thought changes in union goals were necessary:

> I don't think she [Jenny] has got room to stress educational issues. There's just so much — I mean, you can stand up and holler, and say just so many words . . . [and] if your membership is under attack, your first responsibility is to your membership. . . . If their welfare is not . . . taken care of, then . . . the schools certainly will go down,

because you'll have a bunch of disgruntled, unhappy teachers . . . and their output will fall. . . . They're only human beings.

Others felt, however, that leaders could have done more to actively sustain the union's early, broad-based goals and to reduce tensions between teachers and the community. Such respondents suggested that, in spite of external constraints upon the union, there were degrees of flexibility within which leaders exercised choices — that more could have been done to reduce internal factionalism and to promote dialogue with the community had leaders been more secure in dealing with controversial issues and more sensitive to community concerns. One such critic suggested:

> The arguments regarding tenure, for example . . . should be entered into by the union as much as . . . by the citizenry. . . . The conservative citizenry [is] somewhat annoyed at the notion of tenure. The conservative citizenry . . . thinks about merit. Now the union should respond to this, should talk about those issues. Not in arrogant opposition, but as educators. They should be a group of educators, rather than a group of protagonists.

Still others faulted the professional-idealists for having withdrawn from union activism, claiming their continued participation could have influenced the union's direction.

Such alternatives appear plausible in hindsight; whether they were in fact possible or even apparent to those immediately involved in the situation is far from clear. Many respondents speculated whether the district might have followed a different course under different leadership in the union, administration, or school board, but others noted the limitations placed on all these groups by external economic forces, a divided community, and a divided staff.

Undercurrents of regret, disillusionment, and frustration ran through many interviews in Middlebury. The economic crisis, lowered community support for liberal integrationist programs, and routinization of leadership and goals in the teachers' union were all themes evoking expressions of regret. A respondent who had served on the school board in the late 1960s and early 1970s, commenting on her own sense of powerlessness, summarized the dilemma as follows:

> In all honesty, I don't know, at this point in time, how you run a heterogeneous school district, given all the factions in the union, among

administrators, the community, and the school board, and now, with inflation and the budget, and the terrible problems with children not accomplishing what they should. . . .

I think that in Middlebury, as much as anywhere in the United States of America, where people are concerned and idealistic – good, decent, educated people want to make something like this work, and it doesn't – [breaks off]. . . . Because, in the end, when it shakes down, people have different values, . . . different perceptions. It's too heterogeneous. So the decision-making process becomes a soccer game . . . [comparing it to] a homogeneous district, where people do understand what their goals are, more or less. . . . What the answer is – I don't know. . . . I don't know how you can be a good superintendent, a good principal, . . . a good school board member. . . . I don't know how you can be a good union leader.

4

OAKVILLE

The Oakville story is about a group of fairly conservative teachers pressured to unionize by unreasonable school board actions. Oakville is a rural community, which, until the 1970s, consisted of one elementary school. Although situated in a conservative area, the Oakville school was remarkably advanced, well staffed, and well equipped through the early 1960s because of the leadership of an unusually progressive, supportive school administration and board in a period when conservative community elements remained uninvolved.

Growth in the district was slow by comparison to the two other communities studied. However, some population changes, moderate school expansion, and rising taxes contributed to changing the complexion of the school board. A conservative community backlash against the school in the late 1960s resulted not only in budgetary reductions for staffing and programs, as in the other districts studied, but also in gross board interference in school operations and harassment of both principal and teachers. As a consequence, Oakville's rather conservative teaching staff, at the time more anti- than prounion, were pressured toward greater militancy and unionization in efforts to protect themselves. School board refusal to negotiate what teachers perceived as a reasonable contract led, in the early 1970s, to a one-day teachers' strike, which the board quickly settled. This demonstration of teachers' power was an apparent turning point in the board's eventual recognition of their right to collective bargaining. Other factors contributing to this recognition were the board's wish to avoid the bitter divisions witnessed in neighboring districts following long teacher strikes and the informal teacher-community communication facilitated by the district's small size. Greater community acceptance of teacher rights, in the late 1970s, led to further change in the board and more harmonious school board-teacher relations.

This case study highlights the vulnerability of a small public school system to community pressures. It will show, on the one hand, why teachers perceived formal, organized militancy as necessary in protecting themselves against community hostility and, on the other, how the union leadership later operated successfully through informal, personal channels in a more conciliatory environment. By contrast to both Middlebury and Cedarton, and in keeping with the smallness of the district, the study will show how union leaders operated in a personal, informal style, in close cooperation with administrators. It will also show how polarization between teachers, administrators, and the school board was reduced through the appointment of a respected union leader to a key administrative position in the late 1970s. Maintenance of this spirit of cooperation was in part sustained by the school board's eventual recognition of teachers' power.

BACKGROUND

Oakville is a predominantly rural district, lying just beyond the commuter zone from New York City. Its central school, built in the 1930s, housed kindergarten through the eighth grade until the early 1970s when a new building for the junior high school was constructed. High school students are bused to a neighboring district.

Before the 1960s, a large proportion of the area's population was seasonal, while the year-round population — largely blue-collar — remained relatively stable. Because of the large summer population, the ratio of taxable real estate for every child educated in the district was unusually high, relative to other districts in the state. Thus, even though taxes were low, money for education was plentiful. Furthermore, many summer residents were professionals, sympathetic to the improvement of local education services and supportive of large annual school budgets. Those who were unsympathetic seldom bothered to vote in either school board elections or budgetary referendums.

During this period, with ample funding, a dedicated and supportive school board, and imaginative administrative leadership, the Oakville school district was able to develop programs and facilities unusually advanced for that time and geographic location. A 1948 State Department of Education evaluation report cited Oakville's Central School as offering "a type of education far richer than that provided in the average public elementary school" (local newspaper February 1948). The program included, for example, foreign language instruction and instrumental music as early as the third grade and remedial programs in reading and speech. Staffing included both a psychologist and a social worker. In addition, teachers' salaries were, on average, the highest in the region, attracting and maintaining an unusually competent staff. Classes were small, and by all reports, relations between teachers, administrator, and school board were excellent.

Between 1935 and 1971, only two principals (successively) supervised the school. Both men espoused progressive educational philosophies in the Deweyan tradition, and teachers respected both as educators (in contrast to several later administrators, whom respondents characterized as management men, politicians, or incompetents). The second of these early principals, August Roditi,* had himself been a teacher in the local school for many years before his appointment as supervising principal in the late 1950s and was still principal when this research began in 1969. Roditi was regarded as something of a maverick by local residents, for his progressive ideas, to them, represented a departure from traditions they identified with his Italian, Catholic background. Like his predecessor, however, he was highly respected by his teaching staff and school board, until the board changed in the 1960s.

Teachers, on the one hand, and school board members, on the other, had granted both Roditi and his predecessor virtually complete authority over school matters. Relationships between each principal and these two groups had tended, therefore, to be paternalistic, although informal, comfortable, and mutually supportive. Until the mid-1960s, a majority on the school board remained sympathetic to maintaining high quality educational programs and supportive of the principal's recommendations.

During the 1960s, the district's population expanded and changed. More commuters moved into the area, bringing a larger year-round population and an accompanying growth in the school population. This necessitated some expansion of school facilities and considerable expansion of the teaching staff. Large numbers of new — often young and inexperienced — teachers were hired. Many taught for only brief periods, so staff turnover increased, and so did problems related to administrative supervision.

Expansion of the school, along with general increases in the costs of education, brought an annual rise in taxes. While both tax rates and rates of increase each year were still far below those of surrounding districts, property owners began to register complaints, paying closer attention to public educational spending and voting in school board elections. The Oakville School Board, for many years dominated by a liberal, education-oriented faction in the community, began to change after 1962, when conservative elements in the community succeeded in gaining positions on the board. A major issue was made over rising taxes. From 1963 through 1965, the district suffered annual budget defeats, placing the school on austerity budgets. By 1967, a conservative faction committed to reducing school expenditures and espousing a narrower educational philosophy, gained a majority in the five-member school board.

The new school board openly opposed nontraditional school programs as expensive frills that wasted children's time. They cut personnel in art, music, foreign languages, and library, as well as the school psychologist and social worker, and they increased class sizes. Because the board initially opposed construction of a new building to accommodate the rapidly growing student population, the single school building became severely overcrowded. Teacher dissatisfaction began to mount.

A major objective of the new school board — openly stated by the president at a public meeting in the late 1960s — was to replace the supervising principal because of his progressive philosophy. Because Roditi was tenured, he could not be openly dismissed. The board proceeded to harass him, and the board president treated him with open contempt at public meetings — a drastic departure from the deference granted Roditi by earlier boards.

The board also harassed progressive teachers and other teachers who had openly supported Roditi. Teacher harassment included the arbitrary reduction of a teacher's salary, refusal to grant the sabbatical leave due a teacher, denial of tenure to qualified teachers, and a charge of incompetence against a capable tenured teacher. (Such actions began to pose a real threat to job security for other teachers.) In addition, the board criticized the use of certain classroom materials (such as films) widely used elsewhere in the state, and board members even attempted to personally sit in on classes to observe teachers.

This pattern of harassment and encroachment further aroused teachers' anger — particularly because it appeared to be based more on vindictiveness than on genuine conservative concerns. Some respondents also believed board members negatively capitalized upon school-related issues simply to gain public attention for their own political purposes.

TEACHERS' ORGANIZATIONS

Until 1967, when the conservative faction gained a majority on the board, most teachers belonged to the Oakville Teachers' Association, affiliated with NYSTA. Roditi, also a member, attended meetings regularly. Until then, organizational goals related to school matters were essentially accomplished via the principal; he reported association positions on various matters (ranging from salary to facilities and curriculum) to the school board, made his own recommendations, and, as in the early Cedarton, had them generally accepted by the board. Occasionally, teachers' association representatives met directly with board members, but these informal talks never approached anything resembling negotiations until the mid-1960s, when it became obvious the board had changed in character. In 1966, a year before the passage of the Taylor Law, Oakville teachers did attempt to negotiate a contract with the board. As an association leader interviewed in 1969 explained: "That year [1966] instead of just talking, we made demands. It just seemed to evolve into negotiations, and we got a few things written down. . . . It was really a matter of losing faith, I guess."

A small AFT chapter had been formed in the district during the early 1960s, but until 1967, this chapter represented less than 10 percent of the teaching staff. The teachers who had formed it claimed they had done so more because of a unionist ideology than because of particular local issues. Their original interests had been in nationwide issues.

As board harassment built, association leaders turned to their state organization, NYSTA, for assistance. NYSTA offered some suggestions but did not offer sufficient help. The association had expected NYSTA officials to exert moral pressure on the school board and to eventually assist them in spelling out teacher rights in a contract — in effect, to defend them in their local crisis. They were met instead by what they perceived as a neutral, even unreasonable attitude on NYSTA's part. An association activist explained: "Where we needed assistance they sent somebody down and gave us big talks about how you needed to understand the community and work with the community." On another occasion, a NYSTA representative reportedly told them: "Well, if things get too bad, you'll just sell your houses and move out of the community."

After the passage of the Taylor Law (which mandated negotiations) and in view of the board's continuing harassment, association leaders were particularly anxious to negotiate a more adequate contract when their current, two-page contract expired in 1968. This concern, and their disappointment with NYSTA, led them to begin to discuss the possibility of union affiliation. Of particular appeal at this point in Oakville was identification with an organization having a militant reputation. Furthermore, their union colleagues assured them that the Empire State Teachers' Federation (the parent statewide organization, affiliated with AFT) would provide them with more concrete assistance than they had received from NYSTA. Finally, they hoped identification with the union would have the effect of serving notice to the school board that teachers were prepared to fight, perhaps even to go on strike, for a strong contract that would protect them against further harassment. In fact, the word "strike" came up more frequently in 1969 interviews with activists in Oakville than in any of the other districts, indicating it was a real possibility in their minds at that stage.

The decision to affiliate did not come easily, however, for even though association leaders saw advantages to affiliating with a more militant organization, old loyalties and a generalized perception of unions as unprofessional deterred them. Oakville teachers were not, generally, as liberal in the late 1960s as their predecessors, and they tended, as a group, to be more conservative than teachers in either Cedarton or Middlebury (see Appendix, Tables 12 and 13). A 1969 activist commented: "If you even mentioned the word 'union' — well, you were immediately thought of as being some kind of communist."

Negotiations with the board for the 1968 contract proved extremely difficult, and the harassment continued. Finally, in the words of the then president of the association, William Mandryk,* association leaders went "hat in hand" to the local union chapter to discuss possible affiliation. For Mandryk himself, this was not easy. He explained:

> It was a very emotionally upsetting incident for me. I had been very active in the state organization [NYSTA], and I was committed to their way of thinking. Also, I was interested in administration, and I knew that where I would stand the best chance of entering administration was through NYSTA.

This man, nevertheless, was instrumental in changing the organizational affiliation. Within a few days after approaching the union, he called a meeting of the association, and with virtually 100 percent membership attendance, and better than the two-thirds vote needed to amend their constitution, the Oakville Teachers' Association voted to separate from NYSTA and the NEA and to affiliate with the American Federation of Teachers.

In spite of majority support for this change, following that vote, as in Middlebury, a sizeable minority of Oakville teachers withdrew from the teachers' organization because of its affiliation with labor. Unlike Middlebury, this was the only major basis for division among Oakville teachers at that time. Nevertheless, it was a source of concern to the union, for in such a small district, where teachers were under attack, any division weakened their solidarity. Still, over 60 percent of teachers had joined the union.

The only major formal change in the organization, other than state and national organizational alignments, was the exclusion of administrators, and this, in accordance with AFT regulations, Roditi understood. In fact, the principal saw advantages in this arrangement, in that it allowed teachers more direct access to the board and, thus, greater clout.

The president of the existing union chapter assumed presidency of the new, larger union for the following year. In 1969, however,

Mandryk was elected president of the new organization and continued as president through the mid-1970s, playing a principal role in contract negotiations and other activities. Mandryk was a young, highly respected fifth grade teacher who exercised strong personal leadership within the union through the next five years.

NEGOTIATIONS AND BARGAINING ISSUES, 1968-1973

Following their AFT affiliation, Mandryk and other teacher leaders became more militant in their negotiations with the board. An activist who had participated in informal negotiations with earlier boards put it this way:

> We became more stiff-necked, intractable. . . . Everything was done according to rule. We'd have a [state union] representative with us. . . . Hard-line negotiations. . . . Less give and take, more "If I do this, what will you do for me?"
>
> From that point on, everything had to be printed in a contract. . . . Everything was done according to rule.

Empire State representatives assisted the local union in developing a comprehensive set of demands; a representative from the state union also sat in on the actual negotiations.

Union goals in negotiations emphasized, above all, obtaining a contract that would protect existing teacher rights and working conditions. The act of formally defining these in a written contract (they had never been written) was viewed as a major step. Grievance procedures (now mandated under the Taylor Law) as a means for redressing contract violations were a second important step. These goals — that is, defining of teacher rights and responsibilities and establishing some rudimentary grievance procedures — were successfully attained, largely because of the knowledge and skills of the state union representative and the legitimating force of the Taylor Law.

Other union goals for the 1967 negotiations included improvement of salaries and fringe benefits, improvement in school resources and staffing, and greater teacher influence in educational program decisions (all areas where teachers felt the school district had slipped backward since the early 1960s). Union negotiators were somewhat successful in obtaining better teacher salaries and benefits, mainly on the basis of comparisons they had been able to make to salary scales in adjoining districts, but they were unable to gain improvements in resources, staffing, or teacher influence over educational programs.

Oakville union leaders continued to press for improvements in school resources, staffing, and teacher participation in later negotiations, through the mid-1970s. They met, however, with continued board resistance in these areas, both on the grounds of cost and board prerogatives in making such decisions unilaterally. The most teachers were able to obtain in terms of staffing was a stipulation that teacher aides would be provided when classes had more than 30 pupils — not a commitment to limit class size or to provide additional auxiliary services. In respect to program, they obtained an agreement to teachers having advisory participation, via a curriculum committee. But when such a committee was formed, its recommendations to the board were rarely followed.

The union continued to press for improved job protection and measures for due process through the early 1970s. In 1969 and 1970, two apparently capable teachers were denied tenure by the board, in spite of administrator recommendations, and without explanation. Such denial was, at that time, within board prerogatives. To protect teachers against arbitrary dismissal, the union wanted a contract clause specifying that tenure could be denied only on grounds of incompetence. But the board wanted the power to dismiss some tenured teachers and even went so far as to initiate charges against the tenured teacher who had been Oakville's first union president.

No objective bases for determining teacher competence, or incompetence, had ever been spelled out in Oakville. Such determination had been left in the past to the judgment of the supervising principal and had generally been accepted by earlier school boards. During the 1960s when large numbers of teachers were hired annually, neither the supervising principal nor assistant principals had engaged in even routine observations or evaluations. Teachers were so desperately needed that, except in cases of gross incompetence, most were given tenure. As the school population stabilized in the district, it was in the union's interest, in view of board harassment, to spell out procedures for teacher evaluation, providing the staff with greater assurance of due process. Because the board wanted to evaluate teachers, specification of evaluation procedures also served its interests.

Improvements in grievance procedures (legitimized to the board by the Taylor Law and by changes in other districts throughout the state) and specific clauses providing for due process in teacher evaluation were significant contract gains made by the union in the early 1970s. Clearer specification of evaluation procedures for tenured and nontenured teachers alike was a significant gain for the board.

Money items were especially difficult to negotiate — salaries, fringe benefits, and other items strongly affecting district spending, such as class size or special staffing. During the 1970s, the union sought salary increments commensurate with rises in cost of living, but the board resisted. Teachers were generally granted a 4-5 percent increase (on the basis of comparison with neighboring districts and county averages), but this was considerably below the inflation level. As for class size and specialist staffing, the school board consistently wanted to maintain a reduced staff, even cutting some positions. Class sizes increased frequently to over 30, even in the primary grades. Class size increases did not directly cause teachers to lose jobs, for most position cuts were by attrition. Specialist cuts, however, did result in dismissal of some teachers.

Through the mid-1970s, negotiations were always difficult, but in the early years, they were especially so. In 1970, when the union negotiated its second contract, so many issues were outstanding in the late spring that union leaders began to consider the possibility of a strike. In June, the membership voted, almost unanimously, to authorize the negotiating committee to call a strike for the first day of school in September if a satisfactory contract were not reached. Late in the summer, when no progress had occurred, union leaders went so far as to rent office space for a strike headquarters and to begin preparations for a lengthy strike. The board, although faced with a possible strike, continued its stand on the outstanding issues; the board's attitude toward the union was, in the words of a 1970 teacher negotiator, "very negative," and it refused to acknowledge the extent of the union's influence among teachers.

On the opening day of school, in September 1970, Oakville teachers went on strike. The strike had virtually total support from union members. Some teachers simply stayed away;† almost two-thirds demonstrated or actively participated in other ways. In accounting

---

†Staying away may have represented an attempt to accommodate to peer pressures, on the one hand, and fear of board reprisals, on the other. More

for the high level of strike support, respondents explained that the strike represented a reaction by teachers to years of irritation rather than to any particular contract issues. As a union activist put it: "Teachers were angry. . . . There was enough feeling [about the board] to keep everyone out — to rally the troops."

The board, surprised and embarrassed by the extent of teacher support for the strike, was motivated to end it quickly. Roditi was instrumental in moving the board to bend on some key issues. By the end of the first day, therefore, the school board offered the union a contract settlement satisfactory in respect to most outstanding issues, including provisions for reasonable salary increases and some guarantees for due process in protecting teachers.

THE EARLY 1970S

Relations between the Oakville school board and teachers remained strained through the next five years. In 1971 by continued harassment, the board finally succeeded in forcing Roditi's resignation. He was replaced by Thomas McNally,* a man whose ideas were more in keeping with board members' own conservative educational philosophies. McNally tended to remain aloof from the staff. In contrast to Roditi, teachers found him inflexible, lacking in understanding of their concerns, difficult to work with, and of questionable competence as an administrator.

McNally lasted only until 1973, but the period of his administration was one of great tension in the district — continuing tension between teachers and the school board and causing new tensions between teachers and administration. This was also a period of high teacher militancy within the school. Union leaders utilized grievance procedures to the hilt. One commented, "When we thought there was a violation of the contract, we would grieve anything we saw. . . . I remember having as many as 11 or 12 grievances on the table at one time." There was also a high level of personal militancy among teachers. As another union activist put it, "Voices were pretty loud during [McNally's] reign."

---

stayed away in Oakville, in its one-day strike, than in the other two districts, in their longer strikes (see Appendix, Table 3).

During these years, the union also began to become politically active in the community. It hoped to rouse public sentiment to pressure for improvements in school programs and resources and to replace incumbent board members. School board seats held by educational conservatives were contested several times, with close election results, but conservatives unsympathetic to teachers maintained a majority through several elections until 1976.

In 1973, the board replaced McNally with a man named Daniel Johnson.* Johnson was generally better liked than McNally. Teachers found him more outgoing, more accessible, and a more competent administrator than McNally and a more skillful manager than Roditi. Johnson was not, however, fully accepted by teachers. Teachers often referred to him as a management man or a politician — not an educator, like Roditi, who understood their teaching objectives and problems. To many teachers, Johnson, like McNally, seemed more concerned with accommodating board interests and saving taxpayers money than in representing teacher concerns to the board. Several union activists pointed out, however, that most teachers had little conception of the political pressures to which the supervising principal was subject, noting that Johnson came to the district at a time when tensions were high, appointed by a board teachers distrusted, to replace an administrator who had let many things slide.

In the fall of 1973, there were strikes in two neighboring school districts. One of these was in the district where Oakville students attended high school, and the other was in Cedarton. It was these strikes, more than anything else, that resulted in changing the community and board as they witnessed the bitter aftermath — the breakdown of trust between teachers, administration, and community. Oakville union leaders, in contact with leaders of the striking unions through their mutual state affiliation, were, for their own part, aware of how costly these strikes had been, personally, to striking teachers and how slight their concrete gains. While continuing to hold strong local antagonisms, the board, as well as the union, wished to avoid further escalation of these antagonisms into a similarly devastating strike in which no party could expect to make significant gains. Awareness, by all, of the consequences of these other strikes largely accounts for the mellowing of school-community relations that began to occur in Oakville.

In the spring of 1976, two candidates ran for the Oakville School Board on platforms of wanting to improve board-teacher relations. One of these candidates explained in a 1979 interview:

> I refused to look at the whole situation as a black-hat, white-hat type of thing. I would not consider the union or the faculty as "they" and us as "we." I said that as elected representatives of the school district, our concerns were for the best possible educational system within our means. I made very clear that among our faculty almost half were residents of this community and certainly had a vested interest in this school system, so how could we possibly construe them as enemies?

Both these candidates won board seats. Their victories now gave liberals and moderates a 3-2 edge on the board. The change in board composition reopened opportunities for dialogue about school policies within the board. With this change, conflict between the board and union was greatly reduced.

THE UNION IN THE 1970S

Mandryk had resigned the union presidency in 1973, at which time a young sixth grade teacher, Nancy Drusten,* assumed the position. Drusten had been vice president since 1970. Like Mandryk, Drusten appears to have been a strong leader who had the respect of both teachers and administrators. Although some union members viewed Drusten as a weaker president than Mandryk, that impression apparently derived more from Drusten's personal style and from changes in external circumstances than from a lack of forcefulness.

Union activism was concentrated within a very small group in Oakville. Over one-third of teacher respondents on both the 1969 and 1979 surveys identified themselves as having been active within a period of three years before the survey (see Appendix, Table 2), but only six to seven individuals were identified by others as very active in the union in 1979 (by contrast to much larger numbers in both other districts). The small size of the district and the lack of a high school faculty were apparently contributing factors. There was simply a smaller pool from which to recruit new people to allow for more sharing of leadership responsibility; moreover, elementary teachers were often reluctant to assume such responsibility.

Union activists also reported some difficulty in maintaining active member participation in other respects — especially attendance at meetings. Because of poor attendance at meetings dealing with routine matters, the union discontinued regular monthly meetings, holding on the average only three annually in the later 1970s. Although this schedule somewhat improved membership attendance, it reduced the potential for leadership communication with membership in respect to ongoing union activities and issues. Informal word-of-mouth transmission of information was a moderately satisfactory alternative in this small district, but both activists and members complained in 1979 that the union was becoming less democratic than they would like. An activist commented:

> I do feel that we tend to be somewhat closeted. . . . People feel, I think, reasonably free to bring their problems to us, but I think they have a sense that decisions are made privately, over a cup of coffee, and I think indeed that is the way things are done.

This respondent went on to explain, however, that such separation of leadership from the rank-and-file reflected a lack of membership interest in becoming more involved in union affairs rather than a deliberate exclusiveness on the part of its officers.

By 1979, 89 percent of Oakville respondents were union members, in contrast to 61 percent in 1969 (see Appendix, Table 1). There was no competing local organization. Respondents also reported little internal dissension within the union. There was a small, vocal, critical rank-and-file group, who claimed union leaders were lax in contract negotiations and relations with administrators, or too independent in making organizational decisions, but this group did not constitute a real faction in the sense of advocating different union goals or strategies (as in Middlebury). Criticisms were based more on differences in perceptions of what constituted realistic goals.

Another important change in the union in the late 1970s was the degree of leader involvement in the state organization.† During the 1960s and early 1970s, Oakville union leaders had relied strongly

---

†Now called New York State United Teachers (NYSUT) following the 1973 merger of the Empire State Federation of Teachers with the New York State Teachers' Association.

on the state organization for assistance in negotiations and handling of specific grievance cases, but the leaders were not directly involved in any broader activities on the state level. As the 1970s progressed, the president — especially Drusten — became far more involved in external union activities. These included regional or statewide conferences, political lobbying, and informal meetings with union officers in neighboring districts for purposes of exchanging information. Thus, the local chapter was in far greater communication with other locals in the late 1970s.

MIDDLE AND LATE 1970S

Changes in Administration

By the mid-1970s, Oakville finally completed an additional school building to house the upper elementary grades (6-8), relieving some of the crowding of the older building. Each school now had its own principal, and the supervising principal's offices were located in a separate building, further removed from direct contact with the teaching staff. These changes increased the influence of the building principals and decreased the influence of the supervising principal over teachers' daily lives.

Johnson appointed a former Oakville teacher who had been moderately active in the local union as principal in the new middle school. The man, an elementary principal since 1972, another former teacher, described by his colleagues as a survivor, had remained aloof from the union before his administrative appointment and after his appointment avoided controversial issues. He did not, for example, conduct classroom observations of teachers eligible for tenure, even after such evaluation procedures had been detailed in the union contract.

In the late 1970s, Johnson asked his elementary principal to resign, claiming he wanted someone who could exercise stronger leadership in that school. In spite of a pool of more than 200 applicants for the position, Johnson urged Bill Mandryk, the former union president, to apply. Mandryk, by now in the district for about 15 years, had earned a degree in school administration ten years earlier. He had once previously applied for the principalship, but the board had turned him down because of his union activities.

It was with some hesitation, therefore, that he accepted Johnson's invitation to apply again. Johnson then had to convince the school board to support Mandryk's appointment. A favorable board respondent explained, "There was some reluctance on the part of other board members to appoint him because they were concerned about whether he could be impartial, to represent the other side." However, on the basis of Johnson's strong recommendation and with the support of liberal members on the school board, Mandryk was appointed elementary principal in the fall of 1977.

Mandryk was the only administrator, in all three districts studied, who had held high office in the union before his appointment. Some other principals had been former association officers in their districts or elsewhere, but only in Oakville — in the middle school — had a principal or even assistant principal been appointed who had been even somewhat active in a union. Mandryk had been very active and had even led his union out on strike.

In the 1979 survey, Mandryk was more highly rated by his staff than any other administrator in this study. He was one of the two administrators in all three school districts that teacher respondents called an educator. One commented, "He's the first supervisor I've had who understood what I was doing." A few teacher respondents voiced some resentment of Mandryk, commenting that once he became principal, he forgot what it was like to be a teacher. Their criticisms, however, tended to cluster around administrative behaviors essential to the fulfillment of his new role — for example, conducting classroom observations and holding teachers to obligations specified in the contract. Board respondents were highly favorable in their comments about Mandryk as an administrator, noting that his union background proved after all to be a strong asset, not only because he understood teachers and had their confidence, but also because he understood the union contract.

Mandryk's success as an administrator is significant for purposes of this research because it suggests that union activity need not preclude successful entry to a management position in education and that, in fact, it may provide the administrator with a perspective important to the understanding of teachers' viewpoints, thus enhancing his or her potential for exercising constructive leadership in the school system.

Administrator-Staff Relations

During the late 1970s, administrator-staff relations in Oakville greatly improved. The number of grievances filed by teachers dropped dramatically. Only two were filed between 1977 and 1979, and both of these were easily resolved at the district level. Union activists explained a major reason for the reduction in grievances to have been greater administrator sensitivity to the contract. The president, Nancy Drusten, commented, "They [administrators] know that contract as well as we do." Other union activists commented:

> Bill [Mandryk] and Davd [the middle school principal] are not going to violate the contract.
>
> You can't say anything to him [Mandryk] about the contract. He wrote our contract.
>
> Since he [Mandryk] had a hand in writing the contract, he knows it well, and he does not tend to violate it.

These principals, who had been active unionists, who had seen teachers treated arbitrarily, and who had in consequence fought to hammer out solid grievance procedures, now tried to anticipate and avoid potential grievances.

Those complaints that did arise were generally resolved informally at the building level. Union building representatives played an important role in such informal resolutions, bringing potential grievances to the building principal's attention as soon as they developed. Broader problems were handled in a similar fashion, through informal cooperation between the union president and supervising principal. The accessibility of administrators to union representatives and their motivation to avoid formal grievance procedures appear to have been important factors contributing to the relative ease with which most teacher complaints were locally resolved in the late 1970s.

A few union members were critical of the apparently relaxed relationship between union leaders and administrators in Oakville. One attributed the reduction in grievances to union leaders having "let things slide," another to weak union leadership. Several union leaders acknowledged that there was some truth in the charge that they let some things slide. "We get tired, washed out," one explained, noting that their small activist pool did not permit rotation of leadership responsibilities. Administrators, however, unanimously disagreed that the union leadership was weak. All three perceived Nancy Drusten as a strong leader, who, if anything, was overprotective of teachers and their rights. Johnson, the supervising principal, commented: "If an administrator, or I, or the board attempts to do something that doesn't sit well with them, they'll come in strong."

Drusten's informal leadership style may have been a factor accounting for some rank-and-file teachers attributing easy conflict resolution to leadership weakness. A union activist explained:

> I think Nancy is an intensely strong person. Stronger than Bill Mandryk was in that position. . . . She will sit down in a head-to-head with Dan Johnson and . . . work things out, but she'll do it on an individual, person-to-person basis. Bill was more visible [to the membership]. . . . She will go in there and she will know what she has to do and it will get accomplished.

Negotiations in the Late 1970s

In spite of friendlier relations between teachers and the school board, negotiations continued to be difficult during this period. Previously existing pressures on the board to minimize school budgets and taxes were heightened by the national mood of resistance to public spending. These pressures toward frugality were accompanied by further pressures, also supported by nationwide sentiments, to regain more management control over teachers in general. Thus, in 1976 negotiations, both sides were faced, on the one hand, with difficulty in negotiating money issues while, on the other, issues of teacher accountability and productivity more strongly entered the picture. In respect to money issues, teachers wanted substantial salary increases to meet the rising cost of living, and they wanted to keep a limit to class sizes; the board wanted no increases. In respect to accountability and productivity issues, the board wanted to specify how teachers would use existing preparation periods, to have them account for use of personal days,† to take on additional

---

†The concept of personal days — to allow a certain number of unexplained teacher absences for purposes other than illness (for example, legal business,

supervisory duties, and even to teach additional classes. Teachers resisted these proposals as significantly increasing already heavy workloads and infringing upon hard-earned freedoms in respect to their use of time.

The influence of surrounding districts again had its impact locally. Boards elsewhere were demanding more, and unions were being forced to yield more — the beginning of what union leaders referred to as the period of give-backs. In such an atmosphere, the Oakville union's major goal, as in Middlebury and Cedarton, was to prevent erosion of earlier contract gains. Thus, in 1976, leaders settled (in the final hour, in the early morning of the first day of school) for a three-year contract involving no changes except for a clause providing a temporary suspension of sabbatical leaves. The union exchanged the leaves for a small annual increase (4-5 percent, still far below the double-digit inflation rate) in teacher salaries.

In 1978, utilizing an approach that was beginning to be used by union leaders elsewhere (including Cedarton), Nancy Drusten suggested to Johnson, the supervising principal, that the board consider extending the contract for another three years, to avoid another round of lengthy, difficult negotiations. Johnson referred this proposal to the board, and within a matter of days, a settlement was completed, involving only a few minor changes to the contract: a small salary increase for teachers (this time in exchange for a tightening of controls over teachers' use of personal days) and the assignment of some supervisory responsibilities to teaching specialists. (Teaching specialists had never been assigned supervisory duties and thus had fewer hours of assigned responsibilities than regular teachers. Because this change represented greater equalization in assigned workloads, the union did not strongly resist it.)

As in Cedarton, board members, administrators, and union leaders referred to this easy settlement as an indication of improved relations between them. Also as in Cedarton, some rank-and-file teachers complained that union leaders had given away the opportunity to negotiate a new contract in which teachers could have fought for significant gains. Critics complained especially about the low salary increases, restrictions on personal days, and increases in

---

illness, or death in the family) — was a now widely accepted contract provision throughout the state, originally sought in the contract to protect teachers against administrator arbitrariness in approving absences.

specialists' workload. Union leaders, however, pointed out that to have negotiated a new contract would probably have opened the door to greater potential losses than gains for teachers. If, as they believed, the best they could hope for was to maintain existing rights and benefits, it hardly made sense to spend great amounts of time and energy on negotiations and run the risk of renewing old antagonisms, when an extension maintained their present position.

OAKVILLE IN 1979

By 1979 Oakville was a quiet, harmonious school district. The student population, administration, and teaching staff were all relatively stable. Teacher turnover was, once again, minimal, and most teachers had been in the district for more than ten years. School budgets and taxes still represented major school board concerns; classes were much larger than they had been in the early 1960s, and only some specialist positions had been restored. A major difference, however, lay in the style with which 1979 board members conducted themselves. A union leader explained: "Teachers visualize the [board members] as being at least somewhat reasonable at all times." The school board was much quieter and less intrusive in school affairs than it had been in 1969. Board members maintained lower profiles and put more faith in their appointed administrators. Although there were occasional disagreements among the board, teachers, and administrators, relations among them appeared far more comfortable and cooperative than they had been five to ten years earlier. Bill Mandryk commented:

> Everybody's voices have gone down a few octaves since that time. . . . We don't seem to shout as much at each other — teachers shouting at administrators or administrators shouting at the board. Everybody's lowered their voices considerably, . . . which, I suppose, is good for the district. . . . If you look at the districts around us, they're going through all kinds of hell. Oakville . . . has been going quietly along.

The 1979 Oakville School Board president offered this perception:

> I think we have a better understanding of each other's position, a better interchange of ideas. I think the union has a better appreciation of the

district [problems in administering it], and I think the school board and the administration have accepted the fact that we have a teachers' union.

Board acceptance of the legitimacy of the union represented a major change in its relationship to teachers.

No doubt, much of the harmony found in Oakville in 1979 can be attributed to its small size, which allows easy personal contact and mutual accessibility between concerned parties. By parallel reasoning, much of the discord found in 1969 could be attributed to tensions resulting also from the district's small size, which did not protect school activities and staff from personal intrusion by hostile board members. Thus, Oakville's improvement in the quality of staff-board relations in the late 1970s must be credited in part to efforts by particular board members, administrators, and union leaders to change the nature of these relations, in the context of their heightened awareness of problems to be incurred had they allowed earlier tensions to mount.

5

CONCLUSIONS: CHANGES AND IMPACTS

This chapter presents some major themes emerging from the case studies. First, we shall examine patterns of change in the three unions studied, with attention to common developments and differences. Particular focus will be given to changes in union goals and the conditions or forces underlying these changes. We shall then briefly consider some questions concerning the influence of the unions upon the school districts in which they are located.

CHANGES IN THE UNIONS

In respect to changes, we have observed similarities in structural change in all three unions. Between the mid-1960s and early 1970s, all three developed common organizational forms. During the 1970s, all three underwent substantial membership growth so that by 1979 almost all teachers in each district were members.† We have also noted that all three unions expanded during the 1970s to include nonteaching employees.

Another common pattern of change was the development, in all three cases, of stronger connections of the local unions to the state organization — NYSUT. Although we have noted that Middlebury union leaders relied more heavily on consultation with NYSUT, all

---

†Table 1, Appendix, indicates the increases in teacher enrollments in the unions between 1969 and 1979.

three unions utilized the state organization's advisory services on questions pertaining to negotiations and grievances. In addition, local activists, in all three cases, became increasingly involved in NYSUT-sponsored statewide activities, including conferences and legislative lobbying.

We also observed common patterns in respect to changing relationships among the unions and district school boards and administrators. Although there were significant variations in the timing and sequence of stages in these relations, all three districts started with a history of good relations that deteriorated markedly during either the 1960s or early 1970s. In all three districts, tensions between school boards and teachers were generated by conflict over teachers' insistence on their right to collective bargaining, and in all three this conflict culminated in a teachers' strike. In all three, the strike was followed by a period of intensified antagonism and polarization among teachers, school boards, and administrators. Although in two of the districts the antagonisms were more effectively reduced than in the third, in all three, teacher-board relations improved somewhat in later years following the strikes. By 1979, school boards in all three districts had accepted the legitimacy of the union as the official representative of teacher interests and the legitimacy of collective bargaining processes in which teachers and board members negotiated in a spirit of mutual give-and-take.

The Rise of Teacher Militancy

All three of these unions grew initially out of relatively informal, inactive teacher professional associations, affiliated with the National Educational Association (NEA) and the New York State Teachers' Association (NYSTA). Administrators, who had also belonged to these associations, served as teachers' only representatives in bringing teacher concerns before their respective school boards before the mid-1960s. The teachers' departure from these professional associations and their affiliation with the more militant American Federation of Teachers (AFT) came about in response to a combination of circumstances that emerged in each school district during the 1960s and in conjunction with other developments in the state and nation. Especially important among these other developments was the rise of teacher unionism in the nation at large and, especially, in New York City. The United Federation of Teachers, by its early successes in New York, served as a model of what a local teachers' union, backed by organized labor on the state and national levels, could accomplish. But there was no simple and direct relationship between the union movement elsewhere and the rise of the teachers' unions studied here, for this research indicates that teachers in these districts resisted unionization as unprofessional long after the successful establishments of other major unions. It was only after changing circumstances within each district contributed to increased teacher dissatisfaction that the appeal of the union – as a stronger, more militant organization – grew.

Circumstances changed, in all three districts, as a result of population changes accompanying suburban trends in the late 1950s and 1960s. Local populations not only grew in size but also changed in socioeconomic composition. Population increases resulted in rapid school expansion, which in turn led to a variety of new educational problems, increased school bureaucracy, and decreased accessibility of teachers to school administrators. Changes in socioeconomic composition altered the character of local school politics and school boards, thus profoundly affecting teacher-board relations. Incidents involving arbitrary treatment of teachers, including harassment and unexplained teacher dismissals, further contributed to a breakdown of trust among teachers, administrators, and school boards. Changes in teachers' perceptions of their economic and professional status (perceptions influenced by the broader teacher movement) further enhanced their dissatisfaction.

In contrast to interpretations by Cole (1969) and others who have suggested teachers' dissatisfaction with salaries and prestige as the major motivations underlying teacher unionization, this research suggests that teacher frustrations over larger, administrative issues were of equal, if not greater, importance.

The decision to unionize, in each case, was not triggered by any specific concern, but rather by teachers' generalized desire to assert more control over decisions affecting both their welfare and their professional lives. Based on this desire, teachers, in each case, sought collective negotiations with their school boards as a means of asserting such control. The school boards, however, resisted negotiations, at least on the scale that teachers sought. The pivotal issues that eventually pushed a majority of teachers in each of these districts toward greater militancy and affiliation with the union had to do with the right to negotiate and the scope of negotiations.†

Such issues were also pivotal in later motivating teachers' strikes in these districts. The teachers' strikes that occurred in each of these three districts during the 1970s were called not only over particular contract items, but because union leaders felt their contract demands were not being taken seriously by their school board — in other words, that the boards were not negotiating in good faith. Furthermore, the strikes were not called simply because negotiations were going poorly, but because tensions between parties had mounted over months — even years — of unsatisfactory negotiating within a broader context of unresolved teacher concerns. Note, for example, the following description of undercurrents precipitating the Middlebury strike:

> Teachers . . . were upset with the 1972 contract. Now, the next time around, . . . there was simmering and smouldering and an undercurrent of resentment. There had been administrative changes, also. . . . Avery was a disaster. . . . His attitude was to show the teachers who's boss. What teachers wanted was *recognition* [emphasis mine] . . . . The outside evaluation thing became a cause célèbre, but the real issue was, "You can't push us around. Why do you treat us this way?" Now, you can't collectively bargain around such a thing. That's not an issue. So everything else becomes permeated with that, and that's ultimately what it was about.

And these comments by a NYSUT official in 1979 suggest that such problems in teacher-board relationships in fact underlie most strikes:

> Strikes don't happen solely over issues of contract. There are some deep seated problems in those places. And I think if you look at the strikes, like Levittown, . . . Lakeland, . . . Nyack, Eastchester, and the one out on the Island this year, where they were out for 50 days — [they are all] examples of the same thing. . . . And that goes far beyond . . . simply the contract. It's just bad relationships that exist there [that] finally erupt in a strike.

---

†Although New York's Taylor Law (1967) had mandated collective bargaining for all public employees, including school teachers, ambiguities in the law continued to leave much room for interpretation concerning what areas were negotiable and much room for disagreement between teachers and boards. Teachers continued to press for broad interpretations, while school boards pressed for narrower ones.

The Logic of Unionization

The appeal of unionism to teachers, in all three cases, was twofold. In the first place, teachers saw affiliation with the union as providing a kind of shock value in impressing their school boards with how strongly they felt about the right to negotiate. A Cedarton activist commented in 1969, "The union had advantages in that the name itself means 'dissent' — you know, militancy." A Middlebury activist at that time explained, "You know, 'union' is a magic word. . . . The paternal fathers [board members] feared unions. Just the word 'union' was intimidation."

Second, teacher leaders in all three districts saw the state and national union organizations as better able than the teachers' professional associations (NEA and NYSTA) to help them in their struggle for negotiations. NYSTA officials had not themselves fully accepted negotiations as appropriate for teachers, and, because of their own connections with administrative and board networks within the state, they were often reluctant to press for the kinds of things teachers hoped for. Moreover, NYSTA lacked experience in labor negotiations.

Perhaps of overriding importance, however, was the symbolic significance teacher unionization had for teachers in defining their own situation. A Cedarton activist explained this in 1969 as follows:

> I'm in favor of anything which makes teachers join together and realize their own strength, be conscious of it. . . . Conscious of what they can do and cannot do — anything which brings them into a community of interest. You see, teachers everywhere feel this helplessness. . . . Now, we're citizens of a democracy where we know the union movement exists. . . . We know that unions have power, strength. . . . We need the union to give us a little bit of — [breaks off].

The development that most aided teachers in achieving the negotiations they sought — state legislation known as the Taylor Law (Public Employees' Fair Employment Act, enacted in 1967, Article 14 in the New York State Civil Service Law) — ultimately limited the scope of teacher negotiations and the development of the unions in certain important ways. While the new legislation mandated collective bargaining between all public employers and employees, its formal definitions of the areas subject to bargaining adhered more closely than teachers wanted to terms and conditions of employment.

The extent to which this limiting factor actually altered the direction of these unions did not, however, become fully evident until later on.

Early Union Goals

As indicated above, the issues over which teachers in these districts first sought negotiations and later unionized were neither clear-cut nor narrow in scope. Bread-and-butter issues (salaries, fringe benefits, and other money issues) were only one set among a range of other concerns. Such issues were, of course, important, since teachers' salaries in the 1960s were still very low relative to those of other professionals. However, the primary issues that motivated unionization in all three districts went well beyond salary.

The other issues fell into two general categories: due process issues, related to the prevention of unjust or arbitrary treatment of individual teachers by administrators and board members, and professional issues, referring to teachers' level of influence and authority within the schools, relative to administrators.

Although due process issues were of greatest importance in Oakville, where board harassment of teachers had become a chronic problem, they were also central concerns in both Cedarton and Middlebury, where unexpected dismissals had heightened teacher awareness of their own powerlessness in preventing arbitrary treatment of colleagues. To some early activists, concerns about due process were most central to their affiliation with the union. A Cedarton union activist explained in 1969:

> Basically, why is someone "union"? . . . Because he recognizes gross inequities which exist. And this is not only in teaching, . . . [but] anywhere. . . . These people, down deep, are frustrated, angry and disturbed about the problems and discrepancies [between] what they know should be and what . . . exists.

Professional issues were important in Oakville, where teachers were concerned with defending their existing educational system — including services, programs, and teacher involvement in educational processes — against intrusion by a hostile school board. But in

Middlebury and Cedarton, the professional issues were much further reaching. Early activists in these two districts saw the union as an avenue through which teachers could strengthen their influence over a variety of professional and educational matters; in short, as a vehicle for professionalizing teaching and putting teachers on a more equal footing with administrators. Note the following remarks by union officers in Cedarton and Middlebury:

> You asked me why we started. Well, . . . the average teacher involved in founding the union . . . was very much concerned with having a voice — you must have heard this a thousand times — having a voice in actually running the school and helping to make policy decisions. This is to me the major issue; this is the reason why we came into existence. (Early union president in Cedarton)

> We wanted to have a voice — not only in bread-and-butter, salary, welfare, working conditions — but we'd always been told that "professionalism" was a very important part of our role as teachers, and we . . . wanted to have some voice in policy formation. . . . There was a feeling among teachers that the day of unilateral decisions by a board of education, transmitted through the administration, was approaching an end. . . . If we were really to be professionals . . . [we wanted] some meaningful control over our own operations. . . . [Also] I think a very important element in this whole thing was . . . an increasing feeling that [we] knew at least as much as administration about the educational process and what was needed . . . and in many cases . . . perhaps more. (1969 president in Middlebury)

Interest in such professional issues was not unique to teachers in these districts. The teacher influence issue and a new professional ideology, stressing more collegial, less authoritarian relations among teachers, school administrators, and boards, were important themes in the teacher movement elsewhere. The new professional ideology was an extension — not a replacement — of the traditional union ideology, which stressed the bread-and-butter and due process issues mentioned above. Its proponents saw no fundamental conflicts between the old and new ideologies: they claimed both were important and mutually complementary. Landau (1969 president of the Middlebury union) explained:

> It wasn't a question of which was more important — bread-and-butter or . . . professional issues. . . . They were both important. . . . I couldn't

divorce the two. . . . [We felt] that conditions and salaries and fringe benefits had to be improved because we were more than workers in the sense of other responsibilities we had. . . . In other words, I saw it as a total program of which bread-and-butter was a part.

But the new ideology ran counter to more traditional, ill-defined teacher conceptions of professionalism, which stressed social status or respectability rather than authority issues, and teachers holding such views found the new ideology threatening. Others — those who were more traditional unionists — found it inappropriate, and these divisions later proved to be limiting upon the unions.

Nevertheless, while all early unionists did not share the dual vision of union issues described above, it appears to have been the dominant vision among a majority of union activists in all three districts. Table 4, Appendix, shows that while the highest percentage of 1969 respondents in each district reported a union emphasis on salaries, more than 80 percent in all three also indicated an emphasis on strengthening teachers' voice in policy.† More than 70 percent indicated an emphasis on educational programs.

Changes in Union Goals

By 1979, union priorities were clearly upon teacher welfare, in all three districts. In addition to bread-and-butter and due process, job protection took on major importance. Professional issues were now distinctly secondary (see Tables 5 and 6, Appendix).‡ A Middlebury board member remarked in 1979: "I don't know what happened

---

†The apparently lesser emphasis on voice in policy shown in Table 4 for Middlebury, as compared to the other two districts, may not reflect an actual lesser emphasis, but rather more clearly articulated divisions within the union about where the emphasis should lie. There was more internal disagreement on issues within Middlebury than in the other two districts. While the early Middlebury union was dominated by the professional-idealists, who emphasized the new professional ideology, a vocal minority held to the traditional, welfare-oriented position.

‡Note that comparisons of activists' with members' perceptions, as shown in Tables 5 and 6, indicate that on almost every issue activists report a higher level of emphasis than members. Nevertheless, the two groups are consistent in reporting far more emphasis on welfare issues than on program and policy issues. Unfortunately, data are not available allowing for comparisons of these patterns

to make the union so completely involved with . . . [teacher welfare]. It happened all over the place." What happened is clear from the case histories: the unions were subject to strong external and internal constraints that, in all three cases, pressed them into narrowing goals.

The external constraints included school board resistance to negotiations, further refinements in state legislation, an atmosphere of economic crisis, declining student enrollments, and growing public criticism and distrust of school personnel. School board resistance to negotiations meant that where the unions had initially envisioned the struggle for bargaining as a means toward achieving other, broader goals, this struggle became redirected, especially in Cedarton and Oakville, into a struggle for the right to bargain at all. When, with the help of the Taylor Law, the unions won the struggle for bargaining, further refinements in state legislation limited the areas in which boards were required to negotiate policy and management issues. Both the school boards themselves and state legislation, therefore, severely restricted the range of concerns teachers could productively bring to the bargaining table. Without initially conceding the legitimacy of these restrictions, the unions at first directed their major energies toward bargaining in areas where they could anticipate some real gains. And with the boards still at times resisting bargaining even in those areas sanctioned by law, major energies were required in order for teachers to make any gains. A Middlebury activist explained in 1969:

> On a lot of issues we feel are important, they [the board] will simply say, "That's not negotiable. That's not a union issue." . . . Every time we try to make some gain educationally, they say, "That's not a union issue." . . . And so the union is stymied. I know they [the negotiating team] met repeatedly; I know they pushed. . . . I also believe that no

---

with 1969. A refinement in the 1979 survey over the earlier (1969) survey called for distinction between degrees of emphasis (little, some, much) on various union goals, and these distinctions proved crucial in yielding significant differences in the types of issues stressed. Where the distinctions were obliterated by combining categories in the 1979 data to provide comparability to the less refined 1969 data (as shown in Table 4), the resulting tabulation did not show significant differences in emphasis between welfare and professional goals. Because the interviews, in all three districts, consistently referred to a shift away from professional goals, we are relying upon the interviews in assuming that more emphasis was given to these, relative to welfare goals, in 1969 than in 1979.

matter how much they would have pushed, they wouldn't have gotten [more]. I think they assessed the feeling of the people they were meeting with [the board] and pushed where they felt they were going to [be successful]. Some [people say], "We should have pushed them on items they say are not negotiable. We should have insisted." . . . My rejoinder to that is, is it realistic, in this district, under these conditions, to fight for this? I mean, do you fight a windmill? You know we're not going to get [those things] now. But we're pushing for [them] now to give them warning. You start pushing years before you think something is going to come about.

At first, union leaders believed they could simply postpone negotiations on the unacceptable issues into future years, regarding collective bargaining as a long-term process in which each contract would represent a step forward. As the 1970s progressed, however, this possibility receded. The atmosphere of economic crisis, heightened by local tax revolts and declining student enrollments, led boards not to be more expansive, but to cut back on school financing. The atmosphere of public criticism and distrust led them to try to tighten, not loosen, controls over teachers. These situations pressed all three unions into far more defensive positions during the 1970s so that protection of existing staff positions and the contract took priority.

Internal constraints included the unions' need to establish and maintain a large, diverse membership and membership solidarity, traditions associated with the labor movement, and ties to parent organizations. We pointed out in Chapter 1 that unions must concern themselves with sustaining a large, diverse membership that appears unified behind its leaders. Membership size, diversity, and solidarity serve to legitimize leadership positions in both formal and informal negotiations with administrators and school boards, for they demonstrate that the leaders are representative of the entire staff. Moreover, membership size and solidarity further serve to indicate a union's potential to strike. The need to sustain solidarity within a large group, however, requires narrowing organizational goals to those that most members are willing to support, meaning that controversial goals must be deemphasized. Landau, leader of the professional-idealist faction in Middlebury, explained how enlargement of membership affected union goals:

What began to happen was, once we became stronger, a lot of people . . . joined, especially after we got that two-year contract. . . . We increased our membership to 90 percent. I had vague [uneasy] feelings about that at the time but it seemed . . . logical. . . . What happened was that the sharp focused issues had to be blurred to reflect . . . [the membership]. The people who were more conservative, originally, . . . were prepared to jump on the bandwagon, on bread-and-butter issues, because they weren't ideological. But the ideologically conservative people could never get into . . . the role of management and teacher power, . . . which were important issues to me.

Thus, union leaders in the 1970s moved in the direction of emphasizing those issues behind which they could maintain unity, and the goals on which most members agreed were those traditionally associated with the labor movement: goals that enhanced worker welfare and job protection. In fact, traditions associated with the labor movement influenced union leaders to focus considerable energy on such goals, for it was simply taken for granted by most members that such goals took priority. A NYSUT representative explained:

Sometimes the position you are in does not allow you to do what you would like to do as an individual. The district has to do what it has to do, and the union has to do what it has to do, in terms of the positions it has to take. You do get into that. . . . You've got to protect the contract, you've got to protect the members. That's what you're there for. That's what the purposes of the union are, right in the constitution and by-laws.

Ties to larger parent organizations (the AFT and NYSUT), although not mandatory, were important to the local unions in enhancing their skills, knowledge, and power in their dealings with school administrators and boards. While the parent organizations did not impose formal directives on the local unions, they did exert considerable informal influence through advisory assessments of the legitimacy and practicality of local goals and strategies. Advisors from NYSUT were especially influential during the local unions' early stages of development, when inexperienced local leaders relied on them heavily. But advisors often tended to assess local goals in terms of tradition and precedent, and, therefore, their advice tended to further influence the local unions to emphasize the traditional, welfare goals, over nontraditional, professional goals.

District Differences in Sustaining Professional Goals

The early unionists who advocated professional goals did not see these as potentially in conflict with welfare goals, but rather as complementary. With time, however, especially under the new pressures arising during the 1970s, contradictions became more apparent. Questions arose about whether union leaders could give primary consideration to professional goals (for example, maintaining high educational standards in decisions affecting staff allocation and supervision) and at the same time protect the welfare interests of individual union members. The case studies include numerous instances where the two sets of goals came into conflict and where the unions were forced into difficult choices — for example, over issues surrounding staff governance and teacher evaluation in Middlebury and Cedarton and the retroactive pay issue in Cedarton. Such conflicts made it even more difficult to sustain professional goals.

Although all three unions moved toward a greater emphasis upon teacher welfare during the 1970s, this research also shows that the three unions did not move equally in that direction: Cedarton union leaders were considerably more successful than leaders in Middlebury or Oakville in sustaining a balance between professional and teacher welfare goals. Professional goals had not been as strongly emphasized from the outset in Oakville as in the other two districts. But Middlebury, where professional goals had been strongly emphasized in the 1960s, provides an especially significant contrast to Cedarton in this respect.

All three unions put priority on teacher welfare concerns, but the Cedarton union put somewhat less emphasis on these and somewhat more emphasis upon program and policy than the other two unions.† Tables 7 and 8, Appendix, present activists' and members' perceptions of union effectiveness in respect to goals. In keeping with reported differences in emphasis, Cedarton respondents reported their union as significantly more effective in the areas of program

---

†See Tables 5 and 6, Appendix. Note that the differences between unions are consistent for activists and members on welfare issues, but inconsistent on program and policy. On educational program, significant differences are shown among activists, but not among members; on policy, significant differences are shown among members, but not activists — except in the Oakville case. The inconsistencies disappear, however, when we examine activists' and members' perceptions of union effectiveness in Tables 7 and 8, Appendix.

and policy than did other respondents, but significantly less effective in the areas of job security and teaching load. The different patterns of emphasis and effectiveness suggest that there were trade-offs between professional and welfare goals — that is, that the unions could not, in the 1970s, effectively emphasize either set of goals without some sacrifice to the other. The case studies, in fact, indicate that the greater emphasis upon professional/educational concerns in the Cedarton union reflected deliberate, strategic choices by the CFC leaders.

Analysis of Different Union Patterns in Middlebury and Cedarton

The more marked shift in union goals in Middlebury deserves special comment. Although the external and internal constraints identified earlier were clearly factors accounting for changes in union goals, questions arise concerning why the Middlebury union, initially less welfare-oriented than either the Cedarton or Oakville unions, and whose emergence was particularly motivated by professional and educational concerns, should have developed in so much more a traditional direction than Cedarton. (Consideration of Oakville is omitted from this comparison because professional goals were never given as much emphasis in Oakville as in Middlebury and Cedarton.) Because both the Cedarton and Middlebury unions were forced into defensive positions by economic tightening and teacher retrenchment, we wonder why we find more substantial changes from early goals in the Middlebury case.

The inability of the Middlebury union to sustain a highly respected group of teachers in leadership positions was clearly a major contributing factor in its failure to sustain early goals. We have already noted, in the case studies, the importance of leaders' personal commitment to professional and educational values in setting union goals and particularly in moderating the potential for union preoccupation with teacher welfare concerns. Moreover, highly respected, articulate leaders enhanced union capabilities of rallying rank-and-file support for difficult positions on complex or controversial issues. In Middlebury, such leaders had become alienated from active participation, leaving its leadership to those having lesser influence among the members. Assuming quality of union leadership to have been a major factor influencing organizational goals, perhaps we should ask, therefore, not why goals changed, but why the Middlebury union was unable to sustain high quality leadership.

Respondents were always ready with personal, individual explanations: "You get tired. . . ." or "Seth's kids were growing up." But we must ask why similar personal pressures did not appear to interfere with continuity in leadership within the Cedarton leadership or why other potential leaders in Middlebury, who shared the professional-idealist vision for the union, did not assume the presidency when Landau withdrew. We find ourselves left with a larger institutional and organizational question: Why was the union in Cedarton able to sustain a leadership group committed to professional and educational goals, whereas the union in Middlebury was not?

Four major factors appear to account for differences in the ability of the two unions to sustain a professionally committed leadership group:

1. The initial greater idealism of the Middlebury union leadership and membership, in contrast to Cedarton's;
2. The Middlebury union's early rapid growth, in contrast to the more gradual development of the Cedarton union;
3. The greater factionalism within the Middlebury union;
4. The more hostile community in Middlebury.

These factors, of course, were interrelated, as they were also related to the various constraints discussed earlier. The initial greater idealism of teachers in the Middlebury union meant not only that their initial vision of the union was more far-reaching than the Cedarton vision, but also that their ideals for the union meshed with their social, educational, and professional ideals. Many early union supporters saw the union as a mechanism not only for strengthening their own influence in the school system, but also for changing the schools, in keeping with their idealistic vision of a better society. When external economic pressures and school board resistance made early union goals difficult to achieve, the gap between leaders' (and members') idealistic vision and what they could realistically achieve was, therefore, greater in Middlebury than in Cedarton, and this undoubtedly contributed to Middlebury idealists' disenchantment.

The rapidity with which the Middlebury union moved from a formative stage to assuming major responsibility as the organization representing teachers, under the new Taylor Law, meant not only that it grew quickly, absorbing external factions before differences could be clarified, but also that leaders did not have time to explore issues, confronting them in depth. By contrast, Cedarton union leaders had several years in which to explore and resolve internal differences and to clarify differences with other teacher groups outside the union. This period of time appears to have facilitated the development in Cedarton of, on the one hand, a mutually supportive leadership group and, on the other, of clearer union positions on issues involving conflicts of interest between professional and welfare goals.

The greater factionalism in the Middlebury union may have been due in part to its rapid growth and the lack of a time period for clarification and resolution of conflicting interests. It may also have been related in part to the greater idealism of the leadership group. Middlebury teachers were, on the whole, more liberal in social orientations than were teachers in either Cedarton or Oakville. However, Middlebury union leaders in 1969 were considerably more liberal than the rank-and-file (see Tables 12 and 13, Appendix). Note that 65 percent of union activists identified themselves as strongly liberal or radical in 1969, in contrast to 30 percent of the staff as a whole. Factionalism meant that more decisions had to be reached by compromise in Middlebury than in Cedarton. Compromise meant, to the professional-idealists, further obstacles to the realization of original goals. Yet, compromise was necessary, because only with a unified membership could the organization realize any goals.

Early union leaders in Cedarton were also highly liberal, but so was the early membership. Both the greater ideological similarity of leaders and members and the longer time period before their eventual merger with the more conservative teachers' association membership enabled them to develop more internal unity. Internal unity and mutual support were undoubtedly factors in Nelson's ability to sustain his commitment to professional ideals in his union leadership role, over time.

Finally, the presence of a more hostile community in Middlebury — specifically a hostile black community increasingly dissatisfied with the school system and increasingly antagonistic toward teachers — meant that the other external pressures on union leaders in Middlebury were different in tone, if not in substance, from those in Cedarton. An antagonistic school board in Cedarton unified teachers. Black hostility in Middlebury divided them. Blacks' open suspicion of union leaders' motivations as self-interested raised further internal questioning of union purposes in an atmosphere of mistrust that further hindered resolution.

The black criticism — influenced in part by feelings about the 1968 New York City teachers' strike — also raised other conflicts within the Middlebury union. On the one hand, teachers' liberal, egalitarian sentiments predisposed them to sympathize with the blacks' own struggle to assert themselves. On the other, they were deeply offended by antiteacher, antiunion, and anti-Semitic overtones in black charges against them. This situation not only created internal, personal conflicts for union members, but also divided them. By contrast, blatant public criticisms of teachers by white community and school board members in Cedarton (as in Oakville) pulled teachers together in a common feeling of being unfairly attacked.

Thus, the different character of external pressures, coupled with the greater initial idealism of Middlebury teachers for their union, contributed to greater internal factionalism. A less unified membership and more rapid movement of the union to a position of power made it more difficult to resolve complex problems in the attainment of organizational goals.

These tendencies, combined with the external economic and community pressures identified earlier, led to disenchantment with the union and union leadership roles among the professional-idealists in Middlebury. Many withdrew from union activism because they no longer saw the union as a viable mechanism for realizing their social and professional ideals. Furthermore, their commitment to grass roots democracy did not permit them to deliberately recruit a strong centralized leadership group (as in Cedarton). Without the continuing presence of a supportive leadership group sharing professional commitments, it became extremely difficult for any one leader, in isolation, to effectively sustain professional goals within the union, given the external and organizational pressures to emphasize teacher welfare. Instead, routinization of leadership and goals became prerequisite for sustained occupancy of union leadership roles.

By contrast, the Cedarton union's ability to sustain strong, professionally committed leaders derived from their having initially set their sights on a different — perhaps more attainable — vision of what the union could accomplish; pressures upon them to emphasize traditional goals were, therefore, less intensely demoralizing to them than to Middlebury leaders. More gradual organizational development allowed for the emergence of a stable leadership group who mutually explored and resolved complex issues; leadership philosophies encouraged the deliberate maintenance of such a group. The mutual support engendered among Cedarton union leaders, along with a more supportive community environment,† helped to sustain leadership morale and, hence, continuity in leadership positions. Ultimately, the Cedarton leaders' shared commitment to professional standards, their capacity for collective resolution of difficult problems, and their influence with their members seem to have enabled them to more effectively balance professional and teacher welfare concerns within their union.

IMPACT OF THE UNIONS ON TEACHERS

We shall now turn to a consideration of the impact of teacher unionism, examining first its impact upon teachers themselves and second, its impact upon the schools.

Because all three unions gave major emphasis to teacher welfare during the 1970s, let us consider first their relative effectiveness in meeting welfare goals. Then, we shall consider how the unions influenced other areas of teachers' work lives, including teachers' morale and school participation.

In considering the relative effectiveness of the three unions, it is important to bear in mind that neither the individual successes nor failures of the local unions can be attributed solely to local directions and activities, for each union operated within a larger context that in some respects limited, in others, enhanced its ability to meet various goals.

---

†Note, however, that community supportiveness in Cedarton was also fostered by the union in its deliberate efforts to develop and sustain good community relations. Their campaign to inform Cedarton residents about the issues behind the 1973 strike stands in marked contrast to the Middlebury union's efforts in community relations during its strike.

We have already noted the limiting factors in our discussion above. Important as an enhancing factor was the union movement elsewhere, which influenced local bargaining power in two important ways. First of all, significant contract gains by union locals in a few key districts — such as New York City — were important in helping to raise standards throughout the state, since local standards were traditionally based on comparisons with other districts. Thus, in respect to salaries, local union negotiators could cite salary levels in other, comparable, districts as a basis for determining what constituted reasonable increases at the local level.† The same principle applied to other contract benefits, such as the duty-free lunch period and preparation periods achieved in the 1960s. Such gains reflected changing standards elsewhere as much as, if not more than, local union initiative. In fact, such gains were achieved by both associations and unions during that period, as the Cedarton case illustrates.

Second, union political action at the state level contributed to legislation important in protecting teachers' rights. Such legislation, for example, helped to improve grievance procedures, thereby strengthening due process.

In all three districts, teachers reported their salary levels as better in 1979 than in 1969 (see Table 9, Appendix). Note that over 70 percent in all three districts reported salaries as better in 1979. In Middlebury, 53 percent reported salaries to be much better, in contrast to 41 percent in Cedarton and 27 percent in Oakville. (Percentages reporting much better are based on a refinement in the data not included in the Appendix.) Salary levels had, in fact, improved more substantially in Middlebury because of a negotiated cost of living increase earned in the strike settlement and lasting through 1976.‡ In Cedarton and Oakville, negotiated salary increases remained consistently below the inflation rate from 1973 on.

In respect to job security and working conditions, respondents in all three districts perceived a deterioration in their situation since

---

†Note that the local tax base was another factor, however, accounting for variations in what were considered reasonable salary increases. Hence, the Cedarton and Oakville unions could not reasonably demand as much as the Middlebury union on salaries.

‡Because gains made at any one contract period are added to the floor upon which future percentage increases are based, the benefits of the 1973 contract in Middlebury actually continued through 1979.

1969 (see Table 9). In both Cedarton and Middlebury, close to 60 percent perceived job security as worse; in Oakville, 35 percent perceived it as worse. In all three districts, substantial percentages perceived class size as worse, with the Cedarton percentage being the highest. (Of the Cedarton teachers 74 percent reported class size as worse in 1979.) Teaching loads (hours of assigned work) were also perceived as having become worse in Cedarton and Oakville. (Teachers' perceptions of changes in job security working conditions — including class size and teaching load — are also presented in Table 9, Appendix.) As noted in the preceding section, Cedarton union members perceived their union as less effective regarding job security, class size, and workload in 1979 than did union members in the other two districts (see Table 8). Comparison of Cedarton respondents' perceptions of their organization's effectiveness in 1969 and 1979 also yielded a lower rating for the union in 1979 as compared to the teachers' association in 1969, in respect to class size and workload (see Table 8).

At this point, we are faced with a surprising anomaly. In Cedarton, where the greatest teacher retrenchment had occurred, where improvements in salaries and benefits had been less substantial than in Middlebury, and where members gave the union the lowest ratings for job protection, class size, and workload, respondents reported a substantial improvement in teacher welfare, other than salaries and job security (see Table 9). In fact, the 85 percent of Cedarton respondents reporting improvement of general teacher welfare was significantly higher than the percentages indicated in either Middlebury or Oakville — where 70 percent and 73 percent, respectively, reported improvement in general teacher welfare.

The substantial overall percentages reporting improvement in general teacher welfare suggest that the teachers' unions, in all three cases, had an important impact in improving teachers' general sense of well-being, in spite of external economic pressures and staff cuts. Information from the case studies supports this finding in that teacher respondents were in high agreement — in all three districts — in reporting that they felt far more protected, by their unions, against arbitrary, administrative actions than in 1969. Given the severity of external pressures accompanying retrenchment (and, in Middlebury, increased public criticism), respondents perceived union mechanisms for ensuring due process as especially important.

In view of the lower degree of emphasis placed by the Cedarton union on teacher welfare issues,† by contrast to Middlebury, the Cedarton teachers' significantly higher perceptions of improvement in teacher welfare indicates that more than literal economic welfare or job protection was involved. These data, in combination with what our case studies have revealed, suggest that Cedarton teachers experienced a greater sense of stability in their daily work lives because of a more predictable school system and better relations with their school board.

Turning our attention to areas other than teacher welfare, a comparison of the response patterns indicated in Tables 10 and 11 reveals some further interesting differences between Cedarton and Middlebury within the high schools. (The differences in high school climate reported below are especially relevant to this discussion in view of the much greater activity of the Cedarton union at the high school level and of its differing style of activity.) The percentages reporting improvement in staff relations with administrators and school board, in the overall quality of staff, and in teacher participation in decisions concerning the educational program and discipline are all substantially higher in Cedarton by contrast to Middlebury. In fact, the only area listed in Tables 10 and 11 in which Middlebury high school respondents reported greater improvement than Cedarton respondents was teacher participation in decisions affecting teacher welfare.

The comparison provided in Table 11 of high school teachers' perceptions of improvement in the overall quality of the teaching staff in Cedarton and Middlebury is especially interesting. Note that while 44 percent of Cedarton respondents reported the staff to have become better, only 12 percent of Middlebury respondents perceived their staff as having become better. But only 3 percent in Cedarton perceived the teaching staff as worse, while 35 percent in Middlebury perceived it to be worse. These differences are especially important in that the actual teachers in both high schools have remained virtually the same over the past ten years. Thus, it would appear that we are observing ratings of teachers as a faculty — not as individuals. This pattern may reflect differing perceptions of teacher morale and participation in high school affairs, indicated in the case studies and

---

†Including grievances (see Tables 5 and 6).

borne out by accompanying data (in Table 11) referring to their participation in school decisions affecting programs and discipline. It appears that teachers view a nonparticipating staff as a worse staff. This finding is especially relevant to our research in view of the different roles played by the unions in the two high schools. In Cedarton, we found that the union actively promoted collective teacher participation in the affairs of the high school, intervening with administrators to ensure their consultation with teachers in all areas of school decision making; in Middlebury, the union separated itself from such participation. Thus, we find in the Cedarton case that the union has had a positive impact on staff quality, in the perception of teachers themselves. We cannot say in Middlebury that it has had a negative impact — only that it has not had the same positive impact.

IMPACT OF THE UNIONS ON THE SCHOOL SYSTEM

These findings lead also to other kinds of questions about the effects of teacher unionism upon the school systems within which it arose. How, for example, has unionism affected administrative management of schools? To the degree that a union enhances teacher participation in school decisions, how has such participation benefited the school system? If unions have become more effective in protecting teacher rights, has this change adversely affected school systems by protecting incompetent teachers? This research can provide only tentative answers to these questions because its focus has been upon understanding changes in the unions, rather than upon their impact. Nevertheless, the interviews provided some interesting, possibly important, insights regarding the impact of teacher unionism, and these are worthy of attention.

Union Impact on School Management

What has been the impact of teacher unionism upon school management? The data suggest three general areas: effects of working under a union contract, effects of grievance procedures, and effects of the union presence within the schools.

Effects of Contract on Management

Administrators expressed mixed feelings about the effects of union contracts upon school management. All noted that contracts restricted administrative powers and flexibility. A Middlebury principal commented, for example:

> Union contracts really limit the administrative prerogatives. Let's look at some of the things. For instance, there should be one staff meeting per week. Every teacher will have a preparation period every day. The school day is defined as seven hours and fifteen minutes. I think what unions have really done is to kind of reduce the flexibility.... I think there is a preoccupation with working conditions.

Other principals disagreed, however, that union contracts were so seriously restricting:

> Of course I'm bound by the contract. But you don't have to be hidebound. (Another Middlebury principal)

> I see the contract as a guideline, rather than a strict document. (Oakville principal)

> It's never been a "by the contract" sort of thing in this building. (Cedarton principal)

Administrators' sense of having such flexibility depended in large part upon mutual, informal agreements between them and union leaders concerning how strictly contracts were to be read. For example, the Oakville principal cited above commented:

> One of the first things I established with the building representative [was] how we read this contract. Do we see it as black and white, or do we see it as black, white with some grey areas? . . . And we came to a mutual agreement that there are grey areas.

And an Oakville union activist noted: "When you adhere strictly to the contract, letter for letter, it's not going to work. It just can't. It's only when they really abuse something that we have to [object]."

Furthermore, principals who understood the spirit of the contract — that is, those who balanced consideration for teachers' needs with school management needs — generally found their staff allowed them considerably more freedom in reading the contract than those who showed little regard for teachers' needs. Note, for example, the following illustration given by a Middlebury principal:

> When I had a meeting, they went on as far as they had to go. I had my agenda, and they had an opportunity to bring whatever concerns they had, and if it looked like it required more time and if I felt that the group was getting somewhat antsy, I'd reschedule for another time. I understand teachers have [outside] commitments.

It appears to have been those principals who were least sensitive to teachers' needs who found the contract most restrictive.

Many administrators also pointed to distinct advantages to working under a contract:

> I think it's important to have many of these things down, as long as there's some flexibility. . . . I think it's a healthier atmosphere if there are . . . guidelines.

> You may not agree with the contract at all points, but it certainly tells you your limitations — what you can do, and what you can't do.

> I never had a problem with it. I saw the contract — many of the things in there — as clarification for my convenience.

In fact, most principals noted that the contract was helpful in providing guidelines.

Moreover, many administrators observed that the contract, in spelling out staff rights and obligations, served not only as protection for teacher rights but also as a basis for holding teachers accountable for filling their obligations — a point we shall address again shortly.

Grievance Procedures

Some administrators found grievance procedures irritating and unnecessary. A Middlebury principal commented:

> It gets down to, "Don't make a mistake. I'm going to file a grievance." Or, "Gee, you can't do that. You haven't given me enough notice." There's a lot of nit-picking, frustrating things thrown in your path.

But negative administrative reaction to union grievance machinery was surprisingly low. Most administrators accepted grievances as a fact of life in the 1970s. Some even regarded grievance procedures as offering an advantage, by providing objective bases for resolving teacher-administrator disputes that could otherwise have become highly personal. A principal commented, "[Grievances] take it out of the personal realm . . . into an arena where issues can be dealt with."

Grievance procedures can also facilitate resolution of politically sensitive issues. An NYSUT official, noting that district superintendents occasionally encouraged union leaders to pursue grievances beyond the district level, remarked:

> Roberts* [Middlebury superintendent] will be very honest with you. He'll say, "You're going to have to grieve this one." Now that means either that he can't get the board to go along with him, or . . . [that] the board is willing to, but politically they can't — they have to be told what to do by an arbitrator. Then they can say, "Well, the arbitrator said we have to do this."

Another advantage noted by some principals was that grievances taken as far as the school board served to attract board members' attention to important school problems. A Middlebury principal explained:

> In the main, I find it an enabling device, rather than an obstacle. . . . As a matter of fact, when I couldn't get something done, and a teacher complained [for example, because of inadequate support services], I would kind of suggest that they might want to take the route of the grievance and bring it to the attention of the board. . . . It provides an opportunity for the board to become aware. A board can become terribly insulated, just being fed from the superintendent . . . or being fed officially through the union.

The Presence of Unions

The presence of a union within a school sets a different tone to faculty-administrator relations. Building representatives, grievance committees, and other union officers, who act as intermediaries between administrators and teachers, tend to some degree to formalize and depersonalize relationships. In doing so, as we have already noted, union officers are able to protect teachers against vindictive, arbitrary, or discriminatory administrative actions. But what other implications does the union presence have for school management?

In respect to the greater formality in relationships, some administrators, recalling with nostalgia a time when their relations with teachers had been more personal and freer, resented changes brought about by the union. One commented:

> If somebody is concerned about something, they'll go to the union delegate. . . . Now in the past, they'd either complain themselves or they wouldn't complain at all. But now they do it in an anonymous manner. I would rather have a teacher confront me directly.

A union officer, commenting on the principal in his building, remarked:

> When the union rep comes to him about somebody else, he's hurt that it had to be through the union. He has said on occasion to the person, "Why did you go to the union? Why didn't you come right to me?" . . . That's something he can't get used to.

But other respondents pointed out that changes in teacher-administrator relations were inevitable, given larger school districts, increased bureaucracy, and increased budgetary problems. As a Cedarton union activist pointed out:

> Times are different. Attitudes are different. . . . Of course, one ought to be able to relate to people on a personal basis. . . . But with a larger district, with more teachers and more impersonal relationships, and the attitude on the part of the board that everything is strictly business, . . . it would be self-defeating. . . . These are not the old times. Things have changed.

Most administrators also understood that many teachers hesitated to bring complaints to them directly, and that the union, therefore, served an important function in airing and channeling teacher complaints. In fact, several noted that union representatives, in all three districts, had also been helpful in resolving teacher complaints and personnel problems.

Some respondents felt that the presence of the union tended to intimidate administrators. An assistant principal commented, for example, that higher administrators in his district failed to exercise strong enough leadership: "Because of the fear of rocking the boat or upsetting anyone, administrators back off." On the positive side, however, others commented that the union encouraged administrators to think decisions through more carefully and to manage the schools more responsibly. A Cedarton principal remarked, "I'll think twice before I do things, in comparison to the past." A Middlebury School Board member commented, "I think it [the union] forced them to do some things they probably needed to do and to be more careful in doing things they should be doing."

A further effect of the union's presence was to provide a new channel for communication among teachers, administrators, and school boards as older, informal communication systems failed because of increasing size and bureaucracy. We have already noted that the unions, through negotiations and grievance procedures, increased school boards' awareness of everyday school problems and processes. A Middlebury board member commented on the direct effect of collective bargaining:

> In the course of collective bargaining . . . many things are discussed; there's a lot of give and take. School board members are bound to get a lot of information and a lot of criticisms of administrators that they would otherwise not get. . . . It made school boards much more aware of what was going on in the schools, and . . . armed [them] with a great many questions, criticisms, and suggestions for improving the situation in the school districts. School boards became much more critical of their administration and were not willing to accept administrators' word as . . . final.

The boards' increased knowledge of school problems and increased criticism of administrators was, of course, threatening to many administrators, for it undermined their previously unquestioned authority with the boards. On the other hand, increased information, provided through union channels, better enabled school boards to hold administrators accountable for the schools.

The unions also provided regular channels of communication between administrators and teachers. Where teachers had communicated informally and individually with principals in the past, there had been few mechanisms for teachers to communicate collectively with administrators. The union allowed not only for increased official contacts between teacher representatives and administrators, but it also allowed administrators to solicit collective, anonymous faculty responses to proposals, increasing administrators' awareness of staff opinions. Thus, while the unions constituted new structures within the schools that in some respects divided school boards, administrators, and teachers, they also provided new bases for communication and mutual awareness.

The case studies clearly show that effects of the union presence upon school management depend in large part upon the nature of union leadership and how union leaders define their roles. Administrators' perceptions of leaders were especially important in their assessments of union impact. Where administrators saw union leaders as strong and conscientious, they viewed the union presence as an important asset, for administrators maintained that such leaders communicated to their membership the importance of taking responsible, consistent positions and of meeting their own contract obligations. Note, for example, the following statement by a Cedarton principal:

> Union officers can take a stand where they want to. They could come in and say, "My God, you're harassing people. Morale is going down. . . ." Or they can do it the other way. Now, they have a role to play, too. They cannot be perceived as being in bed with the principal. And yet they [union leaders] are among the group who know that the quality of life in this building is directly related to a sense of order and discipline — do things get done on time, is the building organized? . . . At this point, I've come down on a few teachers who have not followed through on attendance procedures . . . and I've had their [union leaders'] support. . . . When someone [who] feels put upon goes to a union officer and says, "Why are they writing me letters saying I should be doing attendance?" the answer is, "Are you turning in your attendance reports? If not, you don't have a leg to stand on. . . ."

Another Cedarton principal, commenting on the effects of the union presence, noted:

> It really depends on the leadership . . . and I think here, in this building, it's been very responsible. . . . If you have good leadership, having a contract helps you . . . because the leaders are going to be willing to tell the rank-and-file, "Hey, this is your responsibility. . . ." It depends on how it's used. . . . Like anything, the unions can be a force for good or for bad.

Teacher Participation in School Decisions

Data presented in an earlier section suggest that teachers believe a participating faculty is a better faculty. The interview data helped to clarify why. First, teachers believed that because of their direct involvement with students and teaching, they had substantive information — information not available to administrators — needed for developing effective solutions to routine school problems (such as discipline).† Martin Landau, former president of the Middlebury union, in describing the schemes devised by the staff council for handling discipline problems in the high school, commented:

> Now, where were the administrators all this time? Were they so stupid they couldn't figure it out? My response over the years was, "Yes, . . ." It was partially that in their own limited sphere, they couldn't come up with ideas, whereas the people who were actively involved and confronted by these problems day in and day out had to come up with some kind of a solution. It wasn't that complicated or difficult.

Second, teachers pointed out that shared ideas not only tended to be better but also were far more likely to gain faculty support than those formed unilaterally by administrators. Landau went on to explain:

> It's so much better to implement . . . with shared ideas. [Usually] the principal comes in and says, "This is the way I want to do it." He can . . . but it would be so much better to lay out the suggestion, kick it around, get reactions, see what problems there might be with it. If he still feels strongly he can go ahead with it, but be prepared to be told "I told you so" if it does not work out. If, on the other hand, there are good suggestions, what has he lost? [He will have] the support of a cross section of people.

Another Middlebury teacher remarked, "[Teachers] are obviously more willing to carry them [decisions] out if they are their own." And a Cedarton high school teacher commented, "No one has ever got this faculty to do anything without the faculty agreeing to it."

Some administrators also noted the value of consultation in gaining faculty support for new policies. Crane (the Cedarton superintendent)

---

† As indicated in the Middlebury and Cedarton case studies.

commented, "Some administrators do it [consult teachers] better than others. And those who don't usually have problems." A Cedarton principal remarked:

> I really believe that the way to run a school is to have teacher input into the operation, because if teachers have a stake in the running, then they can't back out when you say that things go wrong. I want people to . . . take a responsibility for the place, and I . . . feel if people have a hand in running an operation, they feel better about their workplace.

Our data on administrative reactions to teacher participation is, unfortunately, limited. The reasons for this are not entirely clear. In part, it may be because the unions in Middlebury and Oakville had not been active in promoting teacher participation in school decisions during the 1970s. And yet, even in Cedarton, where the union actively promoted teacher participation, and in Middlebury, in reference to the staff council, administrators offered relatively few comments about its value. In only one instance did an administrator fully acknowledge the value of teacher contributions. In respect to the development of a discipline policy in the Cedarton high school, the principal commented:

> Discipline has improved considerably. . . . We developed a strong discipline policy. Very clear, very comprehensive. It has been of immeasurable assistance to us, and I have to say, most frankly, that the quality of that policy can be attributed very largely to the work of teachers who were on that [committee] . . . in putting together [the] . . . policy and in setting the tone with the rest of the faculty.

In fact, most administrators failed to give credit to teachers for ideas that had been jointly developed. Cedarton administrators, for example, typically discussed the successful teacher evaluation policy as if it had been entirely an administrative creation. In response to a question on union contributions to evaluation policies, a top administrator noted only: "and the union cooperated fully. They didn't raise a hassle." A Cedarton principal remarked: "Well, the union has . . . accepted the idea." And another principal commented, "I think they [the union] felt a responsibility to see that a policy was not developed that caused teachers to lose their rights — that was the main issue." Yet, according to reports by school board, union, and some administrator respondents, the Cedarton teacher evaluation policy had been developed over a period of several years by a joint committee of teachers and administrators — a committee created on the basis of the 1973 strike settlement, in response to union demands.

Administrators were also evasive to questions about teacher contributions. Note, for example, this exchange with a Cedarton principal:

> *Principal:* I really feel if people have a hand in running of an operation, they feel better about their workplace.
>
> *Interviewer:* And you might get some ideas, from them, too.
>
> *Principal:* Oh, sure . . . [breaks off].

With that, the principal went on to discuss something else. In response to a question asking about the contributions of the Middlebury staff council in improving discipline in the high school, the principal could not remember any: "It's hard to think back. . . ." Yet teachers active on the staff council had described their own contributions in detail.

Administrators' failure to acknowledge teachers' contribution was puzzling; we can only speculate as to the reasons for this failure. It may have been due to their low awareness of teachers' involvement. This would be a strong possibility in cases where policies involving teachers were filtered to lower level administrators indirectly, through the superintendent (as with districtwide evaluation policies). Or, it may have been that administrators did not consider teachers' contributions to be as important as teachers claimed. Possibly administrators were unwilling to share the credit for mutually developed ideas, wishing to claim them as their own. Or perhaps they failed to understand the value of many teacher ideas, because of a narrow, managerial perspective, as some teachers suggested.

A more likely possibility is that for many administrators, questions related to staff contributions touched too closely on unresolved authority issues — issues they did not fully acknowledge. To recognize the importance of teacher contributions to school decisions could constitute an admission that administrators should not have ultimate authority, but should share that authority with teachers.

Modern school administrators, however, are understandably insecure. They can no longer depend upon the kinds of community and teacher loyalties that sustained their predecessors; instead, they find their authority challenged from both sides, and feel isolated and unsupported in their managerial roles (see Cooper 1978; Mitchell et al. 1981). Furthermore, principals are under pressure from superiors — from superintendents and school boards — to strongly assert their authority over teachers, and especially to prevent any union inroads upon school management beyond those mandated by their contracts. Thus, in the interviews, most administrators made a point of asserting that while they "listened" to teacher suggestions, the final decisions were always their own. They could not, in fact, afford to do otherwise, if they wished to retain their positions. Ironically, however, it was this very insistence on having ultimate authority that tended to escalate tensions between administrators and teachers.

Without more substantial data from administrators, we cannot more fully assess the impact of teacher participation, except from the viewpoints of teachers themselves presented earlier. Our findings do suggest, however, that administrators' failure to acknowledge the value of teacher participation in school decisions may have derived from a preoccupation with asserting their own, uncertain, authority in the schools. Such an interpretation is consistent with the observation by some union leaders that effective consultation did not usually occur without a struggle.

The Issue of Teacher Protection

In protecting teacher rights, does the union protect teachers undeserving of protection — for example, does it prevent the dismissal of incompetent teachers? The public perception is that it does. A Cedarton union officer provided the following example:

> My wife is this way. She doesn't understand what it is that unions do. I tell her, "We're there to protect teacher rights," and she'll say, "You know darn well they've got some incompetent teachers there, and they [the union] won't let them get rid of them."

The issues involved, however, are far more complicated. This research suggests that teacher incompetence is protected, not by the union, but by a combination of other factors in the schools, including administrators' fears of the union.

The major factor protecting teachers has been tenure. In principle, tenure was granted only after a probationary period in which teacher competence was to be evaluated by school administrators. In fact, however, during the 1960s, when these school districts grew rapidly and positions were difficult to fill, many teachers were granted tenure after only cursory review. Some of these would not have received tenure in the 1970s, when the demand lessened and standards became more stringent. With retrenchment, because of budgetary cuts, more recently hired teachers — teachers who had been subjected to the more stringent standards — were not being retained because of seniority rules, while older, tenured teachers tended to be retained, regardless of their capabilities. Thus, the competency issue has centered on these older, tenured teachers. Unions, of course, have helped to create and protect tenure legislation through their statewide lobbying activities, and union contracts have established the principle of seniority as the basis for budgetary cuts. In these ways, unions have contributed to protecting older, tenured teachers. Our focus here, however, is upon the ways in which administrators and unions have met the issues of teacher protection under these broader rules.

Many administrators claimed tenure laws made it almost impossible to dismiss tenured teachers for incompetence — in spite of provisions within the state education law for doing so.† A Cedarton principal reported, "The way the law is set up, you have to prove incompetency. It's virtually impossible to do." In addition, administrators perceived the teachers' union as blocking their ability to establish incompetence under existing legal provisions. An Oakville administrator commented on the union's position in reference to a teacher suspended before a state 3020A hearing, "Behind closed doors, they'll say, 'We know what he's like. But it's up to you. . . .

---

†A school district may charge a tenured teacher with incompetence under Section 3020A of the New York State Education Law (see Hageny 1976). Other grounds for dismissal include: inefficiency, neglect of duty, insubordination, immoral character, physical or mental inability to perform duties. Teachers so charged are entitled to a hearing by a three-member review panel (including one teacher representative) appointed by the American Arbitration Association. Negative decisions by at least two members of the review panel result in the teacher's loss of tenure and dismissal.

We're not going to help you.' And they don't help you. . . . The union protects him." Many administrators and board members echoed the complaint that the unions offered teachers indiscriminate protection:

> They have supported staff we feel they should not have. (Cedarton principal)
>
> They will defend anybody. (Middlebury board member)

But union officers (and some administrators) maintained that such critics misunderstood the nature of union protection, tending to confuse a generalized protection of teachers' positions with protection of their rights to due process. It was due process that the unions emphasized. A Cedarton activist explained, "Lots of times we're forced to take positions that look as if we're trying to support an incompetent person, and we're not. We're just trying to make sure their rights aren't violated." Another Cedarton activist commented, "Even if you think it's a lousy teacher, you have to realize you don't know for sure. . . . You can't make a judgment. So you have to make sure their legal rights are guaranteed." A Middlebury union activist explained that a union's defense in some cases may reflect broader principles that are at issue. For example:

> If it occurs that someone is going to be fired who should be, but it's a violation of the contract, then you have to fight . . . to protect this person, because the next person they go after may be somebody who deserves to keep their job. You have to maintain the integrity of the contract.

As pointed out in the case studies, the unions were forced during the 1970s to play more protective roles than they had earlier envisioned. It became evident that they could not play active roles in evaluating teachers themselves (as Cedarton and Middlebury early union leaders had advocated) and at the same time effectively protect their constituents. Union leaders, therefore, came to define their relationships with school managers as essentially adversarial, especially in personnel matters. Thus, they argued, it was up to administrators — not teachers — to develop a case against any teacher believed to be incompetent, and it was up to the union to make sure that teacher was provided with a defense. Although the unions differed in how far they would go to defend teachers so charged, they agreed in principle that the major basis for such defense should be to ensure that the administrators' case was reasonable, that it was substantial, adequately documented, and handled fairly. Cedarton activists made this very clear:

> What this means is that they can't get rid of any teacher unless they've got really good reasons.
>
> Gone are the days, we hope, when an administrator could say, "Okay, I'll get you," and could fire somebody, and they'd have no recourse. Now we're saying, an administrator can't say, "He was teaching improperly" — [he] has to give instances.

But union leaders made it clear they did not believe their defense of teacher rights should prevent administrative dismissal of incompetent teachers. Nelson* (president of the Cedarton union) explained:

> I tell them, "The union will fight tooth and nail anything not documented, anything not substantiated." But . . . if somebody has the goods, and they come to me as union president, I'll say, "Look, bring him up on charges. We'll supply an attorney, and you're going to win." I would say the same thing in the Son of Sam case. Does that mean he didn't deserve a trial?

Another Cedarton activist remarked:

> It's gotten to the point now where administrators will come to us and say, "Look, this person's an alcoholic. . . ." We'll say, "We see it's a problem. . . . If you can build a case that the person's incompetent, we're not going to fight you. But do it right." . . . That's what people don't see.

And a Middlebury activist remarked, "A principal who can substantiate his charges doesn't have to worry."

Some administrators agreed that dismissal of tenured teachers was possible. A Cedarton principal explained:

> There is a lot the administrator has to go through to develop a case. . . . You'd have to really develop that file, and I'm sure the union would do what they could to protect their members. . . . It would be difficult, but it could be done.

And a Middlebury principal, in response to a question asking if the union prevented the dismissal of incompetent teachers, said:

> Baloney! Anyone who tells you that has not done his homework. . . . If I were to fire someone [for] not doing their job as a teacher, by God I should document it, to make sure that it's not prejudice on my part.

The problem, it would appear, is not that the unions have blocked administrators' ability to fire incompetent teachers, but that administrators haven't effectively exercised their powers. In fact, union leaders in Cedarton claimed they would like administrators to handle incompetency problems better. A Cedarton activist explained:

> They haven't made use of what powers they have. I can tell you of incidents where they have teachers that they should have gotten rid of, and they've got plenty enough evidence to move against these teachers, and they won't do it. . . . And then they claim that they haven't done it because the union will yell at them. Oh, the union will take them to task, but if they're right, we can't get anyplace.

Another reported:

> There are a couple of tenured teachers I think they [should] make a move on, but they haven't. I've had conversations with the principal, and I've said, "Look, when are you going to move on this guy? We're losing [other] good teachers because they don't have seniority, [while] this guy isn't doing anything in class."

Yet the perception that the union prevented administrative action in this area persisted. Part of the problem may have been that union insistence upon adequate reasons and documentation raised deeper problems surrounding teacher evaluation. Before the mid-1970s, evaluations had been conducted very haphazardly in all three districts. Many teachers had not been evaluated at all since receiving tenure, and evaluations for tenure had been only cursory. Administrators were now being asked not only to observe and evaluate large numbers of teachers but to write more careful, thorough evaluations. Many administrators balked. A Middlebury respondent on the school board during the mid-1970s remarked:

Nobody had ever taken these things [evaluation procedures] seriously. Nobody had ever questioned this stuff. And so the administrators' attitude was, "Nobody ever questioned me before. . . ." It drove me absolutely . . . [breaks off].

The demand that administrators conduct systematic, substantiated evaluations required not only greater care in thinking and writing but also the ability to recognize and specify teachers' strengths and weaknesses. These requirements focused upon an important administrative weakness: most did not know how to conduct such evaluations. Ironically, however, administrators' inability to document teacher weaknesses appears also to have been related, in part, to their sensitivity to union criticism. In Cedarton, Nelson explained how administrators' lack of skill may have combined with fear of the union in rendering them ineffective:

By and large, they are incapable of doing it. . . . Part of it may be the innate humanity of not wanting to hurt another person. But more of it, I think, is that a lot of them don't have skills at writing. They're afraid of exposing themselves to the union, because if they write something [inappropriate] that could be challenged. I think there's a tendency to not expose themselves — that if they go along, nobody will bring them up on a grievance.

A Middlebury School Board respondent made a similar observation in noting how unclear some administrators' evaluations tended to be:

We had to make these tenure decisions, and the board [members] were just not going to vote any more for people they thought were lousy. . . . There were a couple of . . . evaluations that were ambivalent, [but] recommended the teachers for tenure. Negative comments were . . . couched, hidden. . . . We brought in the principals for confidential meetings, . . . and it became quite clear the principals didn't want these people. But it was a question of, "Well, *I don't want to make waves for the union.* . . ." [emphasis mine] And that got the board absolutely apoplectic. They wanted to fire the principal who did that. . . .

The poor quality of administrator evaluations was a major complaint, not only voiced by union activists but echoed by board members and even some administrators, especially in Cedarton and Middlebury. Administrators' inability to specify or substantiate teacher weaknesses became the major basis for union opposition to their attempts at teacher dismissal. Nelson explained:

> They criticize for the sake of criticizing, and they don't have substantiation for it. Some of it is nit-picking, little stuff. Some of it is a feeling they can't back up. . . . I tell them, "Look, if you perceive something and it's there, then you'd better find the words to put it down. I will not accept that you 'know' this person isn't well prepared, or something. . . . Show me some incident. If you're going to tell me that every time you go in you see a marvelously well-planned lesson, but you know this person is not well prepared, there's something wrong . . . something wrong with you. If you want the job as administrator, I expect a lot of you. I expect you to be able to write, to be very articulate, and very specific." A lot of them are terrified to do it. Either that, or they go overboard and they're specific that there were three gum wrappers in the third row and the venetian blind is broken. . . . Or, they criticize student behavior as teacher behavior: "In the back, there were two children who were doing drawings in their notebooks."

Other Cedarton activists commented on further problems with evaluations — kinds of problems that led to union objections:

> If we take out a teacher's file and in there there hasn't been an evaluation for ten years, and all of a sudden they're going to fire a teacher for incompetence, we'll ask, "Where does it say they're incompetent? *Nowhere.*"

> If a principal says, "It was a poor class because the teacher didn't involve enough students," and the next evaluation says, "My last [criticism] was cleared up. There was very good participation. But I didn't like the bulletin board," . . . then [we argue] that this teacher has potential, because she has corrected criticism made in the past.

Administrators themselves noted that attempts to dismiss teachers were at times undermined by administrative carelessness. A Middlebury principal implied this had occurred several times in that district "not because of the union, but because of the way . . . we handle things — if someone is not doing their job, many times, it's not documented."

But administrators also noted other kinds of problems contributing to the low quality of their evaluations: lack of time, inadequate staff, and inadequate training for administrative staff in evaluation skills. Some noted other complications, as well. For example, while union leaders generally supported the need for more systematic teacher evaluation, rank-and-file teachers generally disliked them. Many found frequent observations and administrative criticism threatening, and their resistance made the administrators' task more difficult. Furthermore, some administrators pointed out that the retention of incompetent teachers was not due entirely to problems with evaluations, noting cases where political, community pressures had influenced school boards to retain teachers for whom they had recommended dismissal (for example, in the granting of tenure to a mediocre but popular teacher or to a teacher having important political connections). Others referred to cases where the boards voted, on the basis of unpopularity, against tenure for teachers who should have been retained.† Such cases undermined administrator and union efforts to attain greater equity and objectivity in teacher evaluation.

Finally, some administrators referred to the difficulty in establishing consistent criteria for evaluating teaching and providing constructive criticism:

> There's so much that goes into it. . . . You [have to] know what you're looking for. . . . A person has to have that developed. [It takes] a special talent of knowing what to look for and how to criticize [teachers] effectively.

In spite of these difficulties, by the completion of this research, at least one tenured teacher had been successfully dismissed on the basis of the provisions in state law, in each of the three districts studied. In Cedarton, where strong emphasis had been placed on development of a teacher evaluation program, a much larger number (about 15) had been encouraged by administrators either to resign or to retire early on the grounds that well-documented, negative evaluations could become the basis for charges of incompetence. While the union provided advice and a reasonable defense to the teachers involved, it did not attempt to block the administrative actions taken. Finally, also in Cedarton, a still larger number of tenured

---

†On tenure decisions, boards have the legal right to discharge nontenured teachers based on their own judgment, without administrative justification. This had been a major, unresolved strike issue in Middlebury.

teachers made substantial improvement in teaching in response to intensive evaluation and supervision under a plan devised by the union and described in the Cedarton case study.

Overview

By 1979, most administrators and board members interviewed in these three districts understood the importance of the union in meeting teacher needs. A top Cedarton administrator commented:

> They [unions] bring a perspective and a balance that you might otherwise not get. I believe they sensitize administrators as well as boards to [teacher concerns]. I think the matter of unionism in public education is not only desirable, but inevitable, because of the manner in which [informal] teacher groups were treated by boards when the Taylor Law was not there. . . . Boards would often not even meet with teacher groups, and if they did, it was in an arbitrary atmosphere. There was a good deal of that, and I think . . . the very militant attitudes teachers had [earlier] . . . were a direct result of [their] bitterness over the ways in which they'd been treated.

Some indicated that their perspectives on the union changed over time, on the basis of increased information and contacts. A former Middlebury board member reported a considerable change in perspective after his wife joined the teaching staff and later had occasion to file a grievance against an administrator. He wrote the following letter to the union after they won a grievance on her behalf in 1978:

> Some of us are slow learners, but, nevertheless, do finally come to understand complicated issues. In my case, I have come to appreciate not only the staffing and assignment issues raised by the MTF over the years but also the manifest insensitivity and arbitrary nature of school administration. I share with you your frustrations, with a better and clearer understanding.

Most administrators and board members noted that, on balance, the benefits of having a more content and secure teaching staff outweighed possible disadvantages associated with limits to management flexibility. In none of the districts did the majority of board members or administrators view the union as destructive to the educational system. In two of the districts — Middlebury and Oakville — they viewed the presence of teacher unions as neither good nor bad, but a fact of life. In Cedarton, however, many administrators viewed the union as a positive force in the school district.

We have noted in these three case studies the importance of leadership in determining union positions on various matters. Furthermore, in the three districts studied, the union leadership, in spite of certain important differences, was viewed by both administrators and board respondents as basically responsible leadership. The observation that respondents did not note significant negative effects of unionization in these three districts obviously reflects this common quality.

A major conclusion to be drawn from this study is that the impact of teacher unionism will vary, depending on the nature of union goals and leadership. Communities and school boards seem to influence the direction in which unions develop. These case studies suggest that where communities are reasonably receptive and responsive to their unions, the participation of professionally committed, educationally concerned teachers is more readily sustained.

APPENDIX

TABLE 1
Membership in Teachers' Organizations: Percentage Changes from 1969 to 1979

	1969			1979		
Organization	Cdtn	Mdby	Okvl	Cdtn	Mdby	Okvl
Union (AFT)	9	66	61	88	82	89
Assn. (NEA)	75	6	12	5	0	0
Other/none	31	28	27	7	18	11
Total %	100	100	100	100	100	100
Total N	(134)	(103)	(33)	(111)	(61)	(35)

TABLE 2
Union Activism: Percentages of Members Very Active in Unions, 1969 and 1979

	1969			1979		
	Cdtn	Mdby	Okvl	Cdtn	Mdby	Okvl
	43	40	55	28	33	39
Total*	(14)	(67)	(20)	(99)	(54)	(33)

Note: Activism was determined on the basis of two criteria: having been a union officer within three years of survey and regular attendance at union membership meetings.

*Total number of union members responding to the surveys.

TABLE 3
Teacher Participation and Support for Strikes in Early 1970s: Percentage Distributions by School District

Type of Activity or Support	Cdtn	Mdby	Okvl
Negotiating team	10	10	23
Organized demonstrations	18	28	12
Participated in demonstrations	70	36	29
Inactive, but supported strike	1	5	18
Did not support strike	1	21	18
Total N*	93	58	27

*Totals represent only respondents who were in district at time of strike.

TABLE 4
Activists' Perceptions of Organizational Emphasis on Various Issues: Percentages Reporting Emphasis on Each Issue, 1969 and 1979

	1969			1979		
Issues	Cdtn Union	Mdby Union	Okvl Union	Cdtn Union	Mdby Union	Okvl Union
Salaries	100	89	100	100	100	100
Grievances	100	78	100	100	100	100
Job security	—*	—	—	96	100	100
Teaching load	100	82	82	89	78	92
Class size	100	78	82	96	100	100
Changes in educational program	83	70	73	75	56	85
Teacher voice in educational policy	100	82	91	93	89	85
Union solidarity	—	—	—	100	100	85
Total N = 31	6	27	11	28	18	13

Note: Responses of "much emphasis" and "some emphasis" combined for 1979 to permit comparison with 1969, where degree of emphasis was not distinguished.

*Variable not included in 1969 survey.

TABLE 5
Activists' Perceptions of Organizational Emphasis on Various Issues: Percentages Reporting "Much Emphasis" in 1979

Issues	Cdtn Union	Mdby Union	Okvl Union
Salaries	79	89	85
Grievances	75	100	100
Job security	75	100	92
Teaching load	50	50	31
Class size	75	78	46
Changes in educational program	39	11	23
Teacher voice in educational policy	57	50	39
Union solidarity	68	67	46
Total N	28	18	13

Note: Comparisons on "much emphasis" are not possible with 1969 because the earlier survey asked respondents only to indicate whether their organization "emphasized" certain issues and did not distinguish degrees of emphasis.

TABLE 6
Members' Perceptions of Organizational Emphasis on Various Issues: Percentages Reporting "Much Emphasis" in 1979

Issues	Cdtn Union	Mdby Union	Okvl Union
Salaries	73	72	78
Grievances	58	83	78
Job security	61	86	59
Teaching load	25	37	12
Class size	42	64	18
Changes in educational program	7	11	0
Teacher voice in educational policy	38	23	17
Union solidarity	54	56	6
Total N	71	36	18

Note: Comparisons on "much emphasis" are not possible with 1969 because the earlier survey asked respondents only to indicate whether their organization "emphasized" certain issues and did not distinguish degrees of emphasis.

TABLE 7
Activists' Perceptions of Organizational Effectiveness in Various Areas: Percentages Reporting Own Organization as Effective, 1969 and 1979

	1969			1979		
Area	Cdtn Assn.	Mdby Union	Okvl Union	Cdtn Union	Mdby Union	Okvl Union
Salaries	90	95	100	93	100	100
Grievances	83	100	80	100	100	100
Job security	—*	—	—	64	89	100
Teaching load	47	65	40	71	89	92
Class size	42	53	20	50	89	85
Changes in educational program	39	70	70	71	44	69
Teacher voice in educational policy	73	71	80	85	65	69
Union solidarity	—	—	—	96	78	92
Total N	31	27	11	28	18	13

Note: Responses of "very effective" and "somewhat effective" are combined for purposes of this table.
*Variable not included in 1969 survey.

TABLE 8
Members' Perceptions of Organizational Effectiveness in Various Areas: Percentages Reporting Own Organization as Effective, 1969 and 1979

	1969			1979		
Area	Cdtn Assn.	Mdby Union	Okvl Union	Cdtn Union	Mdby Union	Okvl Union
Salaries	96	100	89	96	97	100
Grievances	82	92	100	94	97	88
Job security	—*	—	—	68	81	76
Teaching load	62	67	89	57	86	58
Class size	59	61	44	44	83	61
Changes in educational program	64	67	67	55	47	41
Teacher voice in educational policy	51	69	67	73	59	47
Union solidarity	—	—	—	91	79	47
Total N†	70	40	9			
Total N†	70	40	9	71	36	18

Note: Responses of "very effective" and "somewhat effective" are combined for purposes of this table.

*Variable not included in 1969 survey.

†Totals include only rank-and-file members. Activists are deliberately excluded in order to permit comparisons between members' and activists' perceptions of organizational effectiveness. Activists' perceptions are provided separately in Table 7.

TABLE 9
Teacher Perceptions of Changes in Welfare and Working Conditions since 1969 — by School District: Percentages Indicating Changes in Each Direction

Area of Change	Cdtn	Mdby	Okvl
Teacher salaries			
Better	77	84	73
Same	16	13	17
Worse	7	3	10
Job security			
Better	21	17	24
Same	20	17	41
Worse	59	66	35
Teacher welfare other than salaries and job security			
Better	85	70	73
Same	8	16	23
Worse	7	14	3
Teaching load (hours of assigned work)			
Better	9	12	10
Same	53	69	58
Worse	38	19	32
Class size			
Better	2	5	3
Same	24	55	45
Worse	74	40	52
Total N*	99	55	27

*Total includes only respondents in school district ten years or more.

TABLE 10
Teacher Perceptions of Changes in Relations with Administrators and School Boards since 1969 — by School District and Grade Level Taught: Percentages Indicating Changes in Each Direction

Type of Relations	Cedarton Elem.	Cedarton H.S.	Middlebury Elem.	Middlebury H.S.	Oakville Elem.
Staff relations with building principals					
Better	17	64	24	40	37
Same	36	30	43	34	42
Worse	47	6	33	26	21
Staff relations with district superintendent					
Better	18	39	35	23	11
Same	22	32	43	53	41
Worse	60	29	22	24	48
Staff relations with school board					
Better	42	52	16	6	44
Same	37	39	27	39	44
Worse	21	9	57	55	12
Total N*	65	34	37	18	27

Note: Elementary includes primary, intermediate, and junior high school grades. Cutoff points vary among the districts. For Cedarton, these include first through eighth grades; for Middlebury, first through seventh; for Oakville, first through ninth. High school includes all remaining grades.

*Total includes only respondents in school district ten years or more.

TABLE 11
Teacher Perceptions of Changes in Quality of Staff and Staff Participation in School Decisions since 1969 — by School District and Grade Level Taught: Percentages Indicating Changes in Each Direction

Area of Change	Cedarton Elem.	Cedarton H.S.	Middlebury Elem.	Middlebury H.S.	Oakville Elem.
Overall quality of teaching staff					
Better	36	44	32	12	41
Same	58	53	57	53	48
Worse	6	3	11	35	11
Teacher participation in decisions about educational program					
Better	26	46	24	22	41
Same	52	39	33	44	37
Worse	22	15	43	34	22
Teacher participation in decisions about student discipline					
Better	13	72	22	28	33
Same	74	16	49	44	48
Worse	13	12	29	28	19
Teacher participation in decisions affecting teacher welfare					
Better	65	52	44	61	48
Same	29	45	42	28	52
Worse	6	3	14	11	0
Total N*	65	34	37	18	27

Note: Elementary includes primary, intermediate, and junior high school grades. Cutoff points vary among the districts. For Cedarton, these include first through eighth grades; for Middlebury, first through seventh; for Oakville, first through ninth. High school includes all remaining grades.

*Total includes only respondents in school district ten years or more.

TABLE 12
Ideological Orientations of Union Activists, Comparisons between 1969 and 1979: Percentage Distributions on a Liberalism-Conservatism Scale

	1969			1979		
Orientation	Cdtn	Mdby	Okvl	Cdtn	Mdby	Okvl
Strongly conservative	0	0	0	0	0	0
Moderately conservative	0	5	0	18	0	25
Middle-of-the-road	0	0	20	12	12	50
Moderately liberal	33	30	50	52	59	25
Strongly liberal	67	45	30	18	6	0
Radical	0	20	0	0	23	0
Total N	20	6	10	17	27	12

Note: Rankings are by respondent self-identification.

TABLE 13
Ideological Orientations of District Teaching Staffs, Comparisons between 1969 and 1979: Percentage Distributions on a Liberalism-Conservatism Scale

	1969			1979		
Orientation	Cdtn	Mdby	Okvl	Cdtn	Mdby	Okvl
Strongly conservative	2	1	0	1	0	0
Moderately conservative	20	9	22	23	20	32
Middle-of-the-road	21	16	28	20	11	36
Moderately liberal	40	44	38	47	46	32
Strongly liberal	16	24	12	8	15	0
Radical	1	6	0	1	8	0
Total N*	132	93	32	109	61	34

Note: Rankings are by respondent self-identification.
*Totals represent all teachers in sample, including union activists (except for missing answers).

REFERENCES

Baird, Robert, and John Landon. 1972. "The Effects of Collective Bargaining on Public School Teachers' Salaries and Comment." *Industrial and Labor Relations Review* 25 (April): 410-17.

Barber, Bernard. 1950. "Participation and Mass Apathy in Associations." In *Studies in Leadership*, edited by A. W. Gouldner. New York: Harper.

Blau, P., and W. R. Scott. 1962. *Formal Organizations*. San Francisco: Chandler.

Bruno, James E., and Ira Nelken. 1975. "An Empirical Analysis on Propensity for Teachers to Strike." *Educational Administration Quarterly* (Spring): 66-85.

Bureau of Labor Statistics. 1980. *Directory of National Unions and Employee Associations*. Washington, D.C.: U.S. Department of Labor.

Carr-Saunders, A. M., and P. A. Wilson. 1933. "The Rise and Aims of Professional Associations." In *The Professions*. Oxford. Clarendon Press.

Cole, Stephen. 1969. *The Unionization of Teachers: A Case Study of the UFT*. New York: Praeger.

Cooper, Bruce S. 1978. "The Future of Middle Management in Education." In *The Principal in Metropolitan Schools*, edited by Donald A. Erickson and Theodore L. Reller. Berkeley: McCutchan Publishing Company.

Cooper, Bruce S., and John C. Bussey. 1980. "Collective Bargaining in Public Education and Other Sectors: A Comparative Review of Research." Washington, D.C.: National Institute of Education.

Corwin, Ronald G. 1974. *Education in Crisis*. New York: Wiley.

——. 1970. *Militant Professionalism*. New York: Appleton Century Crofts.

——. 1965. *A Sociology of Education*. New York: Appleton Century Crofts.

Donley, Marshall O., Jr. 1976. *Power to the Teacher: How America's Educators Became Militant*. Bloomington, Indiana: Indiana University Press.

Dreeben, Robert. 1973. "The School as a Workplace." In *Second Handbook of Research on Teaching*, edited by R. M. W. Travers. Chicago: Rand McNally.

———. 1972. "Reflections on Teacher Militancy and Unionization." *Sociology of Education* 45: 326-37.

———. 1970. *The Nature of Teaching*. Glenview, Ill.: Scott Foresman.

Fox, W. S., and M. H. Wince. 1976. "Structure and Determinants of Occupational Militancy among Public School Teachers." *Industrial and Labor Relations Review* 30 (October): 47-58.

Goode, William J. 1973. "The Theoretical Limits of Professionalism." In *Explorations in Social Theory*. New York: Oxford.

Gouldner, Alvin W. 1954. *Patterns of Industrial Bureaucracy*. Glencoe, Ill.: Free Press.

———. 1947. "The Attitudes of 'Progressive' Trade Union Leaders." *American Journal of Sociology* 52 (no. 5): 389.

Grimshaw, William J. 1979. *Union Rule in the Schools*. Lexington, Mass.: D. C. Heath.

Gross, N., W. S. Mason, and A. W. McEachern. 1958. *Explorations in Role Analysis*. New York: Wiley.

Gustman, Alan L., and Martin Segal. 1978. "Teachers' Salary Structures: Some Analytical and Empirical Aspects of the Impact of Collective Bargaining." In *Proceedings of the Thirtieth Annual Meeting of the Industrial Relations Research Association, 1977*. Madison: IRRA.

Hageny, William J. 1980. *School Law*. Albany, N.Y.: New York State School Boards Association, Inc.

Holmes, Alexander B. 1979. "Union Activity and Teacher Salary Structure." *Industrial Relations* 18 (Winter): 79-85.

Jessup, Dorothy K. 1978. "Teacher Unionization: A Reassessment of Rank-and-File Motivations." *Sociology of Education* 51 (January): 44-53.

———. 1971. "The New Unionism: A Study of Teacher Militancy in Six Suburban School Districts." Ph.D. dissertation, Columbia University.

Johnson, Susan M. 1983. "Teacher Unions in Schools: Authority and Accommodation." *Harvard Educational Review* 53 (August): 309-26.

Kasper, Hirschel. 1970. "The Effects of Collective Bargaining on Teachers' Salaries." *Industrial and Labor Relations Review* 24 (October): 57-71.

Kerchner, Charles T., and Douglas Mitchell. 1981. "The Dynamics of Public School Collective Bargaining and Its Impacts on Governance, Administration, and Teaching." Washington, D.C.: National Institute of Education.

Lipset, S. M., M. A. Trow, and J. S. Coleman. 1956. *Union Democracy*. New York: Free Press.

Lipsky, David B., and John E. Drotning. 1973. "The Influence of Collective Bargaining on Teachers' Salaries in New York State." *Industrial and Labor Relations Review* 27 (October): 18-35.

Lortie, Dan. 1975. *Schoolteacher*. Chicago: University of Chicago Press.

―――. 1973. "Observations on Teaching as Work." In *Second Handbook of Research on Teaching*, edited by R. M. W. Travers. Chicago: Rand McNally.

McDonnell, Lorraine, and Anthony Pasal. 1979. *Organized Teachers in American Schools*. Santa Monica, Calif.: Rand Corporation.

Merton, Robert K. 1936. "The Unanticipated Consequences of Purposive Social Action." *American Sociological Review* 1: 894-904.

Michels, Robert. 1962. *Political Parties*. New York: Free Press.

Mitchell, Douglas E., Charles T. Kerchner, Wayne Erck, and Gabrielle Pryor. 1981. "The Impact of Collective Bargaining on School Management and Policy." *American Journal of Education* 89 (February): 147-88.

Nasstrom, Roy R., and Robert L. Brelsford. 1976. "Some Characteristics of Militant Teachers: A Reassessment Based on an Indiana Study." *Journal of Collective Bargaining* 5 (no. 3): 247-56.

National Center for Education Statistics. 1978. *The Condition of Education*. Washington, D.C.: Government Printing Office.

Parsons, Talcott. 1951. *The Social System*. New York: Free Press.

Perrow, Charles B. 1970. *Organizational Analysis*. Belmont, Calif.: Brooks/Cole.

Perry, C. B., and N. A. Wildman. 1970. *The Impact of Negotiations in Public Education: The Evidence from the Schools*. Worthington, Ohio: Charles A. Jones.

Ravitch, Diane. 1974. *The Great School Wars, New York City, 1805-1973*. New York: Basic Books.

Retsinas, Joan. 1982. "Teachers: Bargaining for Control." *American Educational Research Journal* 19 (Fall): 353-72.

Ritterband, Paul. 1974. "Ethnic Power and the Public Schools: The New York City School Strike of 1968." *Sociology of Education* 47 (Spring): 251-67.

Rosenthal, Alan. 1969. *Pedagogues and Power: Teacher Groups in School Politics*. Syracuse, N.Y.: Syracuse University Press.

Selznick, Philip. 1949. *TVA and the Grass Roots*. Berkeley: University of California Press.

Sieber, Sam D. 1967. "Organizational Resistances to Innovative Roles in Educational Organizations." Paper presented at the University of Oregon-UCEA Career Development Seminar, Portland, Oregon.

Thornton, Robert. 1971. "The Effect of Collective Negotiations on Teachers' Salaries." *Quarterly Review of Economics and Statistics* 11 (Winter): 37-46.

Vagts, Christopher, and Robert B. Stone. 1969. *Anatomy of a Teacher Strike*. West Nyack, N.Y.: Parker Publishing Company.

Waganaar, Theodore. 1974. "Activist Professionals: The Case of Teachers." *Social Science Quarterly* 55 (September): 372-79.

Wollett, Donald. 1967. "The Importance of State Legislation." In *Readings on Collective Negotiations in Public Education*, edited by Stanley M. Elam, Myron Lieberman, and Michael Moskow. Chicago: Rand McNally.

ABOUT THE AUTHOR

Dorothy Kerr Jessup teaches sociology at the State University of New York at New Paltz. She received the B.A. degree from Wellesley College and the Ph.D. from Columbia University. Her interest in teacher unionism grew out of her own involvement in political, housing, and school reforms in New York City during the 1950s and 1960s, during which time she served as a school board member in Brooklyn. Her awareness of political and social limitations to reform led her into sociology.